ORGANIZATIONS IN SOCIETY

Glenn Morgan

MACMILLAN

First published 1990 by
THE MACMILLAN PRESS LTD
Houndmills, Basingstoke, Hampshire RG21 2XS
and London
Companies and representatives
throughout the world

ISBN 0–333–43854–X hardcover
ISBN 0–333–43855–8 paperback

A catalogue record for this book is available
from the British Library.

Reprinted 1992, 1993, 1994

Printed in Hong Kong

For my mother

Contents

Preface

This book has been a long time in the making. It derives essentially from ten years' experience of teaching courses on the BA in Organization Studies at Bradford and Ilkley Community College. My first debt, then, is to all the students at Bradford who have had to listen and struggle to understand the early formulation of these ideas. My period at Bradford has also been noteworthy for the opportunity to work with people from a wide variety of disciplinary backgrounds. In particular, I would like to thank the following for their friendship and intellectual support over many years: David Hooper, Tom Johnston, Albert Mills and Liz Shorrocks.

This book would probably still not be finished if I had not been granted a year's study leave by the Governors of Bradford and Ilkley College in 1987–8, and for that reason I owe them a debt of gratitude. In relation to this, I would like to thank Professor David Hickson of the Management Centre at the University of Bradford who helped me get study leave by arranging for me to be a Visiting Fellow at the Management Centre during this period.

David Dunkerley in his role both as External Examiner for the BA in Organization Studies and as reader of this book has been a continuous source of help and encouragement.

Finally, my thanks go to Susan, Ryan, Spencer and Kate for all they have endured over the time of writing this book.

GLENN MORGAN

Introduction

Our society is an organizational society. We are born in organizations, educated by organizations and most of us spend most of our lives working for organizations. We spend much of our leisure time paying, playing and praying in organizations. Most of us will die in an organization and when the time comes for burial, the largest organization of all – the state – must grant official permission. (Etzioni, 1970, p. 1)

Since Etzioni wrote these words, the power of organizations over life and death has continued to increase. In the same period that revolutionary new techniques in medicine have developed which can save, prolong and improve life, the potential for planetary destruction has also increased, both through nuclear warfare and through the damage (both anticipated and unanticipated) inflicted on the earth's ecological system by industrial expansion. These developments are only the latest in a long line which have arisen because of the way in which human beings have learnt how to organize rationally vast social and physical resources across time and space.

The simplest aspects of life in Western industrial societies are dependent upon complex organizations which would have defied the imagination of human beings less than 200 years ago. Take, for example, the activity of shopping. The commodities we in the West purchase will often have been produced or harvested thousands of miles away: oranges from Israel, bananas from Guatemala, tea from India, coffee from Kenya, toys from Singapore, shirts from Taiwan, videotapes from Japan – the list is almost endless. Each of these products has to be produced and then

1

transported through a variety of links to the point of sale. They will be touched by many human hands before they end up in our shopping basket. Each time we purchase these everyday commodities which we take so much for granted, we become the final link in a chain of complex relationships which stretches across many organizations in different parts of the world. The degree of co-ordination of human energy and physical resource which maintains this chain is peculiar to the last two centuries of human development. Whilst there have often previously been empires in which international trade has played a central part (see, for example Wallerstein, 1974, 1980, on the sixteenth- and seventeenth-century European empires, and Perlin, 1980, on trade in seventeenth-century India), at no previous phase of history has this become so essential to the everyday life of society as it has in current Western economies.

Another way in which our lives are linked to the worldwide system of organizations derives from our sense of citizenship. Our life today is so inextricably bound up with our sense of citizenship in a particular state that we tend to take it for granted. My identity as a British citizen places me as part of a set of relationships which make up the British state. This state in turn has relations with other states at a variety of levels – as a member of the European Community, NATO, the West, the Commonwealth. Each of these relationships is reinforced through our learning in school, in the media, and in our personal lives. Not insignificant in this is the growth in Western societies of tourism, through which we familiarize ourselves with concepts of difference and similarity between peoples, as well as the international sporting occasions which are now so much a part of many people's lives. In the course of an ordinary day, then, I may reproduce my understanding of myself as 'British' in many ways e.g. through watching television, reading the newspaper, going to the cinema, arranging my summer holiday, learning French at night, going to the 'British' Museum or the 'National' Gallery. At the economic level, I pay my taxes to the British state, which ensures that, among other things, it can buy the latest military technology and support British troops in Northern Ireland, West Germany and the Malvinas/Falklands, as well as contribute to the maintenance of NATO and the possibility of nuclear war. None of these activities could be possible without organizations.

In eighteenth-century Britain the situation would have been very different. Although there might have been some international trade in commodities like tea and silk, for the vast majority of people outside London, markets were primarily local. Food and clothing, together with all the other necessities of life, were produced and purchased within small local areas. Only gradually during the eighteenth century did anything like a national market emerge (Malcolmson, 1981; McKendrick *et al.*, 1983; Mathias, 1969). Political life was also highly localized for the majority of people, and the state at national level consisted of barely a handful of men (the gender is appropriate). As one recent commentator has said regarding eighteenth-century England:

> What impact did the organs of the Georgian state have on society at large? To twentieth century eyes, the things it didn't do are very conspicuous. Kings and their ministers did not set out to implement manifestos of social justice or interest themselves in reform. They didn't pursue comprehensive and long-term industrial and agrarian policies or promote programmes of education and welfare. 'Providence has so organized the world,' said Lord Shelburne, 'that very little government is necessary' . . . Above all, it was the local offices (the Lord Lieutenants, the Sheriffs and the Justices of the Peace), hogged by the regional elite and backed by law, which dictated the destinies of communities. (Porter, 1983, pp. 131, 138)

Even warfare, a perennial activity in human societies, had had a limited impact on people as a whole. The British Isles had not suffered invasion since 1066, and although there had been outbreaks of war between England and Scotland as well as the Civil War, English soil had rarely been the scene of pitched battles in the 900 years after Hastings. The armies and navies of the period before the nineteenth century were small in comparison to those of the twentieth century. The nationalist outpourings associated with the period of Victorian empire-building and then the First World War drew on ideas of citizenship and nationhood which were only gradually created and reproduced through the late eighteenth and nineteenth centuries. Before this, for the majority of people their involvement in politics and issues of state was highly circumscribed. Their knowledge of other societies was very limited. People lived their lives within limited confines in economic, social and political terms.

Between the eighteenth and twentieth centuries the world has undergone a fundamental transition. Across the globe, lives have become intertwined, both politically and economically. The symbols of this process are all around us. There are few parts of the world where Coca-Cola is not sold. There are few parts of the world where summits between Reagan and Gorbachev were not headline news. There are few parts of the world where the disaster at Chernobyl did not have an impact. The threat of nuclear war hangs over the whole world, South as well as North, East as well as West. How is it that our fates have become so entangled? How have human beings been able to leap the barriers of time and space which only two centuries ago seemed to hold them firmly apart and subject them to their own individual fates? How is it that our lives have become so massively influenced by events taking place thousands of miles away from us? The answer to this lies in organizations.

What are organizations?

As individuals we have limited capacities. As we come together and act in a co-ordinated fashion, our capacities increase not just arithmetically but geometrically. (In other words, when two people work together, their output can be more than the simple addition of what they would have achieved separately. Joining together they are able to utilize each other's strengths and overcome each other's weaknesses. As a result the potential increase in output is qualitatively distinct from a simple additive process.) It is on this simple observation that organizations are built. To state the point so baldly is of course to gloss over many problems, but only if we can see the essential elements of organizations can we begin to get a perspective on the problems. Organizations develop out of a conscious decision on the part of an individual or a group to achieve certain goals through the bringing together in a disciplined fashion of human and material resources. Organizations can be distinguished in this way from other cognate terms. Take, for example, the concept of social institution; a recent encyclopaedia of sociology states that the term institution 'is generally applied to aspects of social behaviour regulated by well-established, easily recognized and relatively stable norms, values and laws' (Mann, 1983, p. 172). Thus when we participate in social institutions such as 'the family', 'religion' or 'education', we have a relatively clear expectation of what such participation involves and the role we should perform. Formal mechanisms to co-ordinate the institution or to punish role deviance are lacking. These institutions have evolved over long periods of time and although sociologists and other commentators may discuss the 'goals' and purposes of the family, etc., this does not make them into organizations. Social institutions may be hierarchically organized; they may embody codes of behaviour and systems of sanctions; but the manner in which these operate lacks the distinctive characteristics of organizations. Even the smallest organizations necessarily involve conscious monitoring and control of the relationship between means and ends on a fairly regular basis. Such monitoring and control implies a conscious disciplinary process whereby organizational leaders adapt internal structures to their perception of external conditions.

A further distinction needs to be drawn between organizations and social movements. Giddens has recently pointed to the neglect of social movements as a phenomenon:

> Social movements can be cogently defined as 'collective enterprises to establish a new order of life'. Unlike organizations, social movements do not characteristically operate within fixed locales and positioning within them does not have the clarity of definition associated with 'roles'. (Giddens, 1984, p. 204)

Social movements may generate organizations – for instance, the 'peace movement' gave rise to the Campaign for Nuclear Disarmament – but they need to be distinguished from each other. The social movement is a wider, looser, social phenomenon.

Organizations involve bringing together human beings and physical resources in a co-ordinated and controlled mechanism in order to achieve certain objectives otherwise impossible. As these central processes of control and co-ordination have become refined and rationalized, so the potential for organizations to expand beyond space and time constraints has increased. This in turn means that not only present but also future resources can be considered and planned for. Thus a directed dynamism is built into organizational functioning; the organization is not simply existing at one particular point in time and space; it has a past, a present and a future which may simultaneously exist across different spatial areas. In this way, organizations link lives that were previously separate into chains of interconnected destinies and fates.

Sociology and the study of organizations

What does sociology in particular have to contribute to our understanding of organizations?

First, sociology has always been centrally concerned with the transformation from pre-industrial society. The social discontinuities of the late eighteenth and early nineteenth centuries became the core object of study for the classical sociological theorists such as Comte, Marx, Weber and Durkheim (see the commentaries by Giddens, 1971, Therborn, 1976, and Nisbet, 1967, for differing perspectives on this). Although the twentieth century has seen a proliferation of sociological concerns, this theme of discontinuity and change has remained central. Giddens has recently restated it in terms of the 'sociological imagination' (the term coined by Mills, 1970); Giddens argues this involves three elements – a historical, an anthropological and a critical sensitivity. By historical sensitivity, he refers to the need to discover our own past: 'Only by such an effort of the imagination . . . can we grasp how differently those in industrialized societies live today from the way people lived in the relatively recent past' (Giddens, 1980, p. 26). Anthropological sensitivity is important 'because it allows us to appreciate the diversity of modes of human existence which have been followed on this earth' (p. 26). Finally, he argues: 'We must be conscious of the alternative futures that are open to us . . . contributing to the critique of existing forms of society' (p. 26). A sociological approach to organizations is therefore concerned with understanding how we got the organizations we have (historical sensitivity), how they differ across the world (anthropological sensitivity) and what alternative types we can imagine (the critical perspective).

Second, sociology is crucially concerned with the relationship between individuals and the social structures in which they live. There has been a continuous debate within sociology between those who argue that, in order to understand society, we must understand the actor's frame of reference, the meanings which the actors hold and how social processes appear to them (this approach is variously identified as 'phenomenological', 'interactionist', 'ethnomethodological') and those who argue that what is necessary is an understanding of the 'objective' features of social structure which stand outside of, if not beyond, the understanding of social actors themselves (an approach associated with functionalism, structural Marxism, and systems theory). These debates have been closely mirrored in the sociological study of organizations (see, for example, Silverman, 1970; Burrell and Morgan, 1979; Astley and Van de Ven, 1983) for reasons that relate to the nature of organizations. As I have already described, organizations involve purposive human action at their very inception, but as they become established they begin to feel like constraints on human action. Bureaucracy is a word synonymous with this feeling that organizations are in some sense 'no longer human'.

Whilst it would clearly be mistaken to believe that this dualism so ingrained in sociology is in decline, it is nevertheless the case that Giddens's recent work in particular has sought to provide a way out by linking structure and action in the theory of structuration (Giddens, 1976, 1979, 1981, 1984). In what follows I shall endeavour to utilize Giddens's framework. In one of the clearest statements of his central argument, Giddens puts the issue like this:

> Anyone who participates in a social relationship forming part of a social system produced and reproduced by its constituent actors over time necessarily sustains some control over the character of that relationship or system . . . actors in subordinate positions are never wholly dependent and are often very adept at converting whatever resources they possess into some degree of control over the conditions of reproduction of the system. In all social systems, there is a dialectic of control. (Giddens, 19822, p. 32; see also Offe, 1985, ch. 1 for a general statement of a similar position)

Thus the sociological study of organizations should never become either simply the study of actors and their meanings or the study of systems, for it is both. The central issue in the study of organizations is precisely the tension between actors as individual subjects with their own goals and interests and the organization as a structure of control and co-ordination which is trying to guide those actors to act 'for' the organization as a system. Even this is an inadequate conceptualization because there is no such thing as the 'organization' apart from actors; it is particular actors who try to induce 'system-like' qualities in the organization; such qualities cannot exist independently of actors. Nevertheless, the key issue remains the way in which organizations seek to control the potential disorganization within themselves that is inescapable from their nature as socially constructed phenomena, and to utilize human resources in a directed and co-ordinated fashion in order to achieve objectives.

Sociology therefore has a specific contribution to make to the understanding of organizations which differentiates it from disciplines such as economics and psychology. The sociological imagination focuses on the dialectic of control between systems and actors as they have emerged in the context of contemporary industrial societies.

Previous approaches to the sociology of organizations

The strengths of such a specifically sociological approach can be seen from a brief review of the main theorists in this tradition. Three main phases can be distinguished.

The classical theorists

No sociology textbook is complete without ritual obeisance to Marx and Weber among the classical theorists. In the case of the sociology of organizations, however, such obeisance goes well beyond the ritualistic. These authors established basic frameworks for the understanding of organizations which remain significant today. (Detailed accounts in relation to organizations are available in Salaman, 1979, and Clegg and Dunkerley, 1979.)

In Marx that basic framework is supplied by the centrality of class and class struggle in social transformation. Within the economic sphere, the central feature of social relations is class struggle over the surplus value generated in the labour process (for the labour theory of value, there are clear accounts in Giddens, 1971, and Mandel, 1968, 1969). Outside the strictly economic sphere, the state and the organizations associated with it are not separate from class struggle, but part of it (see Jessop, 1982, for a comprehensive analysis of various Marxist theories of the state). In the Marxist view the study of organizations is both about the vast expansion in productive forces brought about by capitalism and the social cost of that process in generating class struggle. All organizations need to be understood in terms of the underlying conflict of classes that occurs in capitalism. Marx is little concerned about the nuances of organizational behaviour and the differences that may occur between organizations. For him, these are minor in comparison with their true nature, which is defined by their location in a capitalist society.

Weber's understanding of organizations is more complex than that of Marx, yet retains an underlying unity. This derives essentially from Weber's view that for a variety of historically specific reasons, Western societies from the sixteenth century developed a number of social forms which generated a fundamental change in their structure and gave rise to capitalism and industrialism. One of these changes (a good account of the wide array of such changes can be found in Marshall, 1982) related to the emergence of a new type of organizational form. Weber labelled this as rational–legal bureaucracy because it was based on clearly expressed rules and a hierarchy of officials located within the structure on the basis of their skill and expertise in performing particular roles. Weber distinguished this type of organizational form from those characteristic of traditional societies, which were frequently based on family and friendship and where achievement of goals was frequently of less significance than performance of ritually expressed roles. Rational–legal bureaucracies provided the basis for a huge new outburst of human energy and creativity which had previously been stifled by traditional forms:

> The decisive reason for the advance of bureaucratic organization has always been its purely technical superiority over any other form of organization. The fully developed bureaucratic mechanism compares with other organizations exactly as does the machine with non–mechanical modes of organization. Precision, speed, unambiguity, knowledge of the files, continuity, discretion, unity, strict subordination, reduction of friction and of material and personal costs – these are raised to the optimum in

the strictly bureaucratic organization. (Weber, quoted in Gerth and Mills, 1948, p. 214)

Weber was not naive enough to believe that this was without costs. He lamented the disappearance of elements of the mystical, the magical and the traditional from social life, but he, more than any other social theorist, recognized the significance of organizations and organizational forms. As a break with the past, as a constraint on human action, as a generator of human power, the organization was raised by Weber to a central position in the study of society. It is an agenda of research, a framework of analysis, that retains its significance for us today.

The analysts of bureaucracy

For all their strengths in locating organizations in wider social relationships, Marx and Weber were basically uninterested in any particular organization. A particular organization was treated as somehow representative or symptomatic of all other organizations in a particular society. Such a view was rejected by the analysts of bureaucracy. Central to the emergence of this group is the figure of Robert Merton. Merton is crucial for three reasons. First, as a teacher, researcher and colleague, he appears to have exerted a powerful influence over a number of sociologists who in their turn have made major contributions to the analysis of organizations. For example, Gouldner, Selznick, Blau and Perrow were all connected at one time with Merton and Columbia University in New York where he worked. (For some of Merton's own reflections on these and other relationships see Merton, 1982, 1987.) Second, Merton is important because he developed the idea that sociology would progress better if limited empirically based questions were addressed. Such an approach would in turn generate what Merton called 'middle range theory', which would avoid vacuous over-generalization and instead encourage meaningful debate that was grounded in empirical research about the social world. Third, Merton applied this principle to the study of bureaucracy, arguing that Weber overemphasized the degree to which bureaucracies were efficient. This theme was taken up by Selznick (1966), Gouldner (1954) and Blau (1956) in studies which argued that bureaucracies could be inefficient. Although these studies were harsh on Weber since they did not address his central question regarding the wider process of rationalization (see Albrow 1970 for the definitive review of this debate), they were nevertheless important in opening up the empirical study of organizations. It is of interest to note that in methodological terms these authors owed a great deal to Weber. Gouldner in particular drew on Weber's emphasis on the actor's frame of reference, and all three authors utilized the case study method in which actors' understandings were given full consideration, as opposed to some of the more quantitative approaches to organizations which have developed since.

These quantitative approaches were first systematically developed in Britain, where what was known as the Aston Group (see Pugh and Hickson, 1976; Pugh and Hinings, 1976; Pugh and Payne, 1977, for collections of their writings) began to examine in detail the features that Weber had identified as constituting bureaucracies. Contrary to Weber, they argued that these features did not always go together in the same way; they could appear in different combinations and therefore it was possible to distinguish different types of bureaucracies. Furthermore, they argued that these types fitted with particular environments – there was no one universal model of bureaucracy. As important as the theoretical points they developed was the methodology the Aston Group utilized. This consisted of generating quantitative measures of organization structure and correlating these with aspects of environment and performance in order to develop models of 'fit' between organizations and environments (similar issues were being explored at around the same time in the USA by authors such as Lawrence and Lorsch). This made their approach particularly useful for comparative research where replication and testing of hypotheses in a rigorous manner was required. It also dovetailed with the growing move to quantify social phenomena both as an objective in its own right and as an attempt to heighten the legitimacy of the social sciences. The influence of the Aston Studies has been such that certain authors have even claimed that this is the only way to study organizations (see Donaldson, 1985), though this seems rather extreme and way beyond the claims that the founders of the approach themselves would make. Nevertheless, coupled with the influence of Merton and the American studies of bureaucracy, the Aston Studies were instrumental in generating a sub-discipline within which organizations could be studied in their own right without being treated as derivative of either wider social phenomena such as classes or markets or of individual characteristics such as psychology or consumer behaviour. Together the two strands – American and European – have created a field of organization studies reflected in the two leading journals: in the USA the *Administrative Science Quarterly* and in Europe *Organization Studies*. The two strands have generated great diversity, although there have been periods when a particular orthodoxy seemed to prevail. It was one such period which gave rise to the emergence of critical theorists of organizations.

The critical theorists

In the late 1960s and 1970s the study of organizations seemed to be stuck in the rut of producing more and more quantitative material with less and less theoretical content. What theoretical content existed seemed to come close to a sterile form of functionalism in which organizational structures were justified as 'fitting the organization to the environment'. The potential for change and the notion that workers might resist aspects of structure and managerial authority became invisible. This opened the way to a number of attacks from radical theorists, commencing with Silverman (1970), who attacked the methodological foundations of this view and argued the basic Weberian point that the perceptions of the actors must be taken into account. Later in the decade this methodological issue was taken up in a much more systematic manner by Burrell and Morgan (1979; see also Burrell, 1980), who subjected existing organization theories to an incisive analysis, drawing out their implicit assumptions and demonstrating that these were frequently conservative. Burrell and Morgan argued for a plurality of social and organizational theories, identifying what they termed radical humanist, radical structuralist and interpretive alternatives to the predominance of functionalism. In further work, the authors have continued to emphasize the importance of variety and pluralism to the study of organizations (Cooper and Burrell, 1988; Morgan, 1986). Whilst their work has been criticized for leading to the dead-end of relativism (see, for example, Reed, 1986), it nevertheless does seem to have helped to widen the number of potential approaches to organizations.

Other authors took on the orthodoxy in a different way. A major work in this respect was Clegg and Dunkerley (1979). Although Clegg in his earlier work had addressed some of the philosophical issues considered by Burrell and Morgan (see in particular Clegg, 1975, 1979), Clegg and Dunkerley were more concerned to expose the limited sociological nature of much organization theory and to replace it with an approach more sensitive to issues of class, control and political economy. In later work Clegg has developed this further by examining the importance of different social settings for class formation and organizational transformation (see Clegg, 1981; Clegg, Boreham and Dow, 1986; Clegg and Higgins, 1987).

Often the work of the critical theorists (others in this vein are Benson, 1977, 1985; Heyderbrand, 1977; Salaman, 1979) seemed to come close to the positions being developed by authors with a more orthodox background. (Two significant 'crossover' in-fluences have been Perrow (1981, 1984, 1988) and Child (1984a, 1984b)). However, the ways in which the critical theorists phrased their attacks often appeared polemical and programmatic, and as a result they were ignored in some quarters. For example, in a recent debate between Donaldson (the most aggressive defender of the Aston orthodoxy and most persistent critic of the critical theorists) and a number of other authors in the field, Aldrich (1988) examined the number of references to the main critical theorists in recent journal articles and found them to be few and far between. He concluded that their influence was therefore small. Aldrich's posi-tivism, however, seems to ignore the fact that organization studies is now a much more diverse field than it was twenty years ago, and some of the credit for this must go to those who campaigned for an opening up of the theoretical and empirical issues. However, it is worth noting that much of the current new thinking derives from authors who developed within the orthodoxy such as Perrow, Pfeffer (1982) and M. Meyer (1980), as well as Aldrich (1979) himself, rather than from the critical theorists whose empirical contribution remains limited (much to the delight of their oppo-nents, who thought it never amounted to anything substantive anyway!)

The situation in the late 1980s has thus become one of flux. The sociology of organizations has generated a considerable amount of empirical and theoretical debate since the days when the critical theorists began to storm the barricades of the old orthodoxy. There are now many theoretical positions flourishing, alongside a wide range of empirical research. Any new student in this field may be tempted to see only part of this diversity as the 'real' sociology of organizations. This would be a great pity, as the fundamental issues of change and the role of human agency in creating new organizational forms and social arrangements can be studied from many directions. In this book I shall try to present one perspective on how this diversity can be integrated, enabling the sociology of organizations to play its proper role in the analysis of society as a whole, rather than being simply a sub-specialism only of interest to those poor twisted souls whose idea of fun is counting the number of levels in a managerial hierarchy!

The plan of this book

The aim of this book is to explore the processes whereby organizations are structured and changed by beginning at the intra-organizational level and working upwards to more societal and historical issues. The first three chapters concentrate on the organization of work, bureaucracy and management. The emphasis here will be mainly on capitalist organizations. There are two reasons for this. The first is practical and relates to the fact that the literature on organizations is dominated disproportionately by analyses of capitalist organizations. This in turn can be linked to the second, theoretical reason, namely that in modern Western societies the dynamic sector has traditionally been the economic one. Although these societies consist of other sectors (in particular that associated with the state and that associated with voluntary organizations), it has been the problems surrounding the production of material wealth in the economic sector that have centrally concerned social theorists and managers alike. Only recently has it come to be recognized that state and voluntary organizations are significant in their own right and should not simply be subsumed as sub-categories of capitalist organizations. Most literature on organizations fails to make this clear; it concentrates on capitalist organizations without making this explicit.

In Chapter 4 I attempt to bring out some of the distinctive features of non-capitalist organizations. I draw examples from a number of different types of state and voluntary organizations. At a time when in Britain and many other Western societies there is an increasing tendency to adopt uncritically the methods and style of capitalist organization in state and voluntary organizations, the chapter seeks to establish the notion that there is a legitimate difference between the sectors. The political and communal nature of state and voluntary organizations has in the past provided a certain insulation from market forces. The extent of this has varied according to the role and function of the organization. There are good reasons for this insulation that relate to the nature of citizenship and participation in modern Western societies. The attempt to reduce this insulation threatens to undermine these fundamental values and their articulation in state and voluntary organizations.

In Chapter 5 I return to the issue of how organizations are controlled and co-ordinated. I consider in particular the significance of the location of organizations in sets of market relations. This issue has become increasingly important in the study of organizations over the last two decades. Three approaches are critically examined. I argue that both the population ecology approach (which leaves no room for organizations exerting control over the market) and the market and hierarchies position (which prescribes a limited role for organizations in controlling the market) seriously underestimate the way organizations can control their environment. Developing the third approach that has arisen recently – the resource dependency/interorganizational networks view – I argue that through combining in various formal and informal ways, organizations can minimize the disruptive effects of the market. This in turn leads to the argument that the market is itself a structure of power through which powerful groups within organizations seek to reproduce their own power. In particular, I consider the Marxist view that finance capital takes on an increasingly directive role, limiting systemic environmental disturbance through co-ordinated action and planning. The existence of an inner circle of people who not only control these financial institutions but also other major organizations within the state and voluntary sectors is also examined.

The final substantive chapter, Chapter 6, argues that organizations must be located in their specific historical and social setting. Societies have different articulations of their central institutions. In most Western societies, the capitalist sector is predominant, and state and civil society (within which voluntary organizations are located), although based on distinctive principles of citizenship and participation, are driven by the predominant sector. Nevertheless they have an institutional autonomy which is the outcome of the specific historical development of the West. In Soviet-type societies such as the USSR, however, this institutional separation has not occurred. Instead all organizations have been subordinated to the political control of the Communist Party, and any threat to this principle has threatened the underpinnings of the system as a whole. The Gorbachev era is an attempt to reform this structure from within – to allow organizations to develop semi-autonomously from state control and to develop along new lines. Essentially, these moves look as if they may be taking the USSR down the road towards the institutional separation of the market, the state and civil society, although there remain many resistances to such a project. This analysis points to the need to locate organizational analysis in specific processes of societal and state formation rather than giving in to the free-floating cultural stereotypes of national character which have such power in the media. Through an examination of Japanese organizations, this point is developed further. Finally, Chapter 6 argues that we are currently in a new period of societal change in which national boundaries are increasingly irrelevant and are being undermined by the growth of multinational organizations and international finance.

In Chapter 7 I attempt to identify some of the key choices that face us in the future regarding the nature of organizations and society. I focus on four central dilemmas: democracy versus autocracy in work; co-ordination versus anarchy; plan versus market; and national versus multinational forms. Each of these dilemmas creates choices in which we are all involved. The future will be shaped by the way we respond to these choices and dilemmas.

1 Work in Organizations

Introduction

This chapter is concerned with the control of work in capitalist organizations. Organizations consist of sets of disciplined relationships in which individuals perform tasks assigned to them. The nature of those tasks, the manner in which people are persuaded to fulfil them and the mechanisms of control over them is the main subject of this chapter. The relations of power that produce and reproduce work relations is given central attention, as it is through these relations that key aspects of social life are formed. The argument develops from a critique of Braverman's theory of the labour process; it rejects the idea that there is one particular form of work that is essentially capitalist and develops instead the idea that forms of work control are produced by a complex interaction of different interests within the workplace and different though connected interests outside the workplace. Central to this is the concern of various interests to gain power by taking control over the labour process. These interests, which go wider than the simple capital–labour relation to encompass gender and ethnic groups as well as occupational groups, struggle over the nature of the work task according to powers derived and reproduced both inside and outside the work situation.

Elements of the core task

What are the elements of work in organizations? At this stage we are simply seeking to identify in general terms what is brought together inside the organization to achieve what might be called the core task. Frequently this issue is skated over, and yet by considering it in some detail we can gain a better understanding of what is meant by these terms.

People

The first and most obvious element consists of people. It may seem strange, but many studies of organizations have failed to look at the people in organizations as anything more than mechanical parts in a machine. Take, for example, the classical studies of the Western Electric Company in the USA in the 1930s. The authors of the studies based on this research (Roethlisberger and Dickson, 1964) treated the people in the organization as though they were 'tabula rasa' when they came into the company; they endeavoured to explain everything that happened purely on the basis of the physical and social changes which they, the researchers, instituted. Nowhere did they consider the outside environment and its impact on the workers involved in the study. The fact that there was massive unemployment outside and that workers were desperate to ensure they kept their jobs by co-operating with the researchers was ignored. So too was the fact some of the workers were women, which could have made a difference to the way they reacted (see Carey, 1967, and Rose, 1988, for critical discussions of the Hawthorne Studies). Goldthorpe et al. (1968) attacked this tendency to forget that people had lives outside the factory gates; they argued that people brought into the organization certain attitudes, characteristics and skills which were important to the structuring of work. It is possible to distinguish between (a) people's motivation on entering the organization, (b) their skills and qualifications, and (c) their 'natural' characteristics.

The motivation of people entering the organization includes the degree of legitimacy accorded to authority as well as people's particular reasons for working within the organization. Etzioni's (1970) typology of compliance is relevant here. He argued that there were three main types of power in organizations: coercive, remunerative and normative. From the point of view of members of the organization, there were three main kinds of involvement: alienative (based on a rejection of the organization and its goals), calculative (based on a pragmatic acceptance of the organization for the achievement of personal, extra-organizational goals), and moral (an acceptance of the moral significance of the organization and one's place within it). This led Etzioni to devise a typology of compliance relations (see Table 1.1).

Table 1.1   *Etzioni's typology of compliance relations*

Kinds of power	Kinds of involvement		
	Alienative	Calculative	Moral
Coercive	1	2	3
Remunerative	4	5	6
Normative	7	8	9

In Etzioni's view;

> The nine types are not equally likely to occur empirically. Three – the diagonal cases, 1, 5, and 9 – are found more frequently than the other six types. This seems to be true because these three types constitute congruent relationships, whereas the other six do not. (Etzioni, 1970, p. 108)

Etzioni's typology can be criticized for a number of reasons. First, it is static and tends to assume that attitudes are fixed rather than continually developing in interaction with internal and external features of the environment. Second, it is 'rationalist' in the sense that it tends to assume that people hold one consistent set of attitudes, whereas a number of studies have tended to indicate contradictory attitudes that are frequently situationally determined in the sense that people express attitudes in different contexts that to the external observer appear contradictory: to the person concerned, however, the attitudes 'fit' the different situations. Consistency of thought is frequently a virtue only intellectuals cherish (see, for example, Mann, 1970, on contradictory political attitudes). Recently, however, labour process theorists, following Burawoy (1979), have claimed to discover the importance of consent in the work situation. Authors such as Baldamus (1961) emphasized this a long time ago; the point is the simple one that whilst there are many features of work which promote conflict, there are also features in and outside work which ensure that people come with concepts of co-operation, consent and fairness already instilled in them. (See Hyman and Brough, 1975, for a general discussion of this which emphasizes the need to locate the production of consensus and concepts of fairness within a framework of ideological production in general; for a more limited development of the idea, lacking the more critical societal framework, see Harris, 1987, which attacks Nichols and Beynon, 1977, for ignoring the issue of consent.) The issue of motivation is a complex one which sociologists tend to leave to psychologists and then claim that psychologists fail to recognize the social context of motivation. For a major attempt at tackling the issue from a sociological point of view, which utilizes recent developments in the theory of the subject, see Knights (1989).

People also enter organizations with certain specific sets of skills and qualifications. They may have paper qualifications, they may have experience, they may have a reputation of work in their profession. It may be that the organization does not use these skills: for example, in their study of non-skilled manual workers, Blackburn and Mann (1979) found that most of them used more skills driving to work in the morning than they did when actually at work. Or it may be that the organization uses the skills badly. However, it is the fact that these skills are brought in that is important. Furthermore, the supply of and demand for skills is an essential element in the creation of the labour market in general and processes of labour market segmentation in particular.

Finally, it is important to recognize that there are a host of characteristics which border on the 'natural' which people take into organizations. Take, for example, gender, which is seen in many organizational settings as defining certain natural abilities. Thus women are seen as more caring, men as more aggressive and ambitious. The nature of these characteristics become part of the way in which work is organized. (For a major attempt to place this at the heart of the study of organizations see Hearn and Parkin, 1983, 1987; see also Burrell, 1984, 1987). Similarly, people's 'racial' or ethnic characteristics can be used to define certain 'natural' qualities in relation to their work potential, e.g. stereotypes of the Irish as 'navvies' or West Indians as 'workshy'. It is not that these characteristics are inevitably accompanied by certain behavioural or attitudinal traits, but that in the minds of those who take key decisions the two are linked together. Pfeffer (1983) has recently suggested another set of characteristics that operate in a similar way; these relate to the age of people within organizations. Pfeffer argues that organizations have a particular demographic profile which relates to the date of the founding of the organization, the initial process of recruitment, and the extent of the organization's turnover. The age profile in terms of numbers in each age cohort can have implications for the organization, e.g. in the differences of socialization and educational experience of the different groups and the potential for conflict or consensus that arises from this.

Technology

The definition of technology in work settings is a highly complex task in itself. MacKenzie and Wajcman (1985, pp. 3–4) argue:

> The word 'technology' has at least three different levels of meaning. At the most basic level, 'technology' refers to sets of physical objects . . . But few authors are content with such a narrow 'hardware' definition of technology. An object such as a car or a vacuum cleaner is only a technology, rather than an arbitrary lump of matter, because it forms part of a set of human activities . . . So 'technology' refers to human activities, as well as to objects . . . Thirdly, technology refers to what people know as well as what they do . . . Technological things are meaningless without the 'know-how' to use them, repair them, design them and make them . . . 'technology' as systematic knowledge of the practical arts.

Any task environment involves elements of each of these three notions of technology: it involves a certain hardware element; the hardware has built into it certain organizational constraints about the forms of human activity which can work the hardware; and the technology has certain implications for the structure and distribution of knowledge within the work setting. At this stage I will not seek to identify in more detail types of 'technology' or the determining role of technology on organizational settings – or indeed its opposite, the determinant role of organizational settings on technological developments. The main point is to signal the different meanings embodied in the concept of technology.

Time

Task environments exist in a time dimension. This has been explored in a number of ways.

(a) The discovery of time
A number of authors have pointed out how time itself is a concept that has been refined as part of the changes arising from industrialization. The notion of time being divisible down to its smallest units and human activity being parcelled into hours, minutes and seconds, develops as controls over work in factories increase (see E.P. Thompson, 1971; Gutman, 1977). At the same time the sheer measurability of time is improved through the improved technology of clock-making. Changing conceptions of time are also related to the regularity of time over longer cycles than simply the working day – ideas of the working week and the stability of the work relationship itself had first of all to overcome the irregularity of annual calendars beset with feast days, fairs and Saints Days.

(b) Organizational time
The change in the overall conception of time has had an impact within organizations on the way in which time is spent. McGrath and Rochford (1983, pp. 70–1) have argued that within organizations, three central temporal issues emerge:

> (1) The need for time plans or schedules, that is, for accurate prediction of points of time at which specific action or events will occur or specific products will be available (scheduling), (2) the need for synchronization, or temporal coordination, among the functionally specialized, time-segmented, and spatially segregated parts and activities of the organization (synchronization) and (3) the need for allocation of time (as well as other scarce resources) among different sets of activities, so that the total time available is used in an efficient and rational way to maximize the organization's goals/priorities (allocation).

Clark (1985) has looked at the problem from a slightly different point of view. He introduces a number of concepts to show how time orientations differ within organizations:

> Previously, studies of organization features often aimed to conceptualize phenomena as though its dimensions were so enduring that they were evenly distributed 'in time' . . . The point of departure taken here starts from the observation that many organizations are characterized by temporal differentiation reckoners. . . . Especially important is the examination of those

organizational members whose roles include the construction and operating of the 'strategic time reckoning' system. (Clark, 1985, pp. 21–3)

Within any organization, then, a number of different timescales may be operating. Major investments in plant and machinery may be measured in terms of a commitment over a period of years; market and profit growth is much more likely to be subjected to annual, if not quarterly, scrutiny on the part of shareholders and the stock market, whilst from the point of view of the marketing director, monthly measures are crucial. Clark also introduces the idea of 'organizational timetables and temporal inventories':

> Temporal inventories consist of the actual (or standardized) aggregated man hours available from any particular organizational unit to be deployed and the estimation of the total man hours required to complete certain tasks. These two sets of data are then interrelated to plan future activities, to evaluate existing practices and in the designing of new situations . . . Organizational timetables represent the translation of the inventory into specific flows of people in given sequences and in defined units of time. (1985, p. 25)

Clark's analysis then links the notion of time within organizations to the issue of structuring. Organizational work settings involve 'timing' as one of their dimensions. Where does the 'timing' come from?

(c) Personal time
Finally, it is necessary to consider time from the point of view of the person in the organization. As individuals, people have their own time-clocks running from the moment they are born to the moment they die. As well as time in this personal, biological sense, there is time in a career sense – how is one progressing, if at all, within the organization; how is one passing time at work (Roy, 1973, is a classic study of this process); how does one's time at work relate to one's time outside work? Time at the machine, time in the organization, is a commitment of the whole individual. As Offe (1985) points out in his discussion of the labour market, labour power always comes in the inconvenient form of a human being – you can't have one without the other. As a result there is always

potential tension between the organization and its use of the individual's time and the way in which the individual herself wants to use her time. Similarly, the ticking of the biological clock, whether in its diurnal mode or in its life-time mode with all the processes of decay, depression and elation, can interrupt the smooth passages of time from the point of view of the organization.

Space

Organizational work settings exist in a spatial dimension. This aspect of social life has in general received short shrift in most sociological accounts. Recently, however, there has been a reawakening of interest in this (see Massey, 1984; Gregory and Urry, 1985). I want to explore a number of themes under this heading.

(a) Off-stage/on-stage

Still one of the most fertile discussions of the issue of space can be found in the works of Goffman (1968, 1971). Goffman distinguishes between being on–stage and off-stage. When one is on–stage, one is acting out a role, which can be an organizational role or it can be a more general social role. When one goes off–stage, however, the mask can slip. The restaurant is the classic example of off- and on-stage. The people in the restaurant are served by waiters who cross the boundary into the kitchen; the clientele know little of what happens backstage – all they know is what they can see on–stage. Their feeling of well-being is assured if the waiters are polite and courteous, the atmosphere amenable and the food acceptable. If they saw what was going on backstage to produce all these things, they might not be so assured. If they had to observe the food from yesterday being reheated, the dropped food being recycled, the general state of cleanliness of the kitchen, they might hurry off the stage themselves. What is on–stage within organizations is not fixed; it may change according to circumstances. When the Queen visits, suddenly even the toilets are in some sense 'on–stage' and have to be cleaned to perfection. Time also comes into the notion of being off- and on-stage. After the restaurant closes, the waiters may 'let down their hair' and the cooks etc. come out from backstage in order to mix with the customers who are left. Some work settings have less room for being off-stage than others. For example, airline stewards have very little physical space on a passenger airplane to which they can withdraw and be off-stage temporarily. They have to remain on-stage throughout long tedious and tension-producing flights (see Hochschild, 1983).

(b) Physical setting
Technology and design build into work settings a certain sense of the space that will constrain people. Assembly lines and large factories embody certain work-stations where individuals are expected to stay whilst working. The variability of physical conditions is wide. In the British context there has traditionally been a sharp separation between the office and the factory-floor, perhaps involving the separation of office buildings from the factory; in some instances the offices overlook the factory floor, the superior status reflected physically in the office 'standing above' the workers. The growth of office work itself has generated a further differentiation between the 'typing pool' and other office/clerical workers. This is related to distinctions such as those between open-plan office settings and individualized/closed-off offices. Status is now derived from having an individual office, whilst even in an open-plan setting, people may attempt to partition off their little bit of floor space. From the point of view of the management, the open-plan office increases the visibility of work and allows a greater degree of control over what goes on.

(c) Spatial division of labour
The physical settings which I have so far described all relate basically to face-to-face settings. However, it is important to note that physical settings are now brought together on a much wider scale. Worldwide revolutions in transport and communications mean that control over work settings can rest thousands of miles away from the setting itself. Thus, computer chips designed in London or New York can be produced according to exact specifications in Taiwan or Singapore. The potential for a new international division of labour (Froebel, Heinrichs and Kreye, 1980; Massey, 1984; Henderson and Castells, 1987; Peet, 1987) has opened up a new set of issues as far as the physical location of organizations is concerned. Although there have been organizations on a world scale for many centuries – the Catholic Church

being the most notable and successful example – recent changes have added an increased relevance to the question of how physical settings are determined.

Four main elements go together to make up a work setting within organizations – people, technology, time and space. How are these elements actively put together? At this point I need to return to the concept of power. At its most general level, power is the resource that pulls these elements together and shapes them into a particular organizational division of labour. What form does this power take? Where does it spring from? What are its limits? What are its effects? People, technology, time and space are reshaped and restructured in modern organizations. How are we to understand this process?

Work in organizational settings based on capital-labour relations

An obvious place to commence such a discussion is with the work of Harry Braverman and the labour process debate. Braverman (1973) views power from a straightforward Marxist perspective. Because of the nature of capitalism, workers essentially lack the power to resist capital's attempts to restructure the labour process. The main constraints on capitalists' power derive from organizational problems (how to control the labour process in a way that maximizes profit – a problem that, according to Braverman, Taylorism solves) and technological limitations (i.e. actually having the technology to replace skilled workers – a problem that is resolved by the subordination of technology and science to the requirements of capitalism). Thus the structure of work can be understood in terms of management's attempts within the limits imposed by technology and organization to maximize profit.

Braverman develops his argument from a historical account of changes in the nature of capitalism. In the early stages of capitalism skilled work was outside the control of management. Skilled workers were the only people who knew how to resolve certain problems, such as how to make 'good' iron or steel, how to spin or weave cotton or wool. Since the problems, arising from the variability of raw materials, tools and conditions of work, could not be determined in advance, there was an indeterminacy to the length of time any task should take and therefore an indeterminacy about the cost to the organization of achieving any particular task. According to Braverman, capitalist employers seek to break down this indeterminacy through a process of deskilling the workforce. Three main principles are involved. The first of these is the rendering of the labour process independent of craft, tradition or workers' knowledge. This occurs through management seeking knowledge and information about the work process through 'scientific methods', i.e. through the measurement of work times. This has generated the panoply of techniques known as works study, or time and motion study, where the aim is to devise standard times for certain tasks, independent of either the person who is actually doing them *and* the actual context in which they are done. Second, there is the separation of conception from execution. Through the collection of information about the details of jobs and tasks and the appropriate times for them, management are now able to separate the task of doing from the task of deciding what needs doing. Management are able to plan whole factories in advance and to estimate labour costs on the basis of having times for the tasks in advance of their actual execution. Third, the managerial monopoly over knowledge implies that the design of work itself is now completely under the control of managers. Managers possess the knowledge over the work process; they design jobs in accordance with their 'objective' standards of timing and workers fit as cogs in a wheel into the system created by management.

For Braverman these changes in the labour process derive from capital's need to control the labour force in order to guarantee profit in a competitive market situation. The inner logic of work settings, then, is a logic of deskilling; although this process does not occur at the same rate everywhere, it is nevertheless the central dynamic of work organization in capitalist firms and is premissed on the power of capital to structure the labour process in its interests.

Braverman's analysis has prompted a vast amount of argument over the last decade or so (for some of the main areas of debate see Wood, 1982; Littler, 1982; Thompson, 1983; Littler and Salaman, 1982, 1984). In the context of this book I will be selective in terms of the main areas of argument. In particular, I wish to consider whether Braverman has accurately identified the nature of work

settings in modern capitalist organizations, i.e. the central importance of deskilling.

One of the main attacks on Braverman was launched in Friedman's book *Industry and Labour* (1977). Friedman argued that
deskilling is only one strategy that management may pursue:

> Top managers are often reasonably certain that if they were to do
> certain things, it would provoke a work stoppage. The separa-
> tion of conception from execution by division of labour, mecha-
> nisation or scientific management is not necessarily the best
> strategy for management in organizing the labour process when
> confronted with worker resistance. Techniques which reduce
> managerial reliance on worker goodwill may not be most
> appropriate for insuring against the effects of determined worker
> resistance or for directly reducing expressions of that resistance.
> (p. 25)

Friedman suggests the need to distinguish between two different
forms of management strategy, each of which may be appropriate
at different times or in different market conditions. The first he
calls 'direct control'; this refers to scientific management-type
control over the activity within the workplace. The second he
refers to as 'responsible autonomy'. This second approach does not
demand that management has total control over the labour process
in the way that Braverman suggests. On the contrary, according to
Friedman, this may actually be inefficient in certain circumstances,
because there are always some 'tacit skills' (Manwaring and Wood,
1984) which workers retain and without which the job could not be
completed successfully. This is the essence of 'responsible autonomy'; it does not seek to reduce the areas of discretion but rather to
ensure that they are used 'responsibly', i.e. in the interests of
management. This model therefore has a different combination of
people, technology, time and space. It is particularly associated
with the human relations tradition of management control.

The human relations tradition arose in the USA in the 1930s out
of a series of experiments conducted at the Western Electric
Company; the studies are referred to, after the name of the plant in
which they were conducted, as the Hawthorne experiments (see
Rose, 1988, for a more detailed account of the human relations
school and its impact). Following a series of experiments to assess

the effects of environmental and lighting conditions on work groups, the researchers began to notice that however they altered the physical conditions of the work group, i.e. whether they improved them or made them worse, production was improving. After some time they began to explain this in terms of the relationship that had developed between themselves and the workers they were studying (the so-called Hawthorne effect). Because the workers felt that they as individuals were being given status and esteem, they responded by endeavouring to do their best for managers. The researchers took this as a general message that where people feel that their individual psychological needs are being considered, they will respond better to work.

Since the original Hawthorne studies, this initial idea has received support from psychologists like Maslow (1970) and Herzberg (1966) (with their ideas of self-actualization and the need of human beings for esteem as well as material survival) and it has been developed into a number of applications in work settings (see Warr, 1987b, for a more detailed account). Perhaps the most significant are:

1. The importance of work groups for production; where people feel part of a group their performance may improve, thus the physical conditions must make this possible.
2. The importance of sympathetic leadership and individual counselling on the job.
3. The importance of seeing the totality of the work task and the contribution of the individual to the whole.
4. The importance of providing interesting work.

All of this adds up to an agenda for the structuring of work settings that is very different from that of scientific management. It involves building on people's skills and commitments within the workplace rather than treating them as simply cogs in a machine. In terms of technology, it involves considering ways in which technology can be designed to fit human needs rather than vice versa. In terms of time, it means the recombination of tasks in such a way as to provide people with more meaningful units of work than those characteristic of scientific management. In terms of physical setting, it has considerable implications for designing work settings that provide for collective interaction both during the work period and during breaks. It also necessitates breaking down rigid divi-

sions of status between the shopfloor and the office.
Friedman then places responsible autonomy and direct control
as two management strategies that in essence are providing different models of the work setting and the role of labour within it. For
Braverman, 'responsible autonomy' or human relations is seen as
an adjustment, something which management may resort to in
order to aid in the control of workers. It is a device used by
management to conceal their basic commitment to scientific management and does not actually affect these underlying relations.

Taylor deals with the fundamentals of the organization and the
labour process and of control over it. The later schools of
adjustment of the worker to the ongoing production process as
that process was designed by the industrial engineer . . . Taylorism dominates the world of production; the practitioners of
'human relations' and 'industrial psychology' are the maintenance crew for the human machinery. (Braverman, 1973, p. 87)

The essential point that Friedman brings out, however, is the active
role of workers. Whereas Braverman tends to assume the omnipotent power of capitalists and managers to remake the labour process
with only the constraints of technology and organization, Freidman emphasizes the countervailing power of the workers. A
number of other authors (see in particular Stark, 1980, and Storey
1983, 1985a, 1985b) have argued that workers are able to develop
collective institutions that are capable of resisting the power of
management. Once this point is accepted, then the multiplicity of
forms of the labour process becomes more comprehensible. Instead
of a universal trend towards deskilling, it can be seen that the
labour process can take different forms depending on the powers
which management and workers can mobilize.

Littler (1982), in particular, has made a major contribution to this
discussion. He argues that it is necessary to recognize that there are
many different sorts of management control systems. By this
concept, Littler seeks to expand the analysis somewhat by including as well as the labour process itself the conditions of work which
surround the labour process – in particular, the wages system and
the stability of employment. Littler argues that there are a number
of ways in which different payment and employment systems can
be combined with the labour process. These combinations cannot
be conceptualized simply in terms of a process of deskilling. Littler

distinguishes three main control systems on the basis of his research into nineteenth-century Britain and the USA.

1. *Direct employment and control.* This strategy was pursued in industries where employees were employed for a fixed wage. The work was often menial and routine, with many people (usually men) doing a similar job, e.g. brewing, distilling, sugar refining (and in state employment, the police and the post office). In these industries there was little deskilling, according to Littler, since skill was already low.

2. *Indirect employment and control.* By these Littler refers to those many nineteenth-century industries where forms of piecework were predominant. Frequently employers created a group of internal contractors. Sometimes, as in textiles and metal working, these were highly skilled male craftsmen who took on these jobs. In other industries such as the docks and forms of agricultural work, gang leaders would arise as a result of more complex processes of social interaction. Effectively both groups performed part of the function of management, particularly in terms of controlling the everyday tasks of the workforce. In this sector, deskilling in the period 1890–1920 was in the UK a twinfold attack; for employers the indirect contractor constituted an obstacle to direct control of the labour process; to the unskilled worker, he was increasingly seen as an exploiter.

3. *External contract.* By this Littler refers in particular to what were known in the nineteenth and early twentieth centuries as the sweated trades, such as clothing. These industries frequently worked to tight contractual specifications for larger retailers. Sweated conditions, involving long hours, poor conditions and low wages, derived from high competition within these sectors. Work was based on low levels of training, utilizing existing specialist skill in areas like sewing and stitching which were learnt by women in the performance of their domestic role. Women were employed directly by the employers with some possibilities of bonuses, but these only made a difference to earnings at the margins. Employment was likely to be unstable and dependent upon the manufacturer continuing to get contracts through low prices.

Littler argues that the period which Braverman identifies as central to the establishment of scientific management and the whole deskilling movement was in fact characterized by a much more complex set of changes. In particular, the period from 1890 to 1920 resulted in the gradual emergence of tighter systems of management control, based partially on the increased bureaucratization of the employment system and partially on the gradual displacement of the internal contractor. These changes were not the same as deskilling. Many of the old skills remained of importance; others grew up in new emerging industries. What was different about skilled work after this period was that it was in the main removed from its position of control over other workers. This tendency in turn was also significantly affected by the revolt of semi-skilled workers against their subordination by the skilled workers.

From Littler's argument it is possible to develop some general points regarding the development of the labour process. First, there are a number of possible strategies that management can pursue when it comes to organizing the labour process. This is not the same as stating that each strategy is equally effective; clearly this is not the case, and we therefore need to analyse in more detail the relationship between strategy and context. Just as importantly, however, management strategies may develop not out of rational planning but out of a series of pragmatic adaptations to immediate problems in which power relations within the workforce (e.g. between skilled and unskilled, leader and gang workers, men and women) and between workers and managers, are key issues.

These power relations are crucially embedded in the market in two senses. First, in the Marxist sense, workers in capitalist societies have been stripped of all means of survival other than the sale of their labour power. As Marx (1970) argues, this process of the formation of a landless proletariat is not explicable as a phenomenon brought about by the labour market; rather the rise of a labour market needs to be explained by the use of political action to separate the labourer from the means of subsistence, as occurred in Britain over a long period. This in turn places the labourer in a distinctively powerless situation. Whereas the capitalist and the agents of capital can survive for an indeterminate length of time, using their capital for subsistence if need be, the labourer has no access to any substitute means of survival. He/she is dependent on the employer for work, a wage and subsistence. Although Marx's basic model has been modified by the development of welfare systems, the basic asymmetry of power relations still remains. The labour market is therefore not a sphere of equal exchange between the buyer and seller of labour, but the sphere in which existing inequalities between labour and capital are reproduced. As Marx also foresaw, however, workers can gain a degree of power by collective organization and collective action. Through joining together formally and/or informally they increase their power. It becomes more difficult for a capitalist to ignore a strike than the absence of one worker.

Second, these power relations are embedded in the market in the Weberian sense that the qualities of different commodities, whether they are shoes or labour power, command different prices according to their value. The exact value of commodities varies according to a number of factors. In particular groups will seek to exercise power over the market by distorting supply and demand. Thus there is rarely class struggle in any pure sense, i.e. struggles between classes. Frequently struggles have implications not only for power relations between classes but also within classes; thus occupational groups within classes construct 'shelters from the labour market which protect themselves but restrict others' (see Freedman, 1976, for the concept of 'shelter'). Workers may, for example, seek to limit the amount of particular skills that are available by controlling apprenticeship routes. Employers may try to increase the pool of labour they can use by reducing the scarce skills necessary for production by introducing deskilling technology. Power over the market, however, is not an abstract phenomenon; it also implies power over others – the power of the skilled over the unskilled, the employer over the employee (see Parkin, 1979, for a theoretical discussion of this.) Two aspects of market relations in particular require more detailed consideration for their direct impact on the labour process – product markets and labour markets.

Product markets

The nature of the product market has a crucial impact on management strategy. Product markets put constraints on cost and quality in the labour process. If an organization is competing mainly on cost, then in management terms a number of imperatives arise. These include most obviously the need to keep wages down, the need to maximize use of technology and plant, the need to minimize waste of materials. Whilst no management can afford to be oblivious to quality, cost imperatives place the emphasis of management control on the control of costs. If an organization is competing mainly on the basis of quality, a number of other imperatives arise; these relate obviously to an adequate quality control system, but they also relate to the orientations and skills of the workforce. Management need to ensure that workers are self-monitoring when it comes to quality control; workers are committed to the quality of the output and using both their formal and their tacit skills to maximize quality. Different types of product market conditions – tight versus loose, specialist/quality product versus generalist/mass product – imply potentially different management approaches to the labour process, and they also imply different power relations both for workers as a whole and for particular occupational groups, depending on the way their skills are affected by product market changes.

There are a number of caveats to this. First, management may not be clear about their product market strategy. Second, even if they have a clear view, they may not be able to operationalize it because of organizational inertia derived from heavy investment (both material and psychological) in different past practices. These different practices become institutionalized in both management–labour relations in the labour process and in the technology of the labour process which embodies expectations about management–labour relations. Third, they may not succeed because other firms out-compete them in some way, causing them either to rethink and change their strategy or simply to become a business failure. Fourth, the concepts of failure and success in business terms imply a precision that is in fact illusory. Whilst these themes will be explored in much more detail at a later point, the key issue is that product market processes, issues of cost and profit all need to be interpreted by management, or more likely specific professional groups within management. This process of interpretation is subject to all manner of intra-organizational negotiations and manipulation. Thus, an organization's level of profitability should not be treated as an unambiguous sign of success or failure. For all of these reasons, then, we should not fall into the trap of arguing that product market conditions determine labour process strategy, as the way in which management interprets and adapts to product market changes can reduce the power and influence of particular groups as well as increase the power of others (see, for example, Elbaum and Wilkinson, 1979, and Zeitlin, 1979, for detailed examples of this.)

Labour markets

The nature of labour markets is a crucial feature of management strategy. An initial distinction can be made between tight and loose labour markets. In a tight labour market situation, there will be a high level of competition between employers to attain the sort of labour they require. In a loose labour market situation, there are more people looking for jobs than there are jobs being offered. This basic distinction leads to a further elementary point. Where there is a high level of competition between employers for workers, then workers have a higher degree of choice about where they work and at what wages. Therefore, in general terms, tight labour market situations favour workers. They allow them the opportunity to bargain for higher wages, improve employment conditions and control over the job, and to move around the labour market. Similarly, in general terms, loose labour market conditions favour employers. High levels of unemployment allow them to keep wage rises to a minimum and tighten up on management control in the workplace. These general comments, however, are modified in their actual operation by the following features: the relationship between technology and the demand for labour; the impact of institutionalized relations between employers and workers (i.e. trade union negotiations and the operation of internal labour markets); and the relationship between different types and forms of labour. I will deal with each of these in turn.

The relationship between technology and the demand for labour

Employers only take on workers for specific purposes; if those purposes can be achieved at a lesser cost by the introduction of machinery, then one can expect employers' demand for labour to decline. Thus what was once a tight labour market can become a loose one, not because there is now more labour of a particular sort available, but because there is no longer demand for so much labour. When management come to plan their labour market strategy, they have to think in terms of the relative costs and benefits of employing labour as opposed to machinery to do particular tasks. There is not an unequivocal logic to the replacement of labour by machines. An example might help illustrate the point. In the 1950s the wool textile industry in Britain was faced with an expanding market at home and abroad, joined with growing international competition. The response of the industry was to modernize to a limited extent with the introduction of some new machinery. However, the new technology did not match the highest standards that were available and that were being introduced elsewhere. Instead, the industry concentrated on increasing output at cheap levels of cost by maximizing the running times of its new and old machinery. It did this by employing the cheapest labour that it could find on 24-hour working. During the day, this meant employing women workers, sometimes on short shifts at evening times and at weekend, as well as normal shifts during the day. At night, it meant making use of cheap immigrant labour (see Cohen and Jenner, 1968; Allen *et al.*, 1977; Fevre, 1984; Morgan and Hooper, 1982). during this period, then, the wool textile industry managed to survive; profit levels were high for employers as demand ran ahead of supply. There was no immediate overriding logic in seeking large-scale capital investment for the time being.

Nor is it the case that technology is always available which will allow this replacement to take place. Technology has to be developed, which raises two issues. First, there is considerable evidence that technological development occurs in waves, which limits the potential for certain innovations at particular points in the wave (see Coombs *et al.*, 1987). Second, technology is subject to processes of social construction. Science and technology is controlled by certain interests which push it into certain forms of development (see Noble, 1977, 1984; Mackenzie and Wajcman, 1985 – especially the article by Schwarz). Thus the form of technology which develops cannot be said to have a separate effect on organizations, since it is itself a product of organizations and social interests.

Child (1984b) has identified four main strategies available to managers, deriving in particular from the latest wave of technological development associated with information technology;

1. *The elimination of direct labour.* There are two routes to this. The

first route is via process industries. Here computer controls linked to microelectronic sensors and intelligent data-gathering instruments enable control to be totally centralized. Monitoring the process occurs automatically. When certain values that are being monitored move outside the approved range, then either the system itself takes remedial action to restore equilibrium or, in emergencies, humans are called in to solve the problem. For most of the time, human agents are confined to the job of monitoring. The second route is via flexible manufacturing systems (FMS). These are computer-programmed and controlled integrated production systems which bring to non-process production many of the characteristics of continuous flow production. Probably the best known FMS are those recently installed in many of the major car plants of the world such as British Leyland, where robotic technology has cut out direct labour in certain areas of the plant such as paint shops and welding. As one car company recently put it in its advertising campaign, 'Hand made – by robots'.

2. *Contracting.* This refers to an arrangement whereby the employer pays for an agreed delimited amount of production or period of labour time, but leaves the organization, manning and sometimes the equipping of the task to the worker or group of workers concerned: for example, where staff work at home connected to the office through a telephone line which enables them to communicate with other computers and colleagues. New technology also has the potential to contribute to the new international division of labour. Satellite communications mean that offices and factories around the world can come together almost instantaneously; it becomes possible to monitor production on a much wider scale than could previously have been considered. This, together with falling transport costs, leads to the development of the global factory where firms locate parts of the design, production and assembly of their products to those parts of the world where the quality, quantity and cost of labour and raw materials is most advantageous (Frobel *et al.*, 1980).

3. *Polyvalence.* This denotes a situation in which workers perform or at least are available to perform a range of tasks which cut across or extend traditional skill boundaries. Such possibilities have opened up in a number of areas consequent upon the introduction of new technology. One example is the printing industry, where the technology is now available to take a story straight from the

computer terminal and run it on to the page of a newspaper without the intermediary of a compositor. Thus the worker who is left after the traditional demarcations of journalist, sub-editor and compositor are done away with, will potentially have a much wider area of skill. At the moment, the groups concerned are, of course, still trying to preserve their own specialized niche because of the fear of job loss, but the potential for an increase in skill is there. In manufacturing industry, polyvalence has been tried as a way of overcoming traditional craft demarcations.

4. *Degradation of jobs.* Finally, Child notes that new technology can undoubtedly bring with it deskilling and the reduction in areas of discretion and autonomy on the part of workers.

The relationship between technology, the labour process and labour markets is therefore complex. It is clear that we cannot discern a clear tendency towards deskilling but rather one in which technological influences, themselves constructed and reproduced in particular social settings, empower management and workers in different ways. (For detailed case studies and a theoretical account see Penn and Scattergood, 1985, 1988; Penn, 1985; Penn and Simpson, 1986)

Institutionalized relationships between employers and workers

It is necessary to note that the limitations to managerial action are wider than simply worker resistance and technology. Power relations between managers and workers take on an institutionalized form; that is, certain patterns of action are established which people regard as normal. The stability of these patterns of action varies, depending on many aspects of the internal and external environment. Thus patterns of industrial relations in parts of UK industry in the 1960s, based on strong shop steward representation, which grew out of the increased power of the workforce in an era of full employment and was supported by a benevolent welfare state and an expanding product market, have been fundamentally disrupted by the political economic and social changes of the period since the mid 1970s. These institutionalized patterns constitute the subject matter of industrial relations, which is beyond the remit of this book. Nevertheless there is one key area related to the operation of internal labour markets which needs discussion. The concept of an internal labour market refers to the process whereby vacancies within the organization are filled from within the organization rather than from the external labour market. Clearly an organization cannot be completely self-contained, and therefore must recruit from outside. The extent of this outside recruitment reflects crucial features of the institutionalized expectations of managers and workers. A number of authors (see especially Osterman, 1983, 1984, 1987; Beardsworth *et al.*, 1983; Garnsey *et al.*, 1985; Jenkins *et al.*, 1983; Ford *et al.*, 1983) have examined this issue. They have pointed out that it is necessary to distinguish between various levels in the organizational hierarchy, each of which may or may not operate as an internal labour market. Starting from the manual occupations, it is characteristic of large companies to operate internal labour markets. Thus workers enter at the bottom of the manual hierarchy; as they gain seniority and experience, they find their work conditions and wages gradually improving. At this level, the internal labour market is also crucial in terms of the allocation of redundancies, with those last into the organization likely to be the first out. At the top of the manual hierarchy are skilled craftsmen; this group are less likely to be locked into the internal labour market. They, unlike other members of the manual occupations, have transferable skills which other employers are willing to purchase. Therefore, these occupations are frequently still filled from the external labour market.

In the sphere of non-manual employment, it is similarly possible to distinguish a number of groups. First, there are routine administrative and clerical workers. In general terms this constitutes a port-of-entry position; unlike manual work, there is unlikely to be much of a premium for seniority or experience. This category, as a number of authors have pointed out (Stewart *et al.*, 1980; Crompton and Jones, 1984) is best seen as a position through which different types of workers pass. There are occasionally long-serving male manual workers who, nearing the end of their working life, are transferred to the office; there are management trainees (usually male) who are 'experiencing' this aspect of the organization's work, *en route* to 'higher things'; and finally there are mainly female workers who are fixed into this segment of the organization with few promotion prospects. These in turn can either be young women whom management expect eventually to leave to 'start a family', or older women who have returned to work after a break or a series of such breaks and are seen as not wanting a 'real career'. Thus any internal labour market that operates here is likely to be of very restricted scope, with rewards for experience and seniority being less than for male manual workers in the internal labour market.

Above this group in the white-collar hierarchy are the professionals employed by the organization in various capacities – engineers, scientists, accountants, lawyers, etc. Each of these groups is simultaneously linked to the internal and external labour markets. As the possessor of a professional qualification, the person in this category will be able to sell his/her labour elsewhere than in their employing organization. On the other hand, depending on the size and structure of the organization, there may be greater rewards available from staying within the organization. This may depend upon reducing professional identification by moving more clearly into a management position. This leads on to the final group, managers.

Managers in large organizations are frequently in an internal labour market situation. They are initially employed as trainees within the organization and gain work experience and seniority through working in a number of different parts of the organization. The internal labour market for managers is likely to be the most extended of the internal labour markets operating in the organization in the sense that the gap between the top of the internal labour market, i.e. for the chief executive, and the lower levels of the managerial hierarchy will be much greater than between the top and bottom of the manual internal labour, although at the very top of the organization there may be occasional inputs of 'new blood'. It is characteristic of most large organizations to maintain stability in their managerial workforce through providing opportunities for promotion and reward in internal labour markets.

The structure of internal labour markets is clearly even more complex than this initial model admits. The organization consists of many different career/internal labour market lines of promotion and advance. Being on a line in one part of the organization at manual level does not necessarily mean that one can transfer to the same position on another line in a different part of the organization. This relates in turn to the amount of rational planning that goes into internal labour markets as opposed to the extent to which the key feature of their emergence is a process of unplanned pragmatic compromise between workers and managers. Certain authors, particularly in the USA (see Edwards *et al.*, 1975; Edwards, 1979; and, for a particular empirical example, the article by Stone, 1975) have argued that internal labour markets have developed as a clear response by managers to the need to divide the workforce and introduce 'artificial' distinctions between workers. In this argument, the internal labour market is not technically necessary; since work is becoming increasingly homogenized (an argument which these authors take rather uncritically from Braverman), it follows that, with some initial training, workers in the manual and routine clerical labour markets are perfectly capable of doing all tasks. This, however, potentially leads towards workforce solidarity and might threaten management control. As a result, according to Edwards *et al.*, management introduce promotion ladders to disguise from workers the extent to which they share interests. This argument that internal labour markets derive from a divide-and-rule strategy on the part of management is clearly oversimplified. Not only does it vastly overestimate the coherence and unity of management, but it also fails to take account of the interest in internal labour markets which workers possess.

Nevertheless, it can be argued that the internal labour market is a key way in which employers generate consent to their authority. Workers have an interest in stable employment and wages which is met by the operation of the internal labour market. Thus, as Rubery (1978) has pointed out in the USA, trade unions have been instrumental in pressing for the strict operation of internal labour markets as ways to protect and improve their members' jobs. This point can be made even more strongly by considering how workers seek to control recruitment to port-of-entry jobs. A number of authors (Doeringer *et al.*, 1986; Manwaring, 1984; Grieco, 1987; Dick and Morgan, 1987) have shown that it is not uncommon for workers to aid in the recruitment process through recommending and placing friends and relations in port-of-entry jobs. From the management point of view this gives them ready access to a pool of labour sharing the same characteristics and background as the labour they are already employing. Friends and relatives can help socialize newcomers into the expectations of the firm as well as directly train them on the job. They can also help discipline and control them. Thus the extended internal labour market, as Manwaring (1984) calls it, embodies a set of expectations on the part of workers and managers about how the organization should operate. There is disagreement on the overall significance of internal labour markets in economies such Britain and the USA. For example, in their more recent work Edwards *et al.* have continued to argue that internal labour markets are primarily characteristic of large-scale monopolistic employers, which are able to buy indust-rial peace in this way. Thus there remain many smaller organiza-tions which in their view are unable to afford the operation of extended career ladders. This distinction between the monopolistic sector with internal labour markets and the competitive sector with reliance on the purchase of labour from the external labour market, is the basis of their dualistic view of the economy. However, as has been pointed out, the relationship between internal and external labour markets is far more complex than they allow. Particular organizations may draw on the internal labour market in relation to certain occupations and the external labour market for others. The overall balance of an organization's approach to labour market issues cannot be said to be determined in advance by their location in a particular sector. Indeed, the notion of sectors, particularly as developed by theorists in the dual labour market tradition, is open to severe criticism. It is far more sensible to conceive of manage-ment's strategy towards the labour market as determined in a multitude of ways, and not just by one single factor. In order to examine this further, it is necessary to consider in more detail the relationship between different types of labour.

The relationship between different types and forms of labour

There is a frequent assumption that all employment is full-time work and has an obvious spatial location. In this section I will argue that this view is inadequate and outdated. Most importantly, although there have been strong institutional constraints (sup-ported in particular by male trade unionists) for labour to be sold in blocks of 8–10 hours with variations to be *above* the norm (i.e. overtime) rather than below it (i.e. part-time), there has neverthe-less always been a significant amount of part-time work available. This particularly relates to women's position in the labour market – an issue which will be taken up in more detail later. Part-time work has existed in a number of industries which have drawn on women's labour, e.g. textiles, electricals and clothing, and more latterly secretarial, retail and service working. Over the past ten years in Britain, there has been a rapid expansion in forms of part-time working. Management have been effectively redistributing certain full-time jobs into part-time tasks which can be filled at a lower rate of pay. Furthermore, new jobs that have been created have frequently been created because there was a pool of part-time female labour available.

Other changes in the labour market that have arisen recently need to be noted. One is the increase in the number of temporary employees in organizations who are taken on to do specifically short-term jobs and given minimum employment rights. Another is the number of organizations setting up to do work that previously an organization might have done itself, for example cleaning and catering. Once again, the specialist organization will make maximum use of part-time workers with minimum employment rights. Another sphere of change is in the use of homeworkers. Although it is very difficult to estimate the exact number of people (mainly women) who fall into this category (see Allen and Wolkowitz, 1987; Hakim, 1987b), it is possible to discern two main groupings. On the one hand, and by far the most common, are those women employed to do very menial and poorly paid jobs in their own house. The employer avoids a variety of costs such as heating and accommodation and also avoids the possible problem of workers combining to appeal for better conditions. Frequently, these tasks embody a minimum of technology and skill; they simply require time (in itself a precious commodity for women with small children, as most of this category of homeworkers are). The second category are a group on whom an inordinate amount of attention and misplaced glamour has been heaped. These are homeworkers who are linked to their place of employment through the latest information technology. In this homeworking situation, the work itself is done on a computer and then transferred to the organization's mainframe computer down the telephone line. This opens up the possibility for many tasks which at the moment are carried out in offices to be done at home; these range from simple clerical tasks such as the production of documents and accounts through to computer programming and design. Here again, the employer gains the advantage of lower accommodation costs and of lower chances of worker combination. Whilst, from the point of view of the employee, there is a certain flexibility of hours, he or she is nevertheless being asked to carry certain overhead costs such as office space in their own home. There is evidence to suggest that people working in this situation (again mostly women) are unlikely to gain much job satisfaction, will miss interacting with other people, and will not receive particularly good wages (Huws, 1982).

Summarizing the above discussion on the operation of the labour market, the argument is that it is necessary to see management's response to the need for labour as being based, first, upon the relationship between technology, the labour process and the availability of different types of labour; second, upon the relationship between expectations about the proper way to conduct labour relations (in particular the appropriate role for internal labour markets) and the surrounding economic environment; and third, upon the possibilities of different types and forms of labour that are available. It is worth bringing these together in order to consider the argument regarding changes in Britain over the last ten years. There is a strong argument, first articulated by Atkinson (1984, 1987), that the labour market in Britain is disaggregating and becoming more complex, and at the same time more flexible (though recent work by Pahl, 1984, indicates that the labour market has always been more complex than the traditional male worker stereotype suggests).

Atkinson argues that it is possible to distinguish a number of different groups in the labour force. At its core are the central workers who are employed in full–time, skilled jobs (in professional, managerial, technical, scientific and craft jobs). Firms try hard to retain these workers, offering them as much of the benefits of an internal labour market as they can afford. On the semi–periphery of this group are other workers who are still employed on a full–time basis by the firm, but whose labour is subject to replacement by machinery or new forms of organization. This group are vulnerable to changing product and labour markets in the long term but are safe in the short term. Outside this group are the truly peripheral workers, who can expect little more than occasional bouts of unemployment interspersed with work on temporary or part-time contracts at relatively low wages, with little guarantee of job rights. These groups give the firm flexibility in three senses. It has numerical flexibility in that it is able to rid itself of temporary and part-time workers at times of economic downturn; it can also pick them up again if necessary. It has financial flexibility, partly arising through its ability to lay off workers at short notice but also through its ability to manipulate payments in the internal labour market. Finally, it has functional flexibility since all the workers are expected to move around within the firm if and when required.

Once again, it is necessary to note that there is disagreement about the extent to which this model has become dominant in Britain and the USA. It denotes a degree of management rationality both in the planning and implementation process that I have already treated with scepticism. I shall elaborate on the reasons for this in Chapter 2. It also implies an ability to remake institutional arrangements in a way that potentially overestimates the power of management. Certainly, there have been some well-publicized examples of management 'taking on' unions in the USA and the UK to achieve these forms of flexibility, e.g. British Leyland under Michael Edwardes (see Willmann and Winch, 1985; Edwardes, 1984) and British Coal during the miners' strike of 1984–5. Other authors – in particular Batstone (1984) – have suggested that underneath such dramatic confrontations, institutionalized relationships have remained relatively untouched, at least partly because of the fear that the worm may eventually turn and labour may regain if not the upper hand, then at least a balanced position.

These debates have far-reaching implications with the emergence of 'left'- and 'right'-wing versions of the flexibility thesis. On the right wing, there are many politically influential advocates of the need for flexibility. One of the most memorable phrases of the early 1980s is Cabinet Minister Norman Tebbit's exhortation to the unemployed to 'Get on your bike!', the notion being that, even with four million unemployed jobs were available if people were prepared to look for them and be flexible in the type of job they required. More recently, however, a left-wing version of the flexibility thesis has emerged which argues that the need for flexibility is reducing the power of large monolithic mass production companies to dominate the market. Instead it is opening up the possibility for smaller businesses, which in turn can take a variety of forms. In particular, the authors look to parts of Italy where such small businesses, rather than being models of capitalist exploitation, are models of co-operation between highly skilled workers in co-operatives supported by a beneficient local state which provides ncessary infrastructure and access to capital (see Piore and Sabel, 1984, for an extended analysis aong thse lines; also Piore 1986a, 1986b). In this view, flexibility offers the potential for developing an alternative to capitalist organization. Such optimism over-stretches the empirical evidence (for a critical account of the Italian experience see Murray, 1987; for a measured review of evidence in Britain see Hakim, 1987b; there is a more journalistic account in Leadbetter and Lloyd, 1987, as well as relevant articles in Allen *et al.*, 1986, and Purcell *et al.*, 1986); it also underestimates the theoretical problems (see in particular Pollert, 1988a; 1988b).

Labour market issues cannot, however, be reduced simply to questions of supply and demand. The nature of the labour involved is particularly important. This issue can be examined in relation to the different positions in the labour market occupied by gender, ethnic and age groups. In these examples, we can see how forces external to the organizational interact with those internal to it to reproduce existing patterns of disadvantage.

Gender differentiation in the workplace

It is now usual to distinguish two aspects of the sexual division of labour in occupations. The first is traditionally referred to as the horizontal division of labour between the sexes; the second is the vertical division of labour.

The horizontal division of labour refers to the fact that men and women are to a significant degree in different occupations. Thus, in the British context, women are concentrated in a small number of occupations. They work predominantly in the following occupa-tions: clerical and secretarial; retail; distribution; catering and cleaning; semi-skilled and unskilled occupations in certain types of manufacturing industry (in particular, textiles and light electrical engineering); and service/caring occupations in health, education and social welfare (for details see Hakim, 1979; Martin and Roberts, 1984). Compared to male workers, women are limited in the number of occupations in which they work; there are a large number of occupations and industries where women do not appear at all, for example mining, shipbuilding, and other heavy industry occupations (women do, of course, appear as clerical workers, cleaners, etc. in these industries, but not as direct production workers). There are few occupations, on the other hand, that men do not work in.

The vertical division of labour refers to the way in which, within occupations in which both men and women work, it is likely to be men who move to the top of the ladder. Thus in an occupation like school teaching, although women constitute a high proportion of the population (though this differs depending upon which age group is being considered), the senior positions such as headteacher are more likely to be taken by men than women.

The concepts of horizontal and vertical division of labour are basically macro-sociological terms. They derive from aggregating the multitude of statistics collected on occupational distribution in censuses of employment. They therefore almost invariably under-estimate the degree to which there is gender segregation within a particular organization. There is a great deal of evidence from particular studies (for example Pollert, 1981; Cockburn 1983, 1985; Beechey and Perkins, 1987; Walby, 1986) that there are very few sites where men and women are working side by side. Beechey and Perkins give an interesting example in their discussion of the baking industry. The baking industry is part of the 'food, drink and tobacco industry' in the census of employment; this category has one of the highest proportions of women workers of all industrial groupings. However, when Beechey and Perkins looked at what was actually happening within the industry, they found clear occupational differentiation:

> Bread production is almost totally dominated by men . . . In the plant bakery bread production was 100 per cent male. . . . It was strictly demarcated from confectionery production, which was female. (Beechey and Perkins, 1987, p. 62)

Even in organizations in industries such as telecommunications and textiles, where women were employed in semi-skilled and unskilled occupations, it was invariably in tasks that men were not doing. Thus the amount of job segregation within organizations is frequently underestimated by aggregated statistics such as those from the census of production.

It is also crucial to note the importance of part-time work in women's employment patterns. According to Martin and Roberts, around 40 per cent of women in employment are working part-time, i.e. less than 20 hours per week. Ninety per cent of part-timers in Britain are women, the rest being young men entering the labour market and old men just on the point of leaving the labour market. Part-time work within organizations is almost invariably done by women.

The sexual division of labour

Research has shown that women's position in the labour market is crucially affected by their predominant role in the maintenance of the family and in particular in the upbringing of children. Throughout the period of industrialization most women have been employed full-time. Only during the height of the bourgeois family ideal in the nineteenth century were some women from the middle and upper classes unlikely to have any such experience. By the late nineteenth century with certain professional, clerical and shopkeeping tasks opening up for such women, it became common for most women from all classes to experience paid employment. For example, in textiles, where women were employed on a variety of tasks throughout the nineteenth and twentieth century, it was common for them to return to work after marriage and between children. In the years following the Second World War in Britain, women's employment pattern across the country as a whole moved closer to the pattern that had operated in textiles. Thus instead of leaving employment on marriage, there has been an increased tendency to stay on in full-time employment until the birth of the first child. (This tendency, of course, is related to the gradual disappearance of the so-called 'marriage bar' which many employers in the professional and clerical areas operated (see Walby, 1986) and which meant that women were expected to leave their jobs once they were married.) In the immediate post-war years, women's employment developed into what was called a bimodal pattern. After the family was completed and the children had reached a certain age where they could look after themselves or be looked after by others (usually between school entrance age and about 10), women would begin to re-enter the labour market. Very often, they re-entered in part-time work which allowed them to minimize disruption to their domestic arrangements. Sometimes this work would be a part-time version of the work they were doing previously, though frequently it would involve an effective deskilling, as women took jobs in a completely different sector of the labour market.

Martin and Roberts (1984) have shown that recently there have been a number of changes to this pattern. First, the pattern is no longer bimodal; instead women are tending to return to the labour market sooner after the birth of children and also between the births of children, rather than waiting for the end of the family. Thus the pattern has become more complicated. Second, partly as a result of changes in legal provisions regarding maternity leave and partly as a result of the increased presence of women in professional work (mainly teaching, social work and the health service), where salaries make the employment of childminders a possibility, there are more women returning to their old jobs without a break in their employment status (see the articles in Allatt *et al.*, 1988). It is worth noting here the point made by Crompton and Sanderson (1986) that the women in these professions are also likely to return to employment following childbirth with either a part-time or a temporary contract. Thus professionalization of women does not in itself ensure a smooth return to full-time permanent employment.

The break in women's employment that arises from childbirth is highly significant for their future prospects. It encourages employers to believe that it is not worth investing in the training and promotion of women because they will not be permanent members of the workforce, in spite of the fact that there is no evidence that women are more unstable workers than men. In fact there is reason to believe that men are more likely to switch employers than women, since they are more highly 'career conscious' and therefore from the employer's point of view are a less worthwhile 'investment'. However, this is a much more individual phenomenon than the expected break in women's employment, and therefore seems to lack the same saliency for employers. These beliefs also encourage management to maintain or develop jobs that lack skill or interest in the expectation that women will be prepared to do them because they are only working 'temporarily'.

In professional and white-collar jobs where training opportunities are offered, for example in banking, insurance and financial services and in professions such as teaching and social work etc., women have up until recently worked at the lower levels of the hierarchy and watched men who entered at the same time as them progress rapidly into management. The break in employment from childbirth takes women in these professions out of the labour market at a crucial time. Men of a similar age are able to progress to a significant degree because possible women competitors have temporarily withdrawn. (For discussions of this see Crompton, 1987; Crompton and Jones, 1984; Crompton and Sanderson, 1986; and the articles on particular professions in Spencer and Podmore, 1987). By the time such women return, they have in organizational terms missed the boat for making the sort of management career which would take them to the top. Although there are now more women reducing the break due to childbirth to a minimum, this remains a significant barrier and still forces many women to choose between a family and a career.

The conditions under which this choice is made need to be spelled out. First, it is necessary to acknowledge the powerful influence of educational and socialization agencies in impressing on women (and on men) that a 'woman's place is in the home'. Whilst there are contradictions in many of the images now presented about the nature of femininity, the domestic image remains of central importance, and is something that girls and women cannot avoid. It is a pressure that is mediated through friendship and kinship networks, pushing women into following conventional models. Second, and equally important, the conventional domestic image is powerfully reinforced by the state. Although Britain now has maternity leave, its provisions are the worst of any country in the European Community. Moreover, there are no provisions for paternity leave to allow men instead of women the opportunity to look after newly born children. The expectation embodied in the legislation is that it is women in the first instance who should look after the child. Furthermore, the state provides a very low level of assistance for pre-school children:

> In 1984, there were only 168,327 day care places . . . in England, catering for just 5.3% of the population aged four or less. This is among the lowest provision in the European Community. France, for instance, has far higher provision . . . Childcare in Britain is seen as an essentially 'private' matter, of concern to the state only when children are thought to be 'at risk'. (Beechey and Perkins, 1987, p. 165)

This is further reinforced by the way in which until recently the state in the UK has treated the unemployment of married women (see Walby, 1983).

Third, the choice is significantly affected by the relative levels of pay of men and women. Few women manual workers are likely to be earning as much as their male counterparts. This is because although there is equal pay legislation which has now been extended to provide for equal pay in cases where it can be proven that the work is of equal value (and not just, as in the initial legislation, where it can be shown that men and women are doing the same job), the reality of most workplaces is that there is clear segregation between men's and women's jobs. Thus the tasks of comparison are always highly complex, and women are almost inevitably placed in the lowest skill grades. This reflects partly an ideological process whereby if women are doing a job it is deemed less skilled (see Cockburn, 1985), and partly the reality of workplaces where women are given less training opportunities and more boring, tedious jobs. As a result, women manual workers continue to receive less pay than their male counterparts (a process further exacerbated by the tendency of male manual workers to get much more overtime than women). In office and shop work, women face a similar situation; they will be in routine clerical, secretarial or typing work with very few prospects of advancement and wages generally less than men, who are likely to be placed in trainee management roles either at the start of their employment or much earlier than women. In professional work there is less likely to be segregation, but men's career advancement is likely to be quicker and higher, and therefore salary differentials between men and women will soon open up. All these circumstances mean that couples having children are more likely to reach the decision that the woman should give up work at least temporarily in order to care for the child.

It would be wrong to assume, however, that women's employment position within organizations can be understood totally from the point of view of the sexual division of labour. It is also necessary to consider the operations of the workplace itself. This necessitates considering in particular men workers and the role of management.

The role of men in the workplace

With regard to men workers, there is considerable evidence that they have sought to keep women out of particular jobs and occupations. This has occurred in a number of ways. First, there are formal process of exclusion operated by male trade unionists and work groups. Although these are illegal under present circumstances, they operated in significant areas throughout the nineteenth and early twentieth centuries, and as a result created all-male occupations with distinctively male expectations and cultures which are now very difficult for women to enter. Second, exclusion has occurred through the use of state legislation. The area of 'protective legislation' and its impact on women is highly controversial (see Humphries, 1977, for one interpretation of this). Whereas male trade unionists almost all supported this restrictive legislation, since it both improved their labour market position by reducing competition from cheap female labour and provided them with a servant in their own home, there is little evidence that women themselves were as enthusiastic. Certainly, later in the century when other trades argued for the introduction of similar restrictions in their occupations, feminists were vociferous in their rejection of such proposals (Walby, 1986, p. 139). Nevertheless, the second half of the nineteenth century in particular saw increasing numbers of occupations in the new industries effectively reserved for men. As these occupations stabilized, so did particular forms of workplace culture.

A number of themes are relevant here. Cockburn, for example, has explored the links between masculinity and technology. Referring to the men engineers she interviewed, she says:

> In the main, these men identify themselves with technology and identify technology with masculinity. Technological jobs are often more than just a job to those who do them . . . Men appropriate the technological sphere for masculinity. They also make use of the masculinity of technology to form jobs with one another. They converse about work, technology and sport. (Cockburn, 1985, pp. 171, 175)

The idea that women could have such a close relationship with technology is regarded as laughable by the male engineers. Technology is primarily a male preserve, both in ideological terms and in actual material terms: Cockburn's case studies illustrate that the design, production and maintenance of technology is done by men; women's role is simply to operate it once men have installed it. Other aspects of work are also appropriated by men as part of a culture of masculinity; in particular, hard, dirty work is seen as expressing masculinity. In such a culture it has a positive evaluation, contrasted both with the manual work that women do and the work done by both men and women in offices (Willis, 1978). Also of crucial importance is the way that workplace male cultures are defined significantly through their relation to women as objects of sexuality. Cockburn says:

> the men also relate through competitive swearing and obscenity and a trade in sexual stories, references and innuendo that are directly objectifying and exploitative of women. It serves the purpose of forging solidarity between them. Some men told me frankly that, yes, a woman there, it does cramp your style and spoil the conviviality. The obscenity creates a boundary across which women will fear to step. (p. 176)

If women do step across the boundary, they may find themselves subjected to various forms of sexual harassment, ranging from the symbolically provocative (in the form of 'page 3' nudes), through verbal innuendo, to actual physical harassment (see Hearn and Parkin, 1987, for a detailed discussion of this).

In all these ways, then, men have excluded and continue to exclude women from many occupations. On the other side, men encourage women to take up occupations where they are not competing with men for jobs and where they are working in tasks which fit male images of what women should do. In particular, this means that women are pushed into jobs involving caring for and servicing people in ways which they do for the family in the home. Thus manual tasks such as cleaning, catering and serving in shops do not threaten the male preserve or masculine identity. Professional tasks such as nursing, teaching and social work also fit into this category, as do many secretarial tasks, where being the 'office wife' is a crucial skill (see Barker and Downing, 1985). Some tasks, such as clerical and administrative work, were originally male preserves and are now dominated by women. In these the process of change has involved a redefinition of their nature into 'women's work', which emphasizes particular aspects of the task, such as neatness, presentation of self and work, in such a way as to disassociate them from men and associate them with women. Central to these tasks is the notion of women serving men; thus secretarial and other tasks where men are serviced by women reproduce domestic relationships, even to the extent of the women concerned becoming 'sexual objects'. Office hierarchical relationships therefore have the potential for becoming, at least in a covert way, hierarchical sexual relationships (see Hearn and Parkin, 1987; but see also Burrell, 1984, and Quinn, 1977, for different views on this). The positioning of women in certain occupations and jobs is not simply a result of the sexual division of labour within the family; it is also powerfully constructed within the workplace itself.

The role of management

To fully understand this, it is necessary to consider the process from the point of view of the employers. In this regard, employers have two essential characteristics: they are almost always men, and they are looking to make a profit out of their labour. Whether or not these are complementary is debatable. As men, employers may have an interest in maintaining women in certain occupations, thus stabilizing their own position in the sexual division of labour within the family and maintaining their own idea of their masculinity. On the other hand, as employers, they may want to employ the cheapest labour, whether it is male or female. As Blackburn and Mann say of segmentation theory in general:

> It is not clear that it is in the interests of capitalists to preserve women or indeed any other group as a separate segment of the labour force. If women, blacks, adolescents or any other secondary groups were suddenly interchangeable with white adult males, might not the latter's average wages fall, just as the former's might rise? It is not at all clear that to retain segmentation keeps down the general level of wages and there is no evidence to show that employers believe this. (Blackburn and Mann, 1979, p. 31)

Walby expresses this theoretically as a conflict between patriarchy (the system through which men dominate women) and capitalism (where employers dominate workers). She argues that:

It is a common presumption that capital benefits from the subordination of women by men and that men utilize capitalist relations in the subordination of women ... This position underestimates the conflict between patriarchy and capital and presents an inaccurate picture of historical stasis. Rather, the relations between patriarchy and capital should be seen as historically and spatially variable and riddled with conflict. (Walby, 1986, p. 89; see also Barrett, 1980)

Thus the action of employers in maintaining women's subordination in the labour market needs to be carefully considered. To return to the controversial protective legislation example referred to earlier, employers were in the main opposed to the restriction on women's employment. The reason was quite simply that they saw that it would result in an improved bargaining position for the men and consequently a likely higher wage bill. As capitalists, they potentially faced a financial loss from the legislation, even though as men they might have gained in terms of restabilizing the sexual division of labour.

Recent research seems to indicate that for most of the time, employers act on the basis of male presumptions about suitable work for women. Beechey and Perkins (1987), for example, show how these two features are interrelated in the construction of part-time work. Part-time work, they argue, is not a given; it is not something that has to be there and for which employers have to find a labour force, which is fortunately available in the form of married women with children. On the contrary, 'Certain jobs (particularly manual ones) had been constructed as part-time jobs because they were seen to be women's jobs' (Beechey and Perkins, 1987, p. 145). This becomes apparent when one compares these jobs to men's jobs. It is frequently argued that part-time jobs are constructed in order to give employers flexibility. However, flexibility can be attained in other ways, such as overtime, but Beechey and Perkins found a gender-based definition of flexibility operating:

Employers use gender-differentiated ways of meeting a labour shortage or attaining flexibility. Where men are employed, jobs are invariably full-time, and flexibility is gained through overtime and short-time working, and sometimes through the employment of temporary workers. Where women are employed, on the other hand, flexibility is attained through the creation of part-time jobs. (p. 76)

Similarly, the actual construction of jobs is done with the gender characteristics of the labour force in mind. Cockburn's study of the impact of new technology on work in the clothing and mail-order industries shows how tasks were designed on the basis of there being a female workforce that would undertake them. For example, in the clothing industry, the employers had introduced new technology which would remove certain highly skilled tasks which had previously been a male preserve. Instead, the employers expected that they could utilize female labour:

> [An] advantage to the employer of women lies in the fact that, through the unpaid and unrecognized apprenticeship of a domesticated girlhood, a woman has acquired qualities which the employer can set to profitable work. She is an excellent seamstress, an accurate cutter, and has the diligence and niftiness that makes for a good keyboard or scope operator . . . More women stick at their jobs these days, but employers can sometimes reap an advantage from the fact that many women do leave before they climb up off trainee rates of pay, to be replaced by other cheap school-leavers. Employers can use women's particular characteristics without having to recognize women's special needs. (Cockburn, 1985, p. 71)

Similar examples can be drawn from many other industries and occupations (see, for example, Davies and Rosser, 1986). Jobs are designed in a certain way in the expectation that there will be women willing to fill them. Occasionally this does lead to conflict with men, such as in the clothing industry, where the restructuring of tailoring jobs consequent on the introduction of new technology was effectively deskilling male workers. As Cockburn says,

> If the interests of men as a sex, however, conflict with the interests of profitability, managers must act in the interests of capital. They may have to sacrifice a particular group of male workers. (p. 107)

Nevertheless, this process in which one group of male workers is 'sacrificed' is part of a wider process in which men's domination over women is maintained because the sort of jobs that are created are low-paid, with poor working conditions and few opportunities for training or promotion. Meanwhile, the men who remain are inevitably in either managerial/supervisory jobs or concerned with the design, production and maintenance of the new technology. To conclude this section it is necessary to agree with Cockburn's comment that 'occupations themselves have come to be gendered' (Cockburn, 1985, p. 169). The process whereby this has occurred is highly complex, involving family relations, male organization in the workplace and managerial decision-making, as well as the role of the state (see the articles in Crompton and Mann, 1986, for discussion of these wider theoretical issues). The effect, however, is clear. Within organizations there is a comprehensive process of job segregation. Sometimes this involves horizontal segregation, sometimes vertical segregation, sometimes the creation of part-time and temporary work ghettoes for women. In processes of managerial decision-making over work, the gendered composition of the labour force is a crucial, if often implicit, dimension.

Racism and the labour process

Similar processes can be seen at work in relation to black people, although the specifics of particular Western economies differ (see Castles *et al.*, 1984, on Europe; Piore, 1979, on recent migrants to the USA; on the UK experience see Rex and Tomlinson, 1979; Miles and Phizacklea, 1984; Phizacklea and Miles, 1980; on more general issues see Rex, 1983, 1986; Husband, 1982). In the expansionary phase of the world economy during the 1950s and 1960s, countries like Britain encouraged the entry of black workers to fill the labour market positions vacated by the upwardly mobile, white, male working class. Sometimes to avoid major capital investment, and sometimes to maximize its use (see Fevre, 1984, for a good discussion of this; also Morgan and Hooper, 1982), black workers were encouraged to migrate to European countries.

In Britain in the 1950s and early 1960s white racism based on the imperial legacy and the subordination of black people in former territories of the empire and elsewhere was reinforced and reproduced in a number of settings. Work, housing, politics and trade unionism, informal leisure patterns – all were informally structured on racist lines with black people disadvantaged and discriminated against (see Rex and Tomlinson, 1979; Brown, 1984). Official attitudes, particularly in so far as they were embodied in immigration laws (from 1963 onwards), and the actions of the police went together with press and television in labelling black people a 'problem'. These practices sat uneasily with other notions of democracy, citizenship and formal equality that were also supposedly embodied in British political life. Nevertheless, there was a harmony of interests between different white groups in British society that reproduced racism in spite of growing black resistance (for a general analysis see Centre for Contemporary Cultural Studies, 1982).

Managers used the subordinate position of black people to employ them in poor working conditions, whilst in many cases white trade unionists sat back. Indeed, in the late 1960s and early 1970s, a number of cases came to light where management and unions were hand in glove in denying black people proper training and decent working conditions (see Miles and Phizacklea, 1984 for a detailed account). Black people, together with a number of white supporters both within the labour movement and outside, struggled against these forms of discrimination by industrial action, work within the trade unions, and the development of black community and political organizations.

The recession of the late 1970s and 1980s hit black people particularly hard. Excluded from the better paid, more technologically advanced industries, they were dependent on employment in two main areas. Industries like textiles, foundry work and certain parts of engineering where many black men worked, were badly hit by rising interest rates and foreign competition. Many closed down completely; others reduced their workforce, laying off in particular the less skilled, in which category black people predominantly were. Their other main area of employment was public service, in jobs like cleaning and catering, where a significant number of black women worked (for a more detailed discussion of gender differentiation amongst black workers see Allen, 1980; Phizacklea, 1983). Here government cuts and processes of privatization have further reduced employment. Thus in spite of increased levels of struggle and awareness, symbolized in riots such as those in Toxteth, Brixton and the St Pauls district of Bristol, the situation has if anything deteriorated. From being the bottom layer in the labour market and labour process, many black people have either been excluded altogether, or, in the case of some of the younger ones, have excluded themselves from the labour market on the grounds of a rejection of white racist society.

As with women, it is necessary to note that the processes of exclusion occur through the interaction of extra-organizational phenomena (such as racism in schools and on the street leading, for certain groups, to low levels of educational attainment) and intra-organizational phenomena (such as the operation of racism in selection, recruitment and training). (See Lee and Loveridge, 1987, for a discussion of what they term the 'manufacture of disadvantage'; the contradictory impact of equal opportunities policy is considered in Jenkins, 1985, and Jewson and Mason, 1986.) The organization is not simply a passive recipient of racism; it actively reproduces it in many formal and informal ways. Organizational programmes to tackle racism should not therefore treat it simply as an expression of individuals' attitudes but as a set of institutionalized practices within the organization and in society as a whole.

Age and the labour process

This subject has only just begun to be explored by sociologists. Nevertheless, age is a significant aspect of labour market segmentation. The issue essentially centres on the two opposite ends of the life cycle: youth and old age. Youth has probably been studied more than old age, though neither category has had a central place in the analysis of labour markets and the labour process.

In relation to young people, the recession of the late 1970s and early 1980s had led to a major restructuring of their labour market position (good discussions of the earlier period and the differentiations among young people between boys and girls and 'lads' and 'teacher's pets' are available in Willis, 1978, and Jenkins, 1983). Initially, for both boys and girls in the UK wishing to leave school at 16 the recession led to a rapid contraction of employment opportunities (see Gleeson, 1983, for a collection of papers on this issue). Traditional apprenticeship schemes were massively cut back, whilst the supply of ordinary manual and office jobs for young people also dried up. Successive governments from the mid 1970s defined the problem as one of shortage of skills and training. In the situation of the early 1980s, with unemployment over three million (four million according to some trade union sources), this seemed a bit off the mark. All the training in the world would be of no use if there were no jobs. In order to overcome this disillusion with the scheme, the government in Britain has introduced more and more elements of compulsion into its youth training schemes, so that now young people have little choice but to enrol on government training schemes. Furthermore, such schemes, in spite of protestations to the contrary, seem to reinforce existing segmentations. Black youth invariably end up on the schemes with less likelihood of permanent employment, whilst those on schemes associated with prestige retail companies where permanent jobs are more likely, are invariably white males. Furthermore, in spite of the odd well-publicised exception, there remains strong segregation between boys (in engineering, science and technology jobs) and girls (in traditional 'feminine' areas like shopwork, hairdressing and office work). Whilst the expansion of certain areas of work in the last few years (especially those based on leisure and fast foods) has now provided more work for young people, the nature of the employment and its long-term potential as the basis for independent adulthood is unclear. (These issues are discussed in Willis, 1988; Wallace, 1987; Wickham, 1986; Cockburn, 1987; Roberts *et al.*, 1985; Brown and Ashton, 1987.) The complex nature of the collective social and cultural responses to this among young people is far beyond the scope of this discussion (see Brake, 1980), but the specific nature of this group is increasingly important for employers as a whole, as the current amount of media and political attention on training schemes indicates.

In relation to old age, the amount of literature is still small. Although there are now attempts to create a sociology of old age (see Fennell *et al.*, 1988; Phillipson and Walker, 1986) there is very little work relevant to the labour process. Nevertheless there is certain research that is relevant. In particular, Walker *et al.* (1985) have pointed to the way in which employers use employees' perceptions of their own age in order to manage redundancy situations. This happens in two ways. First, when a redundancy situation arises, the largest redundancy payments inevitably go to the people who have worked there the longest. These are almost always elderly men (elderly women are another 'invisible' group in these situations, often because their employment record may be largely part-time work; interruptions to employment, etc.). Employers can appeal to men further by providing enhanced benefits, which may give an enticing lump-sum payment. Such workers may well be fed up with work after so many years; they may well want to get out whilst they are 'fit enough to enjoy it'. Second, employers appeal to older men on the grounds that they might make way for younger men with families to support. Together these appeals have contributed to the fact that many of the redundancies in the early 1980s were not strongly opposed. Instead men in their fifties gladly took redundancy money, having been partly cajoled, partly persuaded and partly forced out of work. The psychological impact of this, particularly on skilled manual men who have known a lifetime of such employment, has been looked at elsewhere (see, for example, Warr, 1987a). What is important here is how age has been utilized by managers to segment and stratify the workforce.

Conclusion

This chapter has sought to analyse the dynamics of the work situation. The essential point has been that whilst in capitalist societies employers have the central power to structure work, there are a number of constraints upon this power. These vary from worker resistance and collective action through the impacts of product and labour markets, to technology, institutionalized expectations and special differentiation within the workforce. Thus in any particular organizational setting, the need is to analyse in detail the power that is brought to bear and the various sources from which it springs. Rather than seeing any particular structure of work as an expression of the 'real interests' of managers, capitalists, or even particular work groups, we should see it as a temporal (and temporary) construction derived from the different powers in play. As these powers are altered (both from within the organization and from outside) we can expect the structure of work to change and be reproduced in a different way.

In the next chapter I want to examine in more detail the work of management within the capitalist organization in order to develop further the idea that whilst the power of management to control people and co-ordinate the organization has increased greatly, its capability of producing outcomes 'expressive' of that control remains limited, not just because of the countervailing power of the workforce but also because of the contradictions within management and the managerial task.

2 Management and Bureaucracy in Organizations

Introduction

Chapter 1 considered in detail the nature and determinants of work in modern organizations. In this chapter I will look at the ways in which work is co-ordinated within large-scale organizations. Commonsense accounts emphasize the role of management in this process of co-ordination. In particular, management is seen as having responsibility for the setting up and monitoring of systems of co-ordination and control. This view leads in turn to an apparently simple question: what is the best system for an organization? The answer to this has been a central preoccupation of management theorists. Both the complexity of the question itself and the difficulty of either finding answers or getting solutions implemented in the correct way has generated a vast literature.

In the first part of the chapter I will examine in detail the response of certain key authors to this question. My argument will be that these authors are wedded to a particular view of organizations, namely that organizations are the outcome of a rational decision process which seeks to 'fit' the internal environment to the external environment. This view is premised on a systems view of organizations, in which the organization is seen as possessing a series of characteristics, such as adaptability, structure and goals, which are separate from the actors within it. Furthermore (and to an extent paradoxically) the organization is seen as the expression of management's power to manage. Limited attention is given in traditional literature to the constraints on this power.

In the second part of the chapter I argue that what happens within the organization cannot be understood either from a systems perspective or from a rationalist perspective. I look at research on the internal workings of management and bureaucracy, which reveals two important features. First, the conditions under which decisions are reached in organizations are too complex to meet the criteria of rationality. This in turn raises the point that rationality is better seen as a legitimating ideology for management actions than as an actual determinant of those actions. Second, and reinforcing this, is the extent to which decisions in organizations reflect not processes of rational decision-making but rather processes of power, conflict and negotiation over outcomes.

These arguments in turn lead to the point emphasized throughout this book, that organizations need to be considered in terms of social processes of production and reproduction. What is presented both inside and outside the organization as the best fit or the most rational form is in fact no more than a particular structure of social relationships that has arisen at a particular time out of processes of conflict and accommodation.

In the last part of the chapter I consider how and why organizations take on a particular system of control and coordination. Beginning with research on how strategic decisions are taken, I go on to consider models of organizations which take account of the complex relationship between systems, power and culture. Such models return to the point that organizational change cannot be understood other than as a process of social production in which actors shape the present and the future on the basis of their understanding of and implication in the ongoing reproduction of organizational life.

Structure and bureaucracy

Traditional approaches to the study of organization structure usually commence with Max Weber and the theory of bureaucracy. In this section, I will consider in detail what Weber said about organization structure.

Weber's argument was that the emergence of a particular type of rational-legal bureaucracy was crucial to the development of the modern world. This bureaucracy, according to Weber, had a number of characteristics which made it technically superior to previous organizational forms. It is this notion of technical superiority that has been drawn upon by many management commentators as the basis for a theory of organization structure, though Weber's intentions were far more complex and less rooted in pragmatic considerations. By the notion of 'technical superiority' Weber meant to emphasize that in rational-legal bureaucracies, the achievement of narrowly specified goals was the central objective. This is not to say that the goals were always achieved, nor indeed that the mechanisms for achieving goals were static and always the same. On the contrary, the methods for achieving goals have been consistently refined. To achieve the goals, more needs to be known to give an instrumental mastery over recalcitrant aspects of the organization and the environment. Thus Weber's model is dynamic in the sense that it suggests that organizations will change and try to become more technically efficient. It is not that they are perfectly efficient, but that they are continually measuring themselves and being measured by others against the criteria of technical rationality.

A number of authors have challenged parts of Weber's argument, claiming instead that bureaucracies produce their own inefficiencies. Merton (1952), for example, emphasized the extent to which providing an office-holder with security of employment and a clear set of rules could lead to bureaucratic ritualism, by which he meant that rules were followed in order to avoid decisions and have a quiet life. Thus rather than using the rules as a means of achieving the goals of the organization, they became an end in themselves. Blau (1956) argued along similar lines, stating that often formal rules had to be circumvented in order to achieve organizational goals. Other authors analysed what they saw as pathological aspects of bureaucracies. Selznick, (1966), for example, argued that bureaucrats developed their own set of interests separate from the interests that first set up an organization. Thus organization would, after a time, develop new goals to serve the interests of the bureaucrats, rather than its original objectives, a point which Weber's colleague Michels (1921) had developed in relation to the changing nature of Marxist social democratic parties in the early twentieth century. (For a recent discussion of bureaucracy in relation to politics see Beetham, 1987.)

Crozier (1964) developed the pathological notion even further, claiming that the distinctive feature of a bureaucracy is its 'inability to learn from its own mistakes'. This arose because each level in the bureaucratic hierarchy was dependent for information on the layers beneath it, and for orders on the layers above it. Equally, however, each layer wanted to protect its own career position. As a result, information was systematically re-interpreted as it passed up the hierarchy in order not to throw a bad light on the layer passing the information upwards. The information that reached the top therefore bore little relation to the actual situation it was meant to be describing. When orders came down they were based on inaccurate information, but in order to avoid being blamed for failure each layer ensured that orders were rigidly carried out so that failure could be blamed on the originator of the order rather than its implementers. Bureaucracies were therefore trapped in a vicious circle of inaccurate information and irrelevant action.

These criticisms of Weber were frequently based on colourful and well-written case studies. As such they have had a powerful influence on the study of organizations. However, it can be argued that they misunderstood an essential part of Weber's argument. In particular, these authors tended to conflate the bureaucratic 'form' of organization with its substantive content. (See Albrow, 1970, for what is still the best discussion of this problem.) Weber's argument was that it was the form of modern bureaucracies – the fact that they had hierarchies, rules, salaried officials, expert knowledge – that gave them the fundamental advantage over previous forms of administration, namely traditional and charismatic forms. The critics' argument would only stand up if they could show that these features themselves could be replaced and another more efficient form of organization devised. This they are unable to do. Clearly Weber saw that the way in which this form was implemented could vary a great deal and could therefore result in more or less efficiency, but this was not his interest.

It took students of organization a long time to throw off the idea that there was one basic model of organization structure which should be followed by all organizations and could be characterized as a bureaucracy. Although modifications arose, they were essentially designed to improve the bureaucratic model. For example, the French engineer, Henri Fayol, continued to emphasize characteristics such as a unified hierarchical structure of command and direction but elaborated on practical issues such as recommended spans of control and the number of levels in the hierarchy.

The complexity of organizations and the problems they faced as they developed from family firms into giant corporations gradually made traditional ideas of bureaucracy seem increasingly irrelevant or at best limited. In particular, as organizations became more internally differentiated, along functional or geographical or product lines, the old idea that co-ordination could be achieved through unity of command and centralized decision-making became less viable. Similarly, organizations became more interested in professional expertise in areas of finance, law, personnel, engineering and science, and it was not at all clear how these positions could be incorporated in a traditional managerial hierarchy. These problems were indicative of the growing gap between organization theory – with its emphasis on hierarchy, bureaucracy and 'one best way' – and organization practice, where a multitude of pragmatic adaptations to problems existed. From the 1950s, then, a new approach to organizations developed which emphasized diversity of organizational types rather than unity. The old problem remained – how to make the organization efficient – but many more answers were now possible.

Organizational variations and the new approaches

The new approaches that developed in the 1950s were based in the main on large-scale empirical studies of organizations. They were open to different types of organizational form and based on the belief that different forms suited different contexts. The theoretical problem was to specify the determinant elements of the context and the determined components of the structure. For many authors (for example Donaldson, 1985) this is still the heart of the study of organizations.

There are two main strands to the argument. The first, associated mainly with Joan Woodward but also taken up by authors such as Thompson (1967), takes the view that organizations do and should vary according to their basic technology. The second, associated with what are known as the Aston studies (Pugh and Hickson, 1976; Pugh and Hinings, 1976; Pugh and Payne, 1977), argues that the concept of organization structure needs refining and that the key determinants of structure are size and dependency.

In relation to the theme of technology and organization structure, Woodward's original ideas were based on empirical work conducted in south-east Essex in the 1950s. She argued that technology varied along a continuum from small batch unit production through large batch and mass assembly-line production to process production (oil, chemicals, etc.) Each technology had a type of organization structure which fitted it best. Woodward sought to demonstrate this by showing how certain types of organization structure correlated with particular technological configurations. She also tried to go further and argue that organizational success, measured in a variety of *ad hoc* ways, also correlated in the sense that those companies which possessed the type of structure best suited to their technology were likely to be the most successful. Although much of Woodward's methodology now looks exceedingly doubtful, her central message that structure should fit technology and that there was no one best structure, was very widely received.

The Aston studies were far more sophisticated in some ways. They went to great lengths to analyse what exactly was meant by organization structure, arguing that it consisted of a variety of elements. Weber's rational-legal bureaucracy, they argued, was only one possible combination of the elements that made up organization structure. Other combinations would give rise to fundamentally different structures. Furthermore they rejected the view that these combinations could be explained by technology. Rather they focused on size and dependence:

> The larger an organization is, the more likely its employees are to work in very specialized functions, following standardized procedures and formalized documentation; i.e. it will score highly on structuring of activities and have many of the appearances of bureaucracy. The more it is dependent upon only a few owning, supplier or customer units, or even just one – total dependence is where an organization is wholly owned by another which supplies all its needs and takes all its outputs – the less autonomy it will have in its own decision-making, and even those decisions that are left to it are likely to be centralized within itself rather than decentralized. (Pugh *et al*, 1987, 40)

These two main variables of size and concentration of authority could, the Aston team argued, vary independently of one another.

As a result they were able to distinguish four basic types of organization, thus refining the blanket concept of bureaucracy. The four types were: personnel bureaucracies, full bureacracies, workflow bureaucracies and non-bureaucracies. These are shown in Figure 2.1.

Figure 2.1

		Personnel bureaucracies	Full bureaucracies
Concentrations	*High*	Personnel bureaucracies	Full bureaucracies
of			
authority	*Low*	Non-bureaucracies	Workflow bureaucracies

Low   *High*
Structuring of activities

Personnel bureaucracies, the authors argued, were characteristic of central and local government. Because of their responsibility to political masters, authority tended to be concentrated at the top; further down the hierarchy, activities themselves were not highly structured for two reasons: first, key decisions had already been taken at the top; second, selection procedures were also likely to be highly concentrated, thus ensuring strict control over recruitment. This strict control over recruitment usually meant the recruitment of people with professional qualifications and expertise could be expected to get on with their job without a great deal of interference from superiors or rules. Full bureaucracies, on the other hand (which, they argued, came closest to Weber's ideal type) were only a minority of cases. They were characterized by high levels of structuring and high levels of concentration of authority.

Full bureaucracies were typically units within larger organizations, where the larger organization insisted on controlling key decisions as well as maintaining a tight structuring of work activities.

Workflow bureaucracies were typically manufacturing organizations where the actual production process involved standardized and routinized procedures. These organizations were highly structured, but there was a low concentration of authority, and positions lower down the hierarchy had powers of decision-making. Thus, for example, because work activities themselves were highly structured, it was less important to have tight control over selection and recruitment.

Finally, there were certain organizations that seemed to be neither highly structured nor highly centralized; these the authors labelled as 'non-bureaucracies' and were predominantly characteristic of small private companies.

Overall, then, the studies found that only a small number of organizations in the category of full bureaucracies fitted Weber's ideal type. Much more common, they argued, were personnel and workflow bureaucracies, each of which lacked one vital (though different) element of Weber's ideal type. In personnel bureaucracies there was not the formal specification of duties and responsibilities that Weber had expected. In workflow bureaucracies there was not the highly centralized decision-making which he had expected.

The key strength of the Aston studies was that they generated clear and straightforward hypotheses that could be replicated using approximately the same research instrument in other national and international studies of organizations (see Hickson and McMillan, 1981; Lammers and Hickson, 1979). Furthermore, other research, particularly Burns and Stalker (1961) in the UK and Lawrence and Lorsch (1967) in the USA, was developing a similar approach, which together with the Aston studies gave rise to the use of the term 'contingency theory', i.e. the idea that the most efficient form of structure was contingent on certain key aspects of the internal and external environment. In 1981, Hickson and McMillan summarized their findings on this point:

> The consistency of the relationships between variables of organization context and organization structure found in data from 70 manufacturing units in the USA, Britain and Canada supports the 'bold' hypothesis that these relationships, notably those between size and specialization and formalization and those between dependency and autonomy will hold for work organizations in all societies. (Hickson and McMillan, 1981, p. 16)

The main problem with both Woodward and the Aston studies, together with contingency theory in general, is their assumption that managers have the will, cohesion, power and knowledge to shape the organization to the environment. In a seminal article Child (1972) argued that the relationship between size, dependence and structure were treated as determinant by the researchers, whereas a key intervening variable – strategic choice – was ignored. By strategic choice, Child referred to the decision-taking ability of management about matters of structure. Child, echoing the prevailing 'action' critique of organization theory at this time (see Silverman, 1970, for the most explicit version of this critique), argued that top managers shaped organization structure according to their own preference, which in turn were linked to the power politics occurring at the upper echelons of the organization. Thus, in his view, the statistical relationships discovered by the researchers were not adequate at the level of meaning (see Weber, 1949, for an account of this term), i.e. they did not allow one to explain what was happening from the point of view of the actors involved. This could only be done by going into the organization to see what managers were trying to achieve. The original members of the Aston group have since replied to Child:

> These results did not mean a working model immovably fixed by a few major elements. Not only did all of these elements change all the time – for organizations grow in size and abolish some formalized documents and introduce others – but all these and the other elements studied were open to strategic choice. Indeed they had all in some sense been chosen and were continually being chosen. Managers and administrators choose whether or not an organization is to grow or enter into contracts that make it dependent on others. They choose the means of management and control which structure its activities and concentrate its authority. But one choice constrains another – each choice e.g. of size constrains the options open for the next e.g. of the degree of structuring to be adopted. (Pugh *et al.*, 1987, p. 40)

In some ways this is an elegant reformulation of the Aston approach, although the underlying assumption remains similar – that if the organization is going to be efficient, it must adopt a particular structure. Now management are inserted as the agents who must realize the 'rational course of action'. Yet a number of questions remain. How tightly is structure linked to environment? Might there not be many alternative forms of structure open, depending on the way in which management interprets its task? In fact, may not the whole rational model of organization structure be false in a fundamental sense?

This can be examined further if we consider the methodology of the approach used by the Aston authors. Their research tool effectively took a snapshot of the organization at a particular time; it did not attempt to collect information either about the past or the projected future of the organization.

Turning to the way in which the information was collected, the research tool in fact depended on top management; it was they who were asked to respond to the authors' questionnaire, and thus what is presented as an 'objective' snapshot is in fact a 'snapshot' from the perception of a very select group of participants within the organization. Thus the research instrument needs to be treated with care; and so, therefore, must the conclusions. The assumption that the organization structure at any particular time represents a rational fit to certain contextual features such as size and dependence is a large assumption. If we conceive organizations in terms of processes of production and reproduction, we do not have to hold to the rational view but can instead consider how the whole hangs together and generates a semblance of order. Just because an organization survives (leaving aside for the moment what is meant by survival), it does not mean that it survives because management has used its power to fit structure to environment. There are many other reasons for survival, as will be discussed in later chapters.

Thus many of the conclusions of the Aston authors about 'fit' and 'match' remain tendentious and speculative. Once this is accepted, the area of managerial decision-making becomes even more significant, because it is not simply a question of how managers resolve the fit between organization and environment but how they perceive the issue in the first place. Concepts such as 'fit' and 'match' need to be considered as social constructions that are meaningful to actors within organizations but should not be taken as descriptors of what takes place in reality.

Rational and irrational in organizations

Whatever exists within organizations has to be produced by conscious human action. Explanations of organizational phenomena that ignore this and treat the questions of organizations without considering the precarious nature of production and reproduction of social relationships have made a fundamental error in their starting point. In this section I want to show how this simple point undermines much of the discussion of organizations which begins from a rationalist system perspective. Two issues in particular will be considered. The first relates to the problem of complexity in organizational life and the way in which this affects processes of production and reproduction. The second concerns the role of political behaviour within organization.

Anarchy and complexity in organizations

The study of decision-making seems to have gone on in isolation from the study of organization structure. Although the two address similar problems, they come up with very different solutions. Whilst the analysis of organization structure proceeds from the assumption that a 'rational' fit can be achieved with no great difficulty, the study of decision-making has increasingly questioned this view. Early on decision-making theory divested itself of the belief in totally rational decision-making. The idea that decision-makers could take account of all factors and come to a rational conclusion was seen as drastically overestimating people's ability to come to terms (even with the help of computers) with the complexity of the real world. Thus it was suggested that the model of economic 'man' making rational utility-maximizing decisions should be replaced by a model of 'satisficing', where decision-making proceeds not on the basis of making the best decision but of making a decision which is satisfactory or 'good enough'. The argument was spelled out in the notion that organizations and environments are too complex to allow rational decision-making *per se*. Instead, ideas of bounded or limited rationality were developed:

> The argument, due originally to Simon, is that informational and computational limits on decision-making in human institutions require a theory of organizational choice to be a theory of limited rationality. There are limits on the number of alternatives that will be considered and limits on the amount and accuracy of information that will be used . . . Decision-making is seen as problem solving, search and incremental trial and error. (March, in Van de Ven and Joyce, 1981, p. 212)

Lindblom (1959) took the argument further by showing that what occurs is a process of incremental decision-making, whereby previous decisions become the basis for the next action. They are not subjected to critical scrutiny each time a decision comes up; rather, any new issues are interpreted on the basis of what has already happened. Lindblom refers to this as the 'science of muddling through'. In his view decision-makers do not continually make rational decisions; they adopt a strategy of disjointed incrementalism, thus cutting down the size of their problem to manageable proportions.

There are, however, even more radical challenges to the notion of rationality within organizational decision-making. Of particular interest is what is known as the 'garbage-can model of organizational choice'. This perspective was originally developed to explain organizational decision-making in 'organized anarchies', by which were meant organizations in which there were clearly problematic preferences/goals, unclear technology and fluid amounts of participation. Cohen *et al.* argued that:

> These properties of organized anarchy have been identified often in studies of organizations. They are characteristic of any organization in part – part of the time. They are particularly conspicuous in public, educational and illegitimate organizations. A theory of organized anarchy will describe a portion of any organization's activities but will not describe all of them. (Cohen *et al.*, 1972, p. 1)

These authors turn the rational model on its head. Whereas the rational and even the boundedly rational model treats a decision outcome as the result of reasoned processes of information-gathering and evaluation, the garbage-can model turns this round and argues that problems, solutions, participants and decision situations are four relatively independent phenomena that are brought together in a random way:

> An organization is a collection of choices looking for problems, issues and feelings looking for decision situations in which they might be aired, solutions looking for issues to which they might be the answer, and decision-makers looking for work. To understand processes within organizations we view a choice opportunity as a garbage can into which various kinds of problems and solutions are dumped by participants as they are generated. The mix of garbage in a single can depends upon the

mix of cans available, on the labels attached to the alternative cans, on what garbage is currently being produced and on the speed with which garbage is collected and removed from the scene. (p. 2; see March, 1988, for a number of other articles exploring decision-making)

Applying this to any particular organization, the authors are arguing that within the organization, people are committed to ideas that frame their way of thinking. They have certain ways of thinking about what the problems are; they also have ideas about what solutions are effective. There is no necessary connection between the problems one sees and the solutions one favours. The two can be totally independent. People also have only a limited amount of time they can spend on any one decision. Concentrating on one decision means that a person has less time to spend on another decision should one come up in the same time-span. Thus when choice opportunities arise, the people who are actively participating are necessarily limited in number; the way they seek to define the problem and the solutions they offer are similarly not rational products. Rather, the authors argue, the decision-making process is a garbage can full of random products with random results:

> A major feature of the garbage can process is the partial uncoupling of problems and choices. Although decision-making is thought of as a process for solving problems, that is often not what happens. Problems are worked upon in the context of some choice, but choices are made only when the shifting combination of problems, solutions and decision-makers happen to make action possible. Quite commonly this is after problems have left a given choice arena or before they have discovered it (decisions by flight or oversight). (p. 16)

A similarly strong challenge to the notion of rational decision-making comes from the writings of Starbuck, who claims he 'backtracks the trail blazed by Cohen *et al.* and then sets off in a different direction' (1983b, p. 91). Starbuck concentrates on the relationship between action and rationality in organizations. Organizations, he argues, primarily consist of action programmes; actions occur on a regular and routine basis with little reflection about their relevance. Indeed, once they are constructed, action programmes disregard items that are irrelevant to their frame of reference even though such items may have a major effect on the organization:

> Programs construct realities that match their assumptions – by influencing their users' perceptions, values and beliefs, by dictating new programs' characteristics, by filtering information and focusing attention. Most importantly, programs act unreflectively . . . Organizations frequently create action generators – automatic behaviour programs that require no information-bearing stimuli because they are activated through job assignments, clocks and calendars. Consequently organizations act unreflectively and nonadaptively most of the time. Even if actions first begin because of specific needs, they become automatic when assigned to specialists, written into budgets and given floor space. Most likely, however, action generators do not even originate because of specific needs; they are traditional, copied from other organizations, taught in schools of management or legitimated by managerial literature and talk. (Starbuck, 1983b, p. 93)

Starbuck therefore argues that action programmes are set up for a variety of reasons, none of which relates to goal achievement. Once they are set up they gain a momentum of their own. However, according to Starbuck,

> Societal ideologies insist that actions ought to be responses – actions taken unreflectively without specific reasons are irrational and irrationality is bad. So organizations justify their actions with problems, threats, successes or opportunities. (p. 94)

Thus organizations also generate ideologies about the main problems which face them and the reasons for the actions which they generate:

> The ideological molecules called problems resemble crystals; they form incrementally; their elements array in logically congruent patterns; and as rationalization fills the logical gaps, problems grow perfect and hard like emeralds and rubies . . . Organizations have great difficulty dissolving the problems, successes, threats and opportunities that hold central positions in their top managers' ideologies because these molecules are so big and so crystalline. (pp. 95–6)

The ideologies so constructed integrate values with perception. They bracket off certain issues, elevating others to the status of 'facts' or 'values'. These become built in as part of the explanation of organizational actions and justifications. The result is that at one level actions set up for various reasons continue regardless of the circumstance; at another level, ideologies barely linked to the original purpose of the actions justify them, at the same time explaining to the organization what the actions are about. Neither the actions nor the ideology relate directly to the environment. Starbuck summarizes the process thus:

> Many organizations drift along, perceiving that they are succeeding in stable environments, until they suddenly find themselves confronted by existence-threatening crises. Most of the organizations my colleagues and I have studied did not survive their crises ... Nonadaptiveness turns organizations into temporary systems, nearly all of which have short lives. (p. 101; see also March, 1981, for a discussion of resistances to change)

Two aspects of Starbuck's argument deserve further consideration: the first relates to the link between the organization and the environment and particularly the notion of loose coupling. The second relates to the organization's propensity to continue to act in a given way even when it is ineffective.

The concept of loose coupling was first developed by Karl Weick. Weick argued that the link between parts of an organization can be more or less tight; thus department A may be absolutely dependent on department B producing a certain part with certain technical specifications on a certain day. On the other hand, it may not need the parts on a particular day; it may not even need them exactly to meet the technical specifications laid down (perhaps they were a form of over-insurance); indeed, there may be other sources within the organization or even outside for the required part. In the first case, we would talk about a tight coupling between A and B; in the second case we would talk about a loose coupling. This concept may be applied to the relationship between the organization and the environment. Most theories of organization structure assume a tight coupling between structure and environment. Failure to have a certain structure leads to organizational decline. However, it is an essential part of the argument here that there can be a loose coupling between organization and environment. The looseness of the coupling can arise from many factors, some of which will be explored later. (Weick's argument is set out in a number of articles dealing with different aspects: Weick, 1976, 1982a, 1982b, 1985).

As an example, loose coupling can arise from a very favourable market position. Where, for whatever reason, there are few competitors in an area, then success may come anyway, no matter what the structure. There is obviously an argument about whether this could continue in the long term, but for the moment it is sufficient to raise the theoretical possibility of loose coupling. Possibly more important are the interpretive processes that particular actors must go through in order to pronounce an organization a failure. Business failure does not just happen; somebody somewhere must start to perceive that something is failing. However, because this is a process of perception, it can be delayed, diverted and even avoided altogether by people acting in other ways. Thus business failure is not some natural catastrophe like a typhoon; somebody in a position of power and influence has to pronounce it. We can say that there is at the very least the possibility of loose coupling between what is going on within the business, what is happening to it in its outside environment, and what is perceived to be happening to it. This loose coupling opens up the possibility for all sorts of things to be happening in the organization that are irrelevant, irrational or non-functional to organizational goals. Rather than assuming that all these things can somehow make sense in terms of the rational pursuit of the organization's goals, we should consider them from the point of view of the actors involved and subsequently analyse how they relate to the tight or loose coupling of environment and organization.

Second, Starbuck's arguments can be buttressed by Staw's work on escalation costs in organizations. Staw originally formulated his ideas on the basis of an individual's propensity to continue to invest in a course of action even where it did not appear to be achieving its expected results. The effect of this escalation is, according to Staw, to land the person 'knee-deep in the big muddy' (Staw, 1976; see also Staw, 1980, 1984; Staw, Sandilands and Dutton, 1981). In later work, Ross and Staw (1986) have examined this problem from the point of view of the actions of organizations. People and organizations set off on courses of action that at first seem perfectly rational and logical. At some point, however, when the goal has not yet been achieved, the organization/person has to ask if it is worth proceeding. Having decided to proceed in the hope of eventual success, the person/organization becomes even more committed. Ross and Staw argue that there are four classes of variables affecting behaviour in these situations. First, there is the question of the project determinants; that is, the initial reason for setting the course of action may still seem important in spite of mounting evidence against the possibility of success. Second, there are the psychological determinants: people/organizations seek to justify initial failure; they become committed to continuing the course of action because they have convinced themselves it is worthwhile. Third, there are the social determinants – the desire not to lose face or credibility with others because of withdrawal. Fourth, Ross and Staw identify what they call structural determinants:

> Projects can at times become institutionally embedded in an organization, reflecting the web of interrelationships and obligations that extend from a variety of relevant constituent groups. In becoming institutionalized, a relatively permanent structure and system of relationships is erected that favours a policy or decisions. (p. 278)

This argument further supports Starbuck. An organizational action process becomes a goal in itself that needs to be justified. At times of threat, rather than adjusting the action, the organization is actually induced to reinforce it. The organization goes further into the 'big muddy' rather than extracting itself.

Finally, the rationality of the decision process has been challenged by Brunsson, who argues that if decision processes were rational, then no action would ever be taken. Thus organizations have to take decisions in irrational ways:

> Effective decision processes break all the rules of rational decision-making; few alternatives should be analyzed; only the positive consequences of the chosen actions should be considered and objectives should not be formulated in advance. Irrationalities can provide a good basis for organizational actions. (Brunnson, 1986, p. 22–3)

How does this apparent paradox come about? The rational model proposes that all alternatives in a certain decision situation need to be appraised and evaluated. However, the more alternatives that are suggested and examined, the more difficult and complex it becomes to settle on one in particular. Moreover, the negative consequences of course of action should be minimized, otherwise the amount of commitment needed to achieve them may not be given as people hang back in partial expectation of failure. Brunsson describes this disjunction as the difference between two forms of rationality – decision rationality, where the problem is to reach the best decision, and action rationality, where the problem is to act. Decision rationality depends on time and expertise to search out and evaluate different alternatives. Action, on the other hand, depends particularly on motivation and commitment. People will not be committed and motivated if they are told that what they are doing has severe disadvantages and is only slightly better than another course of action which has been rejected. Organizational action requires an element of certainty that cannot be derived from decision rationality. This certainty, Brunsson argues, can come from an organization's ideology:

> Ideologies which are conclusive, complex and consistent can provide a good basis for action, in that they solve a good deal of the choice problem. Such 'strong' ideologies can decide which actions are right, so that analysis is reduced to a minimum and effort can be concentrated on reinforcing actions. (p. 30)

Those organizations where ideologies are ambiguous, broad and non-conclusive leave a much greater part of the choice problem unsolved. Thus organizations of this type tend to use rational decision processes and as a result are less likely to generate adequate action responses to environmental changes. Brunsson's argument leads to the point that organizations should concentrate on developing strong ideologies and value systems, as this will improve their ability to take action. As a consequence, however, they will sacrifice decision rationality. (For another approach to the non-rationality of organizations see Shrivastava *et al.*, 1987.)

The essential point in the above discussion is that much previous analysis of organizations assumed an unproblematic relationship between structure and environment, mediated by managers acting as the embodiment of rational decision-making and utilizing their power to implement decisions. This notion of rational decision-making is severely flawed and does not adequately describe the processes of decision-making within organizations, which are influenced by many factors. It is necessary to move from the level of myth and ideas about how things should work and to consider the actual processes of production and reproduction of organizations. At this level, the complexity of the organization and the environment forces managers away from a rational-decision making model to a more pragmatic approach. There are limits to their power to formulate and implement a rational decision. To assume that structure embodies a rational judgement of how to fit the organization to its environment is clearly false. This can be examined further through considering political behaviour in organizations.

Political behaviour in organizations

Decisions in organizations involve processes of power and conflict between groups within the organization. From this point of view a particular decision or a particular structure is not an expression of the organization's goals but of the ability of particular groups to impose their definition of the situation and their solution to it on other groups within the organization.

Hickson (1987) has developed the argument that within organizations there is a dual rationality. On the one hand, organizations are involved in the solving of problems; to this extent they are always searching for rational solutions. On the other hand, within organizations there are interest groups seeking to further their own goals. All activities and decisions represent a tension between these two elements. No activity is undertaken in organizations unless it can claim to be rational; but the claim and the ability to enforce the claim should not be mistaken for the reality of rationality. The ability to make the claim heard and even more to enforce the claim over others derives from power, not from the superior rationality of the claim. In fact, from the point of view of sociology, it is necessary to be agnostic regarding these various claims and not to advance one rationality over another. As Hickson says, 'The product of two different rationalities is not "necessarily" "rational" in the original textbook sense of the word, since the solving of the problems is shaped by the accommodating of the interests' (Hickson, 1987, p. 186).

Following Lukes's (1973) formulation of the three faces of power, the political processes through which interest groups enforce their goals on the organization can be distinguished at three levels. First, there is the power that is evidenced in an actual decision-making event. Thus A gets what he/she wants whilst B does not because A forces B or C to do something against their interests. Second, there is the power to keep things off the agenda – what has been called the 'mobilization of bias'. These issues are treated as not serious enough to warrant further discussion and debate. Certain groups have the power to define what is legitimate, whilst the arguments of other groups are illegitimate. Third, there is the power inherent in the structure of social relationships – where issues fail to reach the surface not because a powerful group has taken a decision to mobilize against them, but because the normal taken-for-granted framework precludes certain issues. It is this face of power that has caused theorists most problems, since it seems to involve imputing interests to people who may not recognize them as relevant to their particular situation. In other words, can there be a set of 'objective' interests that exist independently of any perceived set of interests on the part of particular subjects?

Hickson *et al.* (1971, 1986) have proposed that questions of lateral power should be distinguished from those of vertical power. In the case of lateral power, what is of interest is the set of relationships between departments, sections, etc. across the organization. Vertical power concerns the power relations between levels in the organizational hierarchy.

Lateral power

As organizations become more complex, structural differentiation occurs and different departments are set up. Even within departments, new specialisms and sub-groups emerge. As differentiation occurs in structural terms, so, it is logical to argue, a potential for a differentiation of interests emerges as individuals within departments come to perceive their own department's survival and growth as distinct, if intertwined with, the survival and growth of other departments. The emergence of distinct departmental or sub-group interests may be aided by a number of factors. There may be a process of geographical dispersion and isolation, or there may be a distinct cultural identity emerging from aspects of the task or the professional or other training and socialization associated with the task. Depending on the way the department links to other departments and how the internal labour market is constructed, individuals may feel more or less tied to the department for their working life. Particular styles of leadership may reinforce departmental identity.

These processes of differentiation and the associated need for integration were a major theme in contingency theory, though in Lawrence and Lorsch (1967) this was treated as a technical problem in need of a technical solution. Hickson and his colleagues (1971), however, recognized that differentiation would lead to power conflicts, and they developed a line of argument regarding the nature of these conflicts that can be usefully explored here.

Hickson *et al.* argued that power relationships between departments were determined by the degree to which a department deals with essential organizational functions. They formulated the following hypotheses:

1. The more a subunit copes with uncertainty, the greater its power within the organization.
2. The lower the substitutability of the activities of a subunit, the greater its power within the organization.
3a. The higher the pervasiveness of the workflows of a subunit, the greater its power within the organization.
3b. The higher the immediacy of the workflows of a subunit, the greater its power within the organization.
4. The more contingencies are controlled by a subunit, the greater its power within the organization. (Hickson *et al.*, 1971, p. 184)

This approach has been labelled the 'strategic contingencies' approach to intraorganizational power. The key problem with this approach, however, lies in some of its taken-for granted assumptions. In particular, the argument assumes that 'uncertainty', 'substitutability', etc. are givens that exist by virtue of the technical inbuilt nature of the organization. Such a view, however, takes for granted power relations that enforce claims to control over uncertainty, etc. Pfeffer, for example, argues that:

> The most critical uncertainty or the most important resource is not a given but is itself socially determined . . . The critical organizational uncertainties are defined by the organization . . . what is missing is an assessment of how certain resources or

uncertainties come to be viewed or defined as most critical or important. (Pfeffer and Salancik, 1978, p. 43)

From these arguments we can distinguish two models: model A, which describes the strategic contingency approach, where positions per se leads to power and model B, Pfeffer's modification where power to define uncertainty lies behind the possession of strategic position which in turn generates power in the organization as a whole. These are shown in Figure 2.2.

Figure 2.2

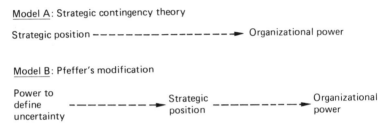

Model A: Strategic contingency theory

Strategic position — — — — — — — — — — — — — —➤ Organizational power

Model B: Pfeffer's modification

Power to
define   — — — — — — — —➤   Strategic   — — — — — — — —➤   Organizational
uncertainty   position   power

Before expanding further on Pfeffer's argument, it is necessary to note another criticism of the strategic contingency theory, that it is excessively static and deterministic, since it assumes not only that strategic position is a given but also that it is a permanent characteristic. On the contrary, it is necessary to think of organizational power relations, as with any other aspect of organizational life, as in a constant process of production and reproduction. Thus in Pfeffer's model the power to define uncertainty is not given for eternity; in fact, organizational departments seek to use the power which they derive in this way to ensure that competing claims to position are defeated. The process of power relations is not linear, but rather a spiralling process, in which claims to power are reinforced or defeated. Whether the spiral is broken into by a successful counter-claim is an empirical question that can only be answered by looking at how these processes of the production and reproduction of power occur in particular organizations.

Pfeffer's critique of strategic contingency theory still fails to answer the key question as to how the power to enforce a claim to uncertainty arises in the first place. He has merely succeeded in pushing the process back one stage. At one level, it could be argued that this is an irrelevant question. Power relations emerge for a variety of reasons that cannot be determined in advance. This perspective is traditionally known as pluralism. In this view, groups – in society, in organizations, in communities – come together on a temporary basis to pursue certain interests. Depending on the nature of the interests, the numbers involved and the commitment of the participants, some groups gain in one setting, whilst others lose. But since these groups are only temporary phenomena, and people move between groups depending upon issues that arise, the result is not permanent rifts but temporary, limited and even, some might argue, functional social conflict. (For the classic statement of pluralism see Dahrendorf, 1959.) Such a view, however, lacks credibility; although it may describe certain processes of conflict, it does not capture the enduring nature of conflicts and power relations within organizations and society.

Another approach is that of Crozier and Friedberg, who utilize 'game theory'. They argue as follows:

> We propose to consider [the functioning of an organization] as the result of a series of games participated in by the various organizational actors. By defining the possibilities for gain and loss, the formal and informal rules of these games delimit a range of rational or 'winning' strategies, which the actors can adopt if they wish their involvement with the organization to serve, or, at least, not to disserve, their personal aspirations . . . To say that players play games in no way implies that there is any initial equality whatsoever amongst them or that there is any consensus as to the rules of the game. (Crozier and Friedberg, 1980, p. 57)

Clegg has made a similar point using the analogy of the chess game:

> To the extent that all pieces were able to negotiate their positions more or less, there is a game with a fixed number of pieces; that piece which ended up ruling on the greatest number of pieces, serving its interests in preference to theirs, would be the most powerful. But obviously, in an ongoing game, then a piece like the Queen would start in a more privileged position than a pawn. (Clegg, 1975, p. 49)

The metaphor of organizations being like games is useful at two levels. At the first level, it poses the central question of where the rules come from. Here the pluralist view is weak; it has no explanation for the underlying rules other than reverting to a consensual model of social relations. At the second level, the 'games' approach emphasizes the active nature of organizational life. As Crozier and Friedberg say (p. 57), 'A constraint imposed by the game does not determine behaviour but rather a range of possible strategies among which the actor chooses'. The rules lay out the possibilities for group advancement; they do not determine it. Thus within any particular organization, there is a wide variety of possible outcomes.

Vertical power

These concepts of rules and games can be further illuminated by considering vertical power relations in organizations. Clearly, a managerial hierarchy implies a differentiation of power between the different levels in the hierarchy. However, the fact of a formal differentiation of powers is not adequate for understanding what actually goes on. A number of studies have shown how individuals and groups at different levels of the managerial hierarchy seek to protect and advance their own interests in informal ways. Pettigrew's (1973) study of the introduction of computer technology into a firm showed how this decision became the subject of intense manoeuvring by managers at different levels of the hierarchy as individuals sought to advance their own career interests through being associated with the computer firm that would win the order. This involved one particular manager's ensuring that the board of directors received all their information and advice through him, even though his subordinates were often in basic disagreement with him when it came to judging the value of the various systems. Thus the final choice was effectively made through the continued sponsorship of one particular computer by a certain manager who was in a key position to filter out any possibly contradictory information reaching the board.

This issue is clearly related within the managerial hierarchy to the career trajectories of different managers. As Nichols and Beynon (1977) make clear in their study of plant managers at Chemco, not all managers show the same level of commitment to their organization. Particularly in middle age, when it becomes clear which managers are going to make it to the top and which have basically reached a level from which they are not going to make further progress, conflicts can emerge as managers who are seeking 'an easy' life before retirement seek to protect themselves from the demands of those higher up the hierarchy. Power relations in a hierarchy, then, are only partially described by the formal structure. Informal relations modify the official power structure. Whilst few managers may use their powers as drastically as, for example, the managers in Crozier's or Pettigrew's studies, it nevertheless remains the basis for alternative power groupings within organizations. The shaping of decisions in the organization is crucially affected by informal relations within the hierarchy.

Rationality and corporate strategy

Even when we look at the highest level of management, that of strategy formulation, we find that the rational model is a myth, a legitimating device that justifies rather than determines actions. The bases of actions lie in the complex power relationships between actors and groups within organizational settings. Thus if we want to understand strategy and leadership in organizations properly, we must look at how these phenomena are produced and not accept them as the rational outcomes of the implementation of organizational goals.

The role of top management within organizations has increasingly been seen as concerned with providing strategic direction. In this view, strategic decisions taken at the top have implications for all those further down the hierarchy. These decisions differ from the routine maintenance of everyday interaction which is the sphere of most management tasks because they specifically involve steps into the unknown. Not surprisingly, there has been a great deal of discussion about how to make known the 'unknown' – in other words to provide a rational framework for strategic decision-making. The most highly developed of these frameworks stems from the Harvard Business School and authors such as Ansoff (1968) and Porter (1985). In the view of these authors, organizations need to develop a clear understanding of their goals, also known as their 'mission'. This should include a broad definition of what the organization wants to achieve. From these goals are derived particular operating policies in the areas of labour, manufacturing, distribution, markets, etc., which in turn must be internally consistent. The strategy must involve an appreciation of factors internal to the organization (e.g. the company's strengths and weaknesses such as its profile of assets and skills relative to competitors, including financial resources, technological posture, brand identification, etc., and the personal values of the key implementers) and factors external to the company (e.g. the competitive structure of the industry and broader societal expectations). Thus the process of formulating strategy involves an appreciation of what the organization is doing now and what is happening in the environment. On this basis, strategic alternatives are formulated and a final decision made on the basis of which of the alternatives best fits the organization's situation to external opportunities and threats.

Porter (1985) has carried this analysis forward to argue that there are certain generic strategies for success which effectively define the main ways in which business organizations can develop. He argues that there are two dimensions to the formulation of strategy. First, there is competitive advantage: firms can achieve this either by emphasizing low cost or by differentiation, i.e. seeking to be unique in an industry along some dimension widely valued by buyers. Second, strategy varies as to its scope – whether the organization is seeking to serve a broad or a narrow segment of the market. The types of strategy that result from taking these two dimensions together are shown in Figure 2.3.

Figure 2.3

	Competitive advantage	
	Lower cost	Differentiation
Broad target	1 Cost leadership	2 Differentiation
Narrow target	3(a) Cost Focus	3(b) Differentiation Focus

Competitive scope

Porter distinguishes three main strategies:
1. Cost leadership, where the firm seeks to be the low-cost producer in an industry.
2. Differentiation, where the firm seeks to be unique in its industry while serving a wide market.
3. The third generic strategy is focus; Porter divides this into two sub-categories; in one sub-category the firm seeks a cost advan-

tage in a targeted segment of the market whilst in the other sub-category the firm seeks to differentiate itself in terms of quality but only for a limited and not the whole market. Porter describes his goal in straightforward rationalist terms: 'Competitive advantage describes the way a firm can choose and implement a generic strategy to achieve and sustain competitive advantage' (p. 26). Pettigrew says of this rationalist framework:

> The rational approach describes and prescribes techniques for identifying current strategy, analyzing environments, resources and gaps, revealing and assessing strategic alternatives and choosing and implementing carefully analyzed and well thought through outcomes. This rational picture of business problem-solving has as its concern the content or 'what' of strategy – the outcome which is sought – and has nothing to say at an explicit level of how to achieve that outcome. In other words, it has no process theory within it of how and why to create the strategic outcomes so perceptively and logically derived from the analysis of competitive forces. (Pettigrew, 1985, p. 19)

When the process of strategy formation is observed in practice, it is clearly different from the rational model. Hickson *et al.*, for example, studied 150 top decisions in thirty different organizations in Britain. In their research they identify three types of decision-making process, none of which corresponds to the rational model. First, they identified sporadic processes in which decisions took a long time to reach – activity was irregular and occurred in bursts. Second, there were fluid processes, 'steadily paced, formally chan-nelled, speedy'. Finally, there were 'constricted' processes where the decision making was narrowly channelled through particular sections of the organization. Sporadic decisions are uneven and widespread; fluid decisions are even and widespread; constricted decisions are closely channelled. None of them is approximate to the rational model. Hickson *et al.* explain the differences in the way strategic decisions are made on the basis of political factors – that is, whose position/power is being advantaged/disadvantaged by a certain decision. Thus the way in which decisions are reached and the decisions themselves cannot be divorced from the politics of the internal structure of the organization.

Mintzberg has pursued a similar line. He argues that strategies are far more complex than the rational model assumes. He argues that rather than seeing strategies as plans for the future which march the organization down a pre-arranged, rationally analysed road, they should be seen as 'a pattern in a stream of decisions' (Mintzberg, 1978). Once strategy is seen in this way, he argues, it is possible to see that the pre-set plan is only part of the process. The pre-set plan (or the 'intended strategy') may be unrealized or realized; the original intention may in fact become unrealizable and another strategy might emerge. Mintzberg argues that the intended strategy and the emergent strategy are two ends of a continuum:

> No organization can function with strategies that are always and purely emergent; that would amount to a complete abdication of will and leadership, not to mention conscious thought. But none can likewise function with strategies that are always and purely deliberate; that would amount to an unwillingness to learn, a blindness to whatever is unexpected. (Mintzberg and McHugh, 1985, p. 196)

Between the planned strategy and the emergent strategy, Mintzberg identifies a number of other types which vary in the extent of imposition of the strategy from above or outside. Thus the entrepreneurial strategy derives from the vision of the organization's founder. Since the strategy is based on an individual's view rather than on the detail of a plan, this strategy can change and become emergent. Planned control over strategy may also be weakened through top management's concentrating less on details than on providing the overall framework of values (the ideological strategy), general guidelines (the umbrella strategy) or a control process (the process strategy). Each of these forms of plan allows for emergent strategies within an overarching framework. Towards the other end of the continuum, however, are the more emergent grassroots strategies such as the consensus strategy:

> The consensus strategy grows out of the mutual adjustment among different actors as they learn from each other and from their various responses to the environment and thereby find a common, and probably unexpected, strategy that works for them. In other words, the convergence is not driven by any intentions of a central management, nor even by prior intentions widely shared among the other actors. It just evolves through the

results of a host of individual actions. (Mintzberg and Waters, 1985, p. 267)

This occurs in what Mintzberg refers to as an adhocracy; that is, where central control is weak it is possible for a strategy to emerge from the grassroots. Mintzberg and McHugh's (1985) study of the National Film Board of Canada illustrates that within the great diversity of the Board's products there were periods when strategies did emerge – not by virtue of central direction, but almost spontaneously as individuals in different parts of the organization strove to give it a sense of identity.

Mintzberg is cautious about the implications of his analysis:

Emergent strategy does not have to mean that management is out of control, only – in some cases, at least – that it is open, flexible and responsive, in other words, willing to learn. (Mintzberg and Waters, 1985; see also Mintzberg and Waters, 1982)

This may be the case, but in effect he is arguing that the notion of a planned strategy is a myth. Clearly planning of sorts occurs: there are large departments of corporate planning, there are many hours of meetings devoted to corporate planning, and there are many reams of paper used up in the presentation of a corporate plan to employees, shareholders and the public. All that is undeniable; what remains questionable, however, is the extent to which these plans embody a neutral rationality expressive of the organization's goals, or whether they are rather the result of long and complex processes of political bargaining and negotiation between groups within the organization. Certainly, one of the most complete and systematic case studies of strategy – Pettigrew's study of ICI – reveals that it is impossible to capture the complexity of the process simply in terms of plan formulation and implementation:

Strategic decision-making and change are here regarded as continuous processes . . . Patterns of strategic change at the level of the firm may be understood in terms of long periods of continuity, learning and incremental adjustment interspersed with hiatuses or revolutions featuring abnormally high levels of change activity. (Pettigrew, 1985, pp. 438–40)

The pattern of strategy formation, he argues, is much more untidy than the rational theorists care to admit:

Forming and implementing strategic change is not a steady, undisturbed progression from one routine to another but rather a slow and incomplete process of breaking down old marriages between strategic context and content in an additive, intuitive and occasionally opportunistic fashion building up a climate of acceptance for change. (p. 457)

In ICI processes of change occurred because of the way in which individuals planted the seeds of relevant ideas at opportune moments which then, with further help (frequently inadvertently and by chance) from internal and external factors, were able to germinate and grow. The result was strategic change, but not as the result of the top-down formulation and implementation of all-encompassing strategic plans, but rather through the long-term evolution of emergent strategies pushed along at particular points by decisive interventions on the part of powerful groups and/or individuals.

The study of processes of strategy formation and implementation lends further weight to the importance of perceiving organizations in terms of processes of production and reproduction. Strategies are negotiated processes and occasionally outcomes which express not a neutral rational assessment of environmental choices and constraints but a socially constructed picture of the past, present and future of the organization in which the power of certain groups within management is key. The goal of organization studies should be to analyse the social processes behind the emergence of strategies, not to treat them as givens.

Conclusions

This chapter began by considering rationalist models of organizations. The key theme in these approaches was that organizations could and should be designed to 'fit' their environment. Such a view, it was argued, depends upon a belief that managers are capable of acting on the basis of a rational plan. However, it has been shown that whilst rationality plays a central part in organizational life as a legitimating factor for all sorts of actions, it cannot be said to determine those actions. Organizational outcomes, whether we are thinking in terms of strategy or structure, are produced through the actions of individuals and groups within the organization. Thus we need to consider in more detail these sets of social relationships. Organizations are social constructs. Their form, purposes, strategies, cultures (see Frost *et al.*, 1985, for a series of papers on the construction of organizational cultures which fits the approach adopted here) do not come fully grown into the world; they are shaped in processes of social relationships embodying power dimensions. If we are to understand organizations better, we need to understand these power dimensions better. I will therefore look in the next chapter at the central role taken within organizations by the power/knowledge discourses of professional groups, for it is in the ability of certain groups to impose their way of looking at things that we can see the emergence of organizational rationalities.

3 Rational Calculation, Professional Power and the Managerial Division of Labour

Introduction

In the two previous chapters I have analysed the internal processes of organizations. A central theme has been the way in which organizations have become progressively rationalized – that is, how they are increasingly subjected to scientific management techniques and bureaucratization. Neither of these concepts, it was argued, should be overestimated. It is not the case that all organizations are Taylorist or bureaucratized in the way Weber suggested; there are too many complexities and foci of resistance and change for that to be the case. Nevertheless, organizations increasingly proceed on the basis that there can be rational calculation about the relationship between means and ends within organizations. This way of thinking involves the development of certain techniques of analysis which become the property of professional groups. These techniques embody forms of power which have specific effects within the organization. They constitute part of the framework of rules about how organizations should operate.

In this chapter I want to look in more detail at the presuppositions embodied in the calculative rationality that is characteristic of modern organizations. These presuppositions have to be put in place by a social process. This process is linked in particular to the development of both accounting rationality and the accounting profession. In the first part of the chapter I focus particularly on this process. I then go on to consider in more detail how this has become embodied in the managerial division of labour.

The essence of the rationalization process

What are the essential elements of rationality and calculation? Rationality does not necessitate the use of a certain model of organization, Taylorist or Weberian. Rather, it involves the rational calculation of the relationship between organizational goals and the means at the disposal of the organization; there may be many models of organization that can be used. It is important that in modern societies these models present themselves as rational. In order for this to happen, however, certain concepts which we take for granted had to be developed and produced. A central role in this process was taken by the transition from qualitative modes of thinking and acting to quantitative modes. In particular, organizations had to be able to measure and think in terms of costs, revenues, etc.; the relationship between means (the utilization of capital and labour) and ends (the goal of profit – indeed, in more general terms, what profit was) had to be clarified. In order for this to happen, the basic ideas of accounting which have become increasingly more organized had to be developed. without these ideas it would be impossible to think about the relationship between ends and means that is essential to all organizational tasks.

Over the last 200 years organizations have increasingly presented 'accounts' of themselves in various forms of financial statements. It is tempting to consider these as social facts – that is, objective statements about the 'health' of the organization. What can be more factual than a profit and loss account? It is surely a technical presentation of facts about the organization.

Accounting's growing complexity is seen as a technical response to the growing complexity of organizational life. However what looks to be a solid edifice needs to be considered as something that has been constructed with a purpose by particular groups in ongoing social transactions. Hopwood elaborates this point:

> Rather than seeing organizational accounts as a technical reflec-
> tion of the pregiven economic imperatives facing organizational

administration, they are now being seen to be more actively constructed in order to create a particular economic visibility within the organization and a powerful means for positively enabling the governance and control of the organization along economic lines . . . Accounting is seen as having played a very positive role in the creation of a manageable organizational domain. A regime of economic visibility and calculation has positively enabled the creation and operation of an organization which facilitates the exercising of particular social conceptions of power. (Hopwood, 1987, p. 213)

The key concept is the idea of visibility. Accounting starts to make visible, to 'call to account' the operation of the organization. In doing so, as Hopper *et al.* (1987, p. 444) say, 'Accounting language pre-empts and influences agendas and meanings'.

The process of construction of accounting knowledge has been traced back over the last two centuries by a number of authors. A key article in this vein is Miller and O'Leary's 'Accounting and the Construction of the Governable Person' (1987). They follow the methodological prescriptions of Foucault by attempting a 'genealogy' of accounting knowledge; they define genealogy in the following way:

It concerns centrally a questioning of our contemporarily received notions by a demonstration of their historical emergence. The point of history in this sense is to make intelligible the way in which we think today by reminding us of its conditions of formation. Whether the terms be efficiency, rationality or motivation, genealogical analysis helps us to appreciate their ephemeral character . . . [Genealogical analysis] does not entail looking for a single point in history which would be the point of origin of our current practices. The emergence of our contemporary beliefs is viewed rather by reference to a complex of dispersed events. Genealogy does not lead us to solid foundations; rather it fragments and disturbs what we might like to see as the basis of our current ideas and practices. (Miller and O'Leary, 1987, p. 237)

Thus in relation to a genealogical approach to accounting, what are of interest are the multiple sources of the changes in discourse and practice that begin to lay the basis for accounting control during the nineteenth and twentieth centuries. In their examination of these issues, Hoskin and Macve argue that although elements of accounting discourse emerged by the fifteenth century, two central concepts – accountability and profitability – did not exist:

> The absence of these two constructs and their subsequent emergence, can, we suggest, be explicated along two related lines. First there is the issue of the temporal orientation of the whole process of accounting. Accounting was not systematically concerned with the future . . . Calculability, i.e. the use of the accounting record as a means for predictive control, whether of money, goods or workers, simply appears to be absent . . . there is a second reason for the lack of a discourse concerned with accountability and profitability – the absence of a full disciplinary technology which could be brought to bear on (and so create) an analysis of both financial and human value i.e. which could render the interrelated but separable values of products and persons calculable. (Hoskin and Macve, 1986, p. 123–4)

How were these discourses created? In their two articles Hoskin and Macve (1986 and 1988) suggest two sources for this change (though, as argued earlier, genealogical analysis is based on the idea of multiple sources of change). The first is the development of certain practices and ideas within the framework of educational practice. In particular, they point to the gradual development of the notion of the examination mark. The distinctive feature of this (which only began to appear around the late eighteenth century – indeed, after examinations themselves) is that:

> A new kind of mathematization was taking place on a number of fronts, which was tending to articulate the principle that human qualities could be quantified . . . It is not just a number but a specific kind of expression of human value, a double sign of human debit and credit . . . Its invention . . . marks the most significant locus of intersection between accounting and education practice to the point where it transforms the latter's power-knowledge possibilities, activating the micro-technology which produces positively and insistently, accountability and profitability. (Hoskin and Macve, 1986, p. 127)

The mark provides the basis for what Foucault calls the 'normalizing judgement' – the norm that individuals can be expected to achieve is now numerically assessed. It is not a guess or a hunch; a person's value in educational terms is now perfectly calculable. Hoskin and Macve argue that the link between the calculation and accounting of the individual in educational terms and accounting and calculation in wider terms can be seen very clearly through studying the West Point Military Academy in the USA. In the period 1817–32, West Point was controlled by Sylvanus Thayer. Thayer introduced a marking system for all aspects of work:

> This is a total human calculability system, where all aspects of performance, academic and behavioural, are constantly measured, evaluated and recorded in a joint numerical–linguistic language which is also a currency. It stretches from the past through the present and into the future. The past as recorded follows one insistently into the future within the institution and beyond; at the same time that future exerts a constant pressure on one's academic and behavioural performance in the present, as does the retrospective recall of the past (for good performance from now on may count against mistakes and failures already recorded). Thayer's cadets were truly rendered 'calculable men'. (Hoskin and Macve, 1988, p. 49)

According to the authors, the regime of calculation which Thayer instituted was exported via the people who went through it into a wide variety of outlets. In particular, they point to the impact of West Pointers on Springfield Armory (which as authors such as Hounshell, 1984, have argued, played a pivotal role in the development of the system of mass production) and on the railroad system (which Chandler, 1977, identifies as the arena of early innovations in managerial control). In both of these areas, West Pointers made major contributions using the techniques of calculation and accounting developed by Thayer. Hoskin and Macve summarize their ideas as follows:

> A whole new eco-system which went wider and deeper than any specific socio-economic system was being put in place, beginning with the sphere of elite education. A new regime of disciplinary organization and human accountability was internalized by the people who underwent that education . . . They were privy to a new wide-ranging set of power–knowledge relations . . . they were trained as disciplinary specialists, their ability and

conduct objectively evaluated through quantified measures. These three things – grammatocentric organization, specialist differentiation and quantified evaluation – they then exported to the world of business via the armories and the railroads. (Hoskin and Macve, 1988, p. 66)

Miller and O'Leary develop this argument in relation to the late nineteenth/early twentieth century, when scientific management and standard cost accounting techniques begin to be developed in earnest. They argued that these ideas were concerned to create norms or standards 'for the doing of work of every kind'. They go on to say:

Cost accounting would expand its domain, to enmesh the person in a calculus of expectations. In thus constructing a notion of the person we have argued that standard costing and budgeting provided a facilitative technology whereby, in time, various interventions to improve the person's performance would become possible . . . The efficiency of the person in the firm . . . is not something which can be observed with the naked eye. Indeed, one might say, it cannot exist until what is to be regarded as normal or standard has first been constructed. But once a norm is to hand, and especially when it gains expression within routinely applicable calculative apparatus like standard costing or budgeting, the person can become a subject for various human sciences. The deviations of the person from the norm, with all of their possible causes and consequences, become available for investigation and remedial action. (Miller and O'Leary, 1987, p. 262)

The argument is that the notion of the individual whose actions have a specific monetary value that can be determined in relation to past behaviour and predicted in relation to the future, is not something that occurs 'in nature'. It is a concept that was constructed from a variety of sources during the course of the nineteenth century. This process of construction is simultaneously a process of power and knowledge. In knowledge terms, the question arises as to how to evaluate the individual – indeed, how to 'know' the individual as an object of specific organizational practices. Boland argues that the end result of this process is that

The subject had now become an object of knowledge in a field that is organized by normalizing judgements. The kind of knowledge that is possible in this field is one in which objects are isolated, classified and located on a scale of differences and similarities. In this field we are looking for an essence that is a norm around which all other observations are imperfect realizations of the essential object. A science of tasks and a science of movements are developed in this field of normalized judgements which are the province of a new breed of experts. (Boland, 1987, p. 269)

The construction of the 'governable person' is a process that occurs in a variety of sites during the nineteenth century. Foucault traced this process in relation to crime and punishment as well as in relation to sexuality (see Foucault, 1979, 1981). Authors such as Hoskin and Macve and Miller and O'Leary have looked at this in relation to the growth of disciplines within education and within the work setting. They all lead to the idea of a disparate series of practices based on notions of the measurability of normality and deviance. The task of measuring is the province of the expert who is simultaneously endowed with the power of defining the normal and treating the deviant to bring it back to the norm. Thus power and knowledge go together; they are working simultaneously through practices on the bodies of people to make them 'normal'.

To return to the nature of rationalization itself, the argument is that accounting within organizations is about the construction of normalizing judgments. It consists of the task of making visible both within the organization and in a different form outside the organization the costs of what people and machines do and comparing this with what they might do (see Hines, 1988, for a novel and enlightening account of these processes). In providing the techniques whereby everything can be evaluated in numerical terms, accountancy provides the archetypal example of the rationalization process in action.

Rationalization in action

In the previous section, I have shown how calculation and rationalization have developed in organizations through the development of norms of accountability. These are the rules on which modern organizations are based. They have to be continually produced in organizational practice by particular actors. The actors with the central role in the maintenance of these processes are the professional experts within organizations. These groups constitute a new middle class or, as certain authors prefer to label it, a service class (Goldthorpe, 1982; Abercrombie and Urry, 1983). This service class has its own causal powers in the sense that it can be seen to be shaping certain key social institutions into a similar form. It is defined by its possession of professional qualifications and its use of those qualifications to shape organizations in line with its understanding of efficiency and to reshape society along those lines.

The concept of professional

Professionals make a claim to a specific body of knowledge regarding a certain object. Thus professionals are expected to undergo a period of training when they learn this body of knowledge. However, being a professional involves more than simply learning abstract knowledge; it also involves the ability to apply it. This notion of application clearly brings out the power dimension of professional knowledge. In medical terms, the professional learns through 'clinical' experience when to act on the body of the client – in other words, when to exert professional authority in order to get the client to do what he/she would not otherwise have done. The professional will justify this as being in the client's best interests – the client does not have the understanding to realize that this action is in his/her best interests and therefore needs the advice of the expert. Why should the client trust the professional? Because the professional is certified as having undergone a rigorous training in the knowledge and practice of their particular skill and also because the professional belongs to a professional body which monitors the exercise of those skills. The existence of the professional body is a crucial organizational feature; the body will be responsible for legitimating the practitioner and presenting the profession's image to the public at large. Complaints about professionals will be dealt with by this body, which has the ultimate sanction of barring somebody from practising if complaints are found proven.

Clearly, as a number of authors have pointed out, there are many differences between professional groups. (There is a huge literature on professions and professionalism; among the most relevant references for this argument are Johnson, 1972; Boreham, 1983; Derber, 1983; Fielding and Portwood, 1980; Larson, 1980; Saks, 1983.) In particular, Johnson has pointed to the different employment relationships in which they are located. The professions of doctor, lawyer and accountant were founded in Britain to serve well-off individual clients who voluntarily came to the professional for help and advice. The clientele was therefore dispersed and fragmented, whilst the profession was united through professional associations and training. Although the situation has become more complicated with the employment of these groups in large bureaucracies as well as private practice, the basic power position based on the professional association has been retained. Others among the newer professions, e.g. teachers and social workers, have found themselves in a different position: they have been employed by the state to work on an involuntary clientele. The nature of their professional expertise has never been accepted in the same way as that of doctors, etc., either by their clients or their paymasters.

In spite of these differences, there is a shared structure to these professional groups. All claim expertise on the basis of their education and training. They all claim power over people based on notions of normal and deviant and their own ability to 'treat' this in some way, and thus they claim to be acting in a disinterested professional manner. This can be referred to as an ideology of 'credentialism' in which power derives from the possession of professional credentials. This group therefore shares an interest in the expansion of credentialism and the accoutrements of professionalism to all aspects of society. Since professionalism is based on concepts of calculability and accountability, we can say that the process of rationalization is carried forward by the expansion of professional groups.

It is important not to mistake the nature of this process. It is being suggested that professional groups seek to expand the extent of 'professional ways of thinking and acting'; this involves an expansion of rationalized power practices. But as Foucault points out, these rational practices are only 'rational' from the point of view of the groups which generate them. They are not rational *per se*. We should be looking, therefore, at how these practices get carried between different sites and legitimated as the rational way to do things. Once we look at these practices we see that specific interests are being served. Furthermore, we should not limit our analysis simply to those groups that have successfully managed to label themselves as 'professionals'; the techniques which lie behind professionalism are rooted in notions of accountability, calculability and rationalization. These features are part of the education of large numbers of specialists in the management field who might not recognize a description of themselves as professional. They certainly will recognize the framework of rational analysis as central to the way they work. This new middle class is legitimated through higher education and professional training which provides it with credentials for professional practice. It takes its skills and techniques into organizations and attempts to shape the organization to fit.

The service class and its techniques do not exist outside the framework of serving the interests of capital (though it is important to recognize that the concept of 'service' involves defining what is in the interests of the person served). How the service class 'serves' capital is a key question.

The question can be considered by looking at recent studies of the early capitalist Josiah Wedgwood. These studies show the central importance of learning to account for costs, a process in which Wedgwood took a central innovatory role. Wedgwood was one of the earliest British industrialists; he developed a production and sales system for his pottery that made him one of the richest capitalists of his day, and built a reputation for Wedgwood pottery that continues to this day. In the second half of the eighteenth century when Wedgwood was developing his business, neither the valorization process (in Marxist terms, the labour process in which surplus value is created) nor the realization process (the process whereby commodities were sold and their surplus realized) was well understood. What Wedgwood initially understood was how to make pottery. The factory he set up was designed for the making of pottery. Although Wedgwood would not have continued to operate if he had not made a profit, the reason he made a profit in the early stages was more luck than rational calculation. Hopwood says of Wedgwood's early career:

Accounting information did not inform his product and pricing decisions or the selection of his methods of work . . . Indeed Wedgwood himself admitted that 'he could do little more than guess at costs' and 'further conceded that his attempts at total costing were out by a factor of two'. (Hopwood, 1987, p. 215)

In these early stages, Wedgwood was able to sell as much pottery as he could make at a substantial profit. However, in 1772 there was a major economic recession which hit the pottery industry as well as every other industry. The result was that Wedgwood was forced to reconsider in detail the processes of production and realization. In the process, he established certain innovations that became the basis for much later work. Wedgwood decided that he might survive the recession if he lowered his prices in order to stimulate demand for his products. The problem was how to reduce prices sufficiently to stimulate demand and at the same time retain a profit. Wedgwood set about the painstaking task of constructing the costs of his products. In doing so he uncovered 'a history of embezzlement, blackmail, chicanery and what Wedgwood called 'extravagance and dissipation' (McKendrick *et al.*, 1973, p. 61). The result was that Wedgwood reorganized his accounts office, sacking his head clerk who had been responsible not just for stealing from him but also for various sexual misdemeanours. (This is an early example of the way industrialists sought to banish sexuality from the work setting: Burrell, 1984.) Crucially Wedgwood had developed the basis for a form of cost accounting within the organization which in turn could be applied both to the valorization process and the realization process:

A basis for a more systematic consideration of marketing policies was created . . . The newly emergent facts of the economic provided a basis for re-appraising the organization of the manufacturing processes, the advantages of large volume production and the calculation of piece rates, wage rates and bonuses . . . The inner workings of the organization had been made amenable to a new form of economic analysis. (Hopwood, 1987, p. 217)

Wedgwood soon realized that since so much expenditure was fixed, for example in the areas of machinery, rent and to a degree wages, it made sense to try and produce the maximum amount possible at any particular time, since in this way fixed costs could be spread and overall prices lowered. It is also of interest to note the explicit distinction Wedgwood made between the cost of an article and its actual price in the shops:

> Outside periods of depression, Wedgwood was well aware that in an imperfect market, with explicit strategies for product differentiation, there was no necessary relationship between cost and price. As McKendrick points out: 'The phrase "The prices Mr. Bentley will regulate as he thinks proper" occurs so frequently in letters on pricing that one soon recognizes it as a familiar refrain.' As Wedgwood himself put it, 'When I fix a price upon any new article, please to remember that I have regard to the expence of workmanship than the apparent and comparative value with other things so you'll correct it by the latter which is often most essential' . . . In McKendrick's words, Wedgwood judged 'the cost of production, the difficulty of making, and the number he could easily make, and then Bentley would decide at which market to aim them, at what price to charge them and in what quantities to make them'. (Hopwood, 1987, p. 217)

Wedgwood showed how the early capitalists could begin to overcome the uncertainty of capitalist production, though it is important to remember the following points made by Hoskin and Macve:

> Wedgwood's initiative remained a one-off (cost accounting remained to be 'rediscovered' a century later) and even within his own factory it is not clear that the innovation led to any sustained efficiency and productivity from the workforce. Its main value lay in the identification and removal of the most corrupt factors while it had a certain preventative role in limiting the recurrence of the worst offences. (Hoskin and Macve, 1986, p. 124)

Certain key elements were involved which needed to be integrated. First of all, there was the process of production itself – making the commodity. Wedgwood was a highly skilled potter in his own right as well as possessing an aesthetic and design sensibility that helped give his work a ready market, even in the segmented and localized marketing systems of the eighteenth century. Second, however, Wedgwood was concerned to produce at a profit. This involved two things: ensuring an accurate measurement of costs, and ensuring control of the labour process. Third, once the commodities were produced, they needed to be sold. Here again there were a number of relevant issues: the question of price and the relationship between costs and prices; and the problem of gaining a market and the use within this of rudimentary techniques of advertising. In relation to this McKendrick quotes the following passage from Wedgwood:

> The great people have had these Vases in their Palaces long enough for them to be seen and admired by the Middling Classes of People, which class we know are vastly, I had almost said infinitely, superior in number to the Great and though a great price was, I believe at first necessary to make the Vases esteemed Ornaments for Palaces, that Reason no longer exists. Their character is established and the Middling People would probably buy quantitys of them at a reduced price. (McKendrick *et al.*, 1983, p. 55)

The interrelationships between these different elements in the capitalist enterprise also open up the possibility for a disjuncture between them. In Wedgwood's day, the owner–manager effectively controlled all these functions. As organizations became more complex, so these functions became separated into departments and thus the institutional basis for differentiation was established.

Professionals, circuits of capital and management

Before considering this further, it is necessary to consider another circuit of capital that further complicates the picture presented. So far I have considered valorization and realization, but there is also the circuit of financial capital itself. When the capitalist wishes to set up a business and commence the purchase of constant and variable capital, he (or she) will almost certainly need some sort of loan or credit mechanism to allow him to get started, since profits will only be realized at a substantially later stage. The means whereby capital is raised result in a further series of complications. How is the capital to be obtained? Various alternatives have been developed (and these will be considered in more detail later): a bank or other type of loan and the sale of shares and debentures are the two most common. Under what circumstances are outside investors likely to agree to hand over their capital? This involves the calculation of costs and benefits and the assumption that profits can be realized in the future on the basis of predictions now. Thus this third circuit involves the link between the organization and outside sources of capital and finance, both short-term and long-term.

The process whereby these circuits of capital become articulated with the managerial division of labour is complex. As capitalist organizations become larger, the chances of individuals overseeing all aspects of the process in the way which Wedgewood did, became less. Instead, the potential arises for each of the circuits of capital to have its own relative autonomy, and with this its own associated group of occupations. Whilst all of these circuits and functions go up to make what Carchedi (1977) calls 'the global function of capital', there is no reason to assume that they work together harmoniously. Indeed, we can expect that each of the occupations associated with the various circuits develops its own power/knowledge practices and enters into competition with other occupations to have its particular discourse accepted as the dominant one for the 'global function of capital'. Thus whilst each discourse centres on a particular aspect of the managerial division of labour and develops the tools of rational calculation within its own domain (e.g. accounting, advertising, production engineering, etc.), the key question is which discourse is predominant and can claim successfully to speak on behalf of capital as a whole.

This issue has been raised by Armstrong (1984) in his discussions of competition between organizational professions. Armstrong considers the implementation of scientific management in organizations and argues that Braverman makes an unequivocal identification of the deskilling impetus with the needs of capitalism *per se*. With only passing reference to the question as to why techniques of scientific management are so widely used in non-capitalist societies such as the Soviet Union (which is dismissed as a 'hybrid formation', 'a reflexive, imitative and, one hopes, transitional form') Braverman (1973) claims that scientific management's role was 'to render conscious and systematic, the formerly unconscious tendency of capitalist production' (p. 121). It is the search for profit and the capitalist's unerring instinct as to the one best way to make a profit which leads him (it usually was *him*!) to scientific management techniques. Unfortunately, as has been shown in earlier chapters, this was not obvious to managers or capitalists. Thus in the United States there was much initial resistance to Taylorism among employers and managers. Similarly in Britain, Taylorism only gradually became accepted and then in the form of the Bedaux system and only within particular industries. (See Littler, 1982, for a detailed account of the Bedaux system in the UK.) On the continent, the progress of Taylorism was even slower, whilst in Japan it was never popular. (See Littler, 1982, and Stark, 1980). Does this constitute a failure on the part of capitalists to recognize where their true interests lie, or is something else behind it?

The answer lies in considering the division of labour within management that was beginning to emerge around this time. Stark, for example, has suggested that Braverman failed to realize that Taylorism was very much an engineer's ideology about work. This is not too surprising when one considers that Taylor himself was originally trained as an engineer. In fact, Taylor was to a significant degree expanding into the human arena principles that had been developed in materials engineering. Armstrong says:

> The approach to the physical process of production grew out of engineers' previous experience of machine design. Workers' movements were analysed and redesigned so as to achieve the most economical sequence, an approach which inherently pre-supposes the subordination of manual to mental labour and close directive supervision. Moreover there is an analogy between the reduction of skilled to simple labour and the earlier development by mechanical engineers of interchangeable parts as a solution to the problem of coordinating production. (Armstrong, 1984, p. 99)

Armstrong argues that engineers should be seen as one possible grouping within the global function of capital (this term being used to 'denote the assemblage of roles which, in modern capitalism, performs the functions once carried out by the individual capitalist' (p. 98). In this view engineers aimed through Taylorism to improve their own position within this global function. They aimed to become the dominant occupational group whose expertise defined the interests of all managers. They planned to do this by developing their own specific skills of analysis and calculation, originally used on inanimate machines, and applying them to other aspects of the organization.

Given this view, it is not surprising that other managers resisted the engineers' claims to be central to the organization. The 'collective mobility project' of the engineers was intimately wrapped up with the success of Taylorism, according to Armstrong, but because there were other possible contenders for the mantle of central professional group within the global function of capital, its success was not guaranteed. On the contrary, what occurred following the original thrust of Taylorism, although it is only gradually being uncovered, seems to have been a complex reconstruction of management functions. Within engineering itself, there seems to be general agreement (see Armstrong 1984, 1987a, 1987b; Child *et al.*, 1983; Noble, 1984; Glover, 1985; Glover and Kelly, 1987) that the attempt to achieve overall hegemony failed. Armstrong argues that in Britain and the USA in particular, engineers' claim to a special and general expertise that was relevant to human as well as material engineering failed. The human elements of engineering were rapidly separated from the position of engineer as such. Separate professional groups quickly began to arise, particularly in the work study movement, claiming a specific expertise in human engineering. Other functions set out by Taylor for the engineer began to be taken over by accountants. Engineers sank back to being purely technical experts. Their role was to solve the technical problems as put to them by the managers of the large corporations. Engineering solutions themselves had to be taken up in a way that was profitable and met the criteria of the accountants. Without the endorsement of higher managers, engineers were powerless; their work was crucially shaped by their relatively subordinate role within the global function of capital. Nevertheless, what engineering had done was to place some of the tools of the natural sciences on the agenda of management. They may have sought to provide a solution that was not accepted (scientific management) and a leadership that was rejected (their own), but they undoubtedly did contribute to a growing process of rationalization that was occurring in companies.

Accountancy in the global function of capital

This process becomes clearer when one looks at the role of one of the other main groups within the global function of capital. In the USA and the UK this group took over from engineers in formulating a collective mobility project which was to give them a hegemonic position among the other competing groups in the global function of capital. This group was the accountancy profession.

Accountancy, I will argue, is a set of professional practices which spans the three main circuits of capital. Accountancy is crucial to the provision of capital through its role in auditing and approving measures of a company's profitability, thus giving outside investors information on which to base their decisions about lending, etc. Accountancy is essential to the production process through the practices associated with cost and management accountancy. Finally, accountancy is critical to the realization process itself – the calculation of profits and the manner of distribution of surplus to the various agents involved. (See Cooper and Hopper's (1987) introduction to a selection of critical papers on accounting for wider discussion of these issues.) In order to establish these points, I shall now look in more detail at the practice of accountancy.

In the nineteenth century, accountancy in Britain had a limited but nevertheless crucial importance. In particular, it gained power from its position as an intermediary between the large capitalist institutions through the role of auditing. In publicly quoted companies there was a legal obligation to produce annual reports for shareholders which indicated the financial health of the company. The role of accountancy firms was to attest that these accounts were a proper statement of the firm's position. Other capitalist institutions could then use these accounts as a guide to whether to invest, lend or deal in any way with the company. A legal monopoly over the auditing function gave accountancy a powerful position, particularly where, as in Britain, there was an active secondary market in shares. In other countries, where the secondary market was less significant and capital for new investment was more likely to come through banks than via new share issues, the accountant did not gain such a role (Armstrong, 1987b; see also Macdonald, 1984, on accountants in Scotland). At this stage, however, the role of accountants was mainly limited to the task of providing information to significant others outside the organization in order to aid the circuit of financial capital. As Armstrong (1984, p. 102) says, 'The adaptation of auditing techniques to the problem of internal control within capitals, as opposed to that of regularizing relations between them or between capitals and the state, had not yet begun'.

Linked to this was the role of accountants in bankruptcy proceedings. Under the 1862 Companies Act, when a company was insolvent an official liquidator for the company had to be appointed by the creditors. This position was almost invariably given to an accountant, who then had the job of advising the creditors on the full position of the company and winding it up or restructuring it in such a way as to maximize returns to the creditors. As well as being a highly profitable part of accountants' business, this also drew accountants more into the field of business policy than mere auditing. This was to be an important basis for later expansions of the accountants' role.

At this stage in the nineteenth century, the costing of internal organizational operations was beginning to expand under the impetus of Taylorism. Internal costing was a process that was often undertaken by engineers. The major accounting firms of the time had little interest in the development of cost accounting:

> The future of cost accountancy as a body of knowledge was, at this time, open. It could conceivably have been incorporated into the knowledge base of the engineering profession . . . Alternatively it could have given rise to a profession independent both of engineering and accountancy. However, although an Institute of Cost and Works accountants was formed, this only occurred after World War 1 when the third possibility had materialised: the reintegration of cost accountancy with the main body of accounting knowledge . . . At the outbreak of the First World War . . . many of the essential techniques of cost accounting had been pioneered but . . . their adoption was proceeding very slowly. (Armstrong, 1987b, p. 419)

Two factors in particular increased the role of accountants in the internal affairs of the organization and brought them into a much more central role in the internal affairs of organizations. The first was the role of war. In the 1914–18 period, and even more so in 1939–45, governments sought to integrate business into the war effort. Firms were allocated production for the war effort. This necessitated a switch of physical resources in return for which the firms expected guaranteed profits. Government, on the other hand, had to resist profiteering. According to Armstrong:

> The solution adopted was to determine, on the basis of access to

contractors' accounts, the production costs of a huge variety of products in a large number of factories . . . In order to cope with the problem, eminent city accountants were appointed to senior positions in the war ministries – in the much neglected area of cost accountancy. (1987b, pp. 423–4)

Until this time the calculation of internal costs had proceeded in a very haphazard manner. The government looked to the established profession of accountancy to aid them in calculating the true costs of the manufacturers. According to Loft (1986, p. 146) there were about 340 chartered and incorporated accountants from the City of London working for the Ministry of Munitions in the calculations of costs. Accountancy became a reserved occupation, so great was the demand for those who knew something about costing. As for the manufacturers, they were keen to ensure that they would not lose out, and so they too began to employ cost accountants in greater numbers. According to Loft,

In retrospect after the war it was felt that costing investigations were not so effective as they could have been, one of the problems being the lack of training of those carrying them out . . . The government's war-time regulations implicitly presupposed manufacturers to have a formal knowledge of the costs of their business activities . . . Unfortunately for the government, many manufacturers did not have these figures available and in the attempt to acquire them there was a 'coming into the light' of cost accountants and cost accounting. (p. 148)

The war propelled traditional accountants to take cost accountancy much more seriously.

The second major factor that thrust accounting more into dealing with the internal affairs of organizations was the slump and depression of the inter-war years. During this period many major British companies ran into profitability crises due to the overvaluation of sterling and the decline in world trade consequent on the Wall Street Crash and the rise of protectionism. The Austin Motor Company, for example, went into receivership. Others like Dunlop and Unilever came close to this fate, while still other companies sought to join forces and create a large combine that could survive the storms of the period, for example ICI. Armstrong describes the responses of those involved, i.e. shareholders and managers, in the following way:

In all cases the crises appeared in fundamentally financial terms (profitability or liquidity) . . . Since accountants were already, as auditors, trusted to interpret these on behalf of shareholders, investigations into the crises tended to be carried out and the remedies proposed by accountants . . . Apart from restructuring the external finances of the companies, these accountant investigators universally recommended some form of centralised budgetary monitoring and control system. (Armstrong, 1987b, p. 424)

The rationalization movement of the period was also significant in installing accountants and financial techniques in central positions in organizations. Rationalization referred to the process whereby existing companies were brought together into one large company. The single large company, it was believed, would be better able to survive. In industries like steel, shipbuilding, mining, textiles and chemicals – all industries badly damaged by the fall in world trade – employers, trade unions and shareholders were keen to join together to rationalize. They sought government support for this in the tangible sense of providing a protectionist trade policy, behind which the newly rationalized companies could supposedly build themselves up again on the basis of the home market. The form that rationalization took, however, was mainly a financial reconstruction:

The merged companies were often organized, on the advice of accountants, as holding companies. In this form of company organization, the component plants or operations are held together by shareholdings owned by a common parent company so that the basic monitoring instrument remains the audit . . . the holding company form, with its weak and exclusively financial headquarters control, remained typical of large British companies until at least the 1960s. (Armstrong, 1987b, p. 426)

Taken together, the reconstruction of certain companies and the rationalization of others took a particular form in Britain during the inter-war years:

It constituted . . . a 'top-down' system of controlling large enterprises, connecting, however crudely, the apex of the corporate pyramid to the productive process itself. As such it represented a major incursion by the accounting profession into the function of the extraction of surplus value from the labour process. Partly because of their possession of relevant techniques, significant numbers of accountants began to be recruited into senior managements at about this time. (Armstrong, 1987b, p. 425).

The holding companies that developed lacked the tight financial integration of the multidivisional corporations emerging at this time in large numbers in the USA. They were characterized by a number of features. First, there was no attempt to reorganize the companies within the holding company in order to provide a unified marketing or production strategy. The companies that had been brought together sought to retain their identity and independence. (For more details, see Loveridge, 1981.) Second, the units within the holding company reported to the centre effectively on a year-by-year basis through the provision of an audit. There was no attempt to introduce a continuous series of financial information that would be available to the head office for examination at any time. Third, the leadership of the company was primarily oriented not to production or even marketing, but to the problems of the overall financing of the company and its relationship with creditors and shareholders. Fourth, although internal cost accounting procedures were improving and developing, there was no major impetus from the central offices to ensure that all units of the company operated equally well.

These trends were continued and reinforced during the Second World War when government control of industry became even tighter. In the post-war period in Britain, accountants consolidated their position within firms through the expansion of cost accountancy or management accountancy. A further important factor was the establishment of new types of company organization. As organizations grew larger, it became less possible for top management to consider the detail of operation of every plant. Instead, companies were divided into divisions, each of which was a profit centre. From the perspective of corporate management, what was of concern about divisions was their relative profitability rather than their physical production processes, which were the responsibility of divisional management. Thus, increasingly, the company's affairs were to be translated into monetary terms. Once again it was up to the accountants to devise information systems capable of performing internal auditing functions, so that corporate management could assess on a frequent basis the relative profitability of the division. The growth of multidivisional forms was a further factor enhancing the position and power of accountants. Although the multidivisional form took time to become established, it nevertheless represented, in Armstong's words, 'a further subordination of operational to financial decision-making: a downgrading of production and the engineer in favour of the headquarters accountant/executive'.

By the 1970s in Britain, accountants were entrenched in a hugely powerful position within companies as well as in the regulatory bodies of industry. This was further increased in two ways. First, there was the area of government regulation of industry. One obvious aspect of this was the company taxation system, which had grown in the post-1945 period. As governments sought to impose new forms of taxation, so company accountants increased as firms sought ways of tax avoidance. Increased government intervention in the form of aid packages granted on certain conditions also necessitated accountants to work out the relative merits of any such scheme. Second, there was growth in the financial markets from the early 1970s. The floating of sterling and the other major currencies in the early 1970s, the internationalization of banking and stock dealing, and the growth of financial institutions like pension trusts, unit trusts, investment trusts, etc., have all called for increased accountancy skills in the manipulation and interpretation of financial information. The massive expansion of share dealing associated with these trends and the emphasis placed on financial information and performance indicators places accountants in a central position. Companies need to be able to show rapid growth in order to protect their shares. As has been shown frequently in recent years, this is done quickest and more spectacularly by takeovers and mergers. Accountants play a central role in enhancing their company's profitability in this way as well as in advising on the various ways of financing such deals.

Within capitalist firms in Britain and the USA, accountancy has risen to a position of dominance in the managerial division of labour. What are the implications of this? It is possible to explore this issue by returning to a consideration of the way in which accountants supplanted engineers and the consequence of this. As has already been suggested, in Britain and the USA the 'collective mobility project' of engineers failed for a number of reasons. Engineers failed to establish a powerful professional association capable of gaining for them a monopoly (legal or otherwise) over particular tasks central to the organization. Instead, professional engineers were divided according to their particular skill – mechanical, civil, chemical, electrical, etc. – and were unable to present a united front. This initial fragmentation was aggravated by the expansion of engineering under the guise of Taylorism into the work of human engineering. Another group of engineers arose, this time with work study specialisms and later developing into ergonomics, organization and method, operational research, etc.; this group gradually severed its connections with the technical side of engineering and gravitated instead towards forming closer links with other groups within management such as accountants. Thus engineers were left in a subordinate position comparable with that which Taylorism had aimed to extract them.

This subordinate position has been the subject of much recent debate. Child *et al.* (1983) (see also Glover, 1985; Glover and Kelly, 1987) have argued that a significant part of any explanation of Britain's economic decline must derive from this subordination of engineers to the bureaucratized constraints imposed on engineers by other more powerful professional groups, particularly accountants. This is reinforced, they argue, by four mechanisms:

1. The tendency of British managing directors to be drawn heavily from the sales and finance functions.
2. The high evaluation of accountancy functions, which excludes those in production from higher management.
3. A preoccupation with short-run profits allied to a reluctance to bear the risk and delayed pay-off of investment, the result being to reduce the standing of production in the firm not only through curbing the expansion of production facilities but also because of the blame attached to production for the delivery, quality and cost problems arising with old plant.
4. The appointment of non-production people as non-executive directors of companies – usually people with banking or civil service/army connections.

Child *et al.*'s argument is reinforced by Noble's work (1977, 1984), which indicates the subordination of technical engineering design functions to the control of the corporation and the state. Decisions to advance production are taken on the basis of a clear financial assessment of the design. Engineers are subject to the control of decisions by non-engineers. According to Armstrong,

> Engineering activity, though esoteric and inaccessible to lay judgement in itself, must end in a physical product or process which *can* be judged by outsiders (unlike, say, the work of accountants which ends as a balance sheet drawn up by themselves). In the face of this, the profession's ideology must somehow sustain the position that the subordination of engineers to non-engineers is still undesirable. This it nobly attempts, arguing that technological innovation in British industry suffers due to the caution of senior managers ignorant of the 'engineering dimension' . . . and that the quality of design work suffers when supervised by non-engineers. . . . Nevertheless the 'problem' of the openness of engineering to lay judgement remains. (Armstrong, 1984, p. 108)

In a later paper, Armstrong has elaborated on the relationship between engineers and accountants:

> It is argued that in British usage, the term 'management' has become identified with the administration and control of capitalist enterprises rather than with the intellectual component of the work of producing goods or sevices . . . This idea of management is structurally based in the high priority which British managements have typically had to assign to such aspects of enterprise strategy as procuring long-term capital and marketing . . . Because it is the senior industrialists who operate within this frame of reference, the corresponding conception of management has become a selection principle which operates against the managerial credibility of engineering. (Armstrong, 1987a, p. 424)

Armstrong emphasizes the centrality in British organizations of the notion of corporate strategy revolving around financial aspects. Financial information abstracts from the specifics of organizational operations and in so doing provides the basis for a universal model of management. Top management in Britain has become increasingly concerned with being successful, not simply in the obvious sense of selling products or services for a profit, but also in the sense of having a 'good' relationship with financial institutions and shareholders. Success in the market-place does not guarantee safety from hostile takeover bids, which nowadays can be launched by companies much smaller than the ones they are seeking to take over, if they can get support from key financial institutions in the City. Thus the essential skills needed at the top of British companies relate to this ability to mediate between the pressures of the system of secondary share-dealing and the pressures of achieving successful growth. As previously argued, this mediation has been increasingly accomplished through takeover and merger rather than through endogenous self-generating and self-sustaining growth in the market. From this point of view, engineers have a low status:

> The engineers' claim to positions of corporate power tends to be couched in terms of a productivist ideology. Whilst natural enough as an expression of the anchorage of professional engineering in productive labour, this is unlikely to impress a managerial elite whose conception of management is something concerned with corporate strategy . . . Judged from such a standpoint, engineering experience and expertise are at best irrelevant and at worst a disability in aspirants to senior management positions. Since the engineering profession cannot escape from its anchorage in intellectual productive labour, and tends to press its case for managerial status in productivist terms, it appears from the point of view of the dominant management culture to emphasize the wrong priorities. (Armstrong, 1987b, p. 430–37)

Nichols (1986) has made similar points, arguing that the so-called 'productivity' problem in British industry arises not from workers but from the inability of British managers to manage 'effectively' at the point of production. He argues that they lack the production engineering skills characteristic of German and Japanese managers, a point which is reinforced by studies of what managers do. The picture in the UK and the USA is one of managers as 'networkers', i.e. concerned essentially with people and planning rather than production problems. (On what managers do see Hales, 1986, for a general review; Stewart, 1983, on the UK, and Mintzberg, 1973, and Kotter, 1981, on the USA are important empirical studies; on the production of managers through managerial education see Whiteley *et al.*, 1981; Whiteley, 1988; for a further critique of

British managers see Anthony, 1986.)

This characteristic subordination of engineers to accountants and the overall domination of accountants within capitalist organization settings is peculiar to the UK and USA. In West Germany the role of the two groups is different. In West German companies, professional engineers dominate managerial hierarchies, and the idea of management as a universal task concerned with the control and manipulation of abstract financial information is relatively insignificant. There management and management education is concerned with the management of a particular production process. Thus whereas in British management education there is a distinction between prestigious 'abstract' subjects such as financial management and lower-status 'concrete' subjects such as production engineering, in Germany the two are intertwined. As a result, there is not the basis for the development of professional rivalries and the separation of interests characteristic of the US/UK relationship between engineers and accountants. It is not just that engineers are accounts-literate, which is a reform of British management education often proposed by engineering bodies, but that to be a manager in the German context is about having both a technical and a financial capability.

Why have these differences arisen? A full consideration of national differences must await the final chapter, but it is possible to present some relevant points briefly. In Britain and the USA, as has been outlined, accountants built on the base of their private practice in the area of auditing to expand their roles as the key intermediaries between the financial institutions and industrial companies. In Germany, by contrast, industrial companies and banks did not adopt such arm's length relationships. Banks became closely associated with particular companies, lending to them at stable rates over the long term. In return they expected to be kept well-informed, frequently through directorships on the companies with which they had such relationships. In these circumstances they were less reliant on abstract financial information and more concerned about the future growth and production potential of the organization than their counterparts in Britain. Why German banks developed in this way in turn relates to the late industrialization of Germany and the way in which the state used the banks to provide long-term capital to industry, rather than relying on the market mechanisms of share-dealing.

Conclusions

In this chapter I have looked at the emergence of organizational professionals, variously called the 'new middle class' or the 'service class'. I have argued that they are the bearers of the process of rationalization. Their training in the various techniques of control and calculation, initially established in the nineteenth century on the basis of a series of new concepts related to individuals, norms, costs, benefits, revenue, etc. and expanded in the twentieth century through the development of higher education institutions and professional bodies, has placed them in central positions in organizations. Whilst the basis of techniques of calculation and rationality are shared among professional groups, there are nevertheless rivalries between them. Thus the service class is not a totally homogeneous entity. Rivalries deriving from the specific area of professional competence and the organizational setting in which it is exercised means that there are differences and conflicts between these groups. Of central importance here is the role of the accounting profession itself. My argument has been that in the UK and, to a lesser extent, the USA, this profession has gained a dominant role in defining the structure of capitalist organizations.

The abstract values of rationality and calculation to which these groups appeal are realized in specific techniques and ways of thinking which are constructed on the basis of particular interests. Professional knowledge in Foucault's terms derives from the 'will to power' on the part of its proponents. It can never be abstract and value-free.

Finally, it needs to be remembered that this process occurs within the framework of a capitalist society. These groups are servants of capital; though they have their own specific professional interests and though they may be influential and instrumental in the definition of capitalist goals, they remain servants rather than masters. It is to this theme that I shall turn in chapter 5, where I show the continued central importance of the mechanisms of the market and, associated with this, the central importance of the capitalist class and the way in which it affects societal-wide co-ordination across the institutional spheres of economy-state and civil society. In the next chapter I wish to consider this issue in relation to non-capitalist organizations.

4 Rationalization and Institutionalization in the State and Civil Society

In this chapter I discuss the way in which certain ideas about the legitimate ways to structure work relations in organizational settings spread from one type of organization to another. There are two main points to the argument. The first is that there is a process of institutional isomorphism occurring in modern societies that draws organizations towards the structures developed in capitalist firms. This process depends on the idea that all organizations can share a similar structure, not in the sense of the same patterns of job design or management system, but in the sense that they can all use the same techniques of rational calculation. This has given rise to the view that a rationalized set of practices is common to all organizational and professional functioning. However, the argument I shall make, which is congruent with points developed in previous chapters, is that there is a 'loose coupling' between the public presentation of many organizations which is based around the legitimized values of rationalization and their actual internal work relations.

The second point is that the carriers of this myth into organizations are organizational professionals, particularly those trained in accountancy, but also others such as personal managers and works study people, who have imbibed credentialist ideas. Their role has been to try to structure all organizations along the lines of those developed in the capitalist sector. The disjuncture between the myths, the organizational professionals and work within these organizations is the object of concern.

Institutional isomorphism

The concept of institutional isomorphism has been developed by DiMaggio and Powell. They argue that:

> Once disparate organizations in the same line of business are structured in an actual field, powerful forces emerge that lead them to become more similar to one another . . . The concept that best captures the process of homogenization is ismomorphism . . . Isomorphism is a constraining process that forces one unit in a population to resemble other units that face the same set of environmental conditions. (DiMaggio and Powell, 1983, p. 143)

The authors distinguish two types of isomorphism. First, there is the type that arises from competitive pressures, i.e. from a number of organizations seeking to get the best fit between themselves and the market. Competitive isomorphism, as they call it, is a theme which has been developed in other approaches to organizations, particularly those concerned with the operation of the market. (This will be considered in more detail in Chapter 5.) Second, however,

> Organizations compete not just for resources and customers, but for political power and institutional legitimacy, for social as well as economic fitness. The concept of institutional isomorphism is a useful tool for understanding the politics and ceremony that pervade much modern organizational life. (p. 150)

The authors go on to identify three mechanisms of institutional isomorphic change:

> 1) coercive isomorphism that stems from political influence and the problem of legitimacy; 2) mimetic isomorphism resulting from standard responses to uncertainty; and 3) normative isomorphism, associated with professionalization. (p. 150)

Coercive isomorphism, the authors argue, 'results from both formal and informal pressures exerted on organizations by other organizations upon which they are dependent and by cultural expectations in the society within which organizations function' (p. 150). This is particularly relevant to the nature of work in state organizations such as hospitals, schools, the civil service, etc. To state the point in general terms, the development of techniques of control and power within capitalist organizations has become central to people's perceptions of legitimate organizational structure. The tendency to create systems of accounting and control within which managerial strategies shape work performance criteria according to measurable characteristics and achieve success or failure according to measurable criteria about the 'financial health' of the organization, has become a powerful image. It increasingly exerts an effect, particularly on state organizations, where work relations, although not based on capital–labour are nevertheless to a significant extent money-based. State organizations can be coerced into adopting such practices by governments bent on expanding the influence of capitalist relations.

DiMaggio and Powell also distinguish mimetic processes towards institutional isomorphism:

> Uncertainty is a powerful force that encourages imitation. When organizational technologies are poorly understood, when goals are ambiguous, or when the environment creates symbolic uncertainty, organizations may model themselves on other organizations. The advantages of mimetic behaviour in the economy of human action are considerable; when an organization faces a problem with ambiguous causes or unclear solutions, problemistic search may yield a viable solution with little expense . . . Organizations tend to model themselves after similar organizations in their field that they perceive to be more legitimate or successful. (pp. 151–2)

Once again, this has particular relevance for state organizations. It can be applied particularly, for example, to the question of nationalization, where ambiguities about the goals have existed. Borrowing from other organizations is frequently done, but as DiMaggio and Powell say, 'The ubiquity of certain kinds of structural arrangements can more likely be credited to the universality of mimetic processes than to any concrete evidence that the adopted models enhance efficiency' (p. 152).

The third type of process leading to institutional isomorphism is that which stems from the process of professionalization. According to DiMaggio and Powell:

> Two aspects of professionalization are important sources of

isomorphism. One is the resting of formal education and of legitimation in a cognitive base produced by university specialists; the second is the growth and elaboration of professional networks that span organizations and across which new models diffuse rapidly ... Such mechanisms create a pool of almost interchangeable individuals who occupy similar positions across a range of organizations and possess a similarity of orientation and disposition that may override variations in tradition and control that might otherwise shape organizational behaviour. (p. 152)

This theme of the role of professionals has already been developed. In the UK accountants in particular occupy a central place. The professional training of accountants provides them with techniques of control that can be applied in the state sector just as in the private sector. Although there may be the need for certain modifications, or rather for a calculated expansion of accounting and management information systems, they can still be created. Spaces in public sector management can be colonized by management trained in an ethos predominantly governed by the requirements of the private sector. The result is that elements of that ethos are transferred into the public sector by the professionals themselves.

The dominance of management education by the private sector model of the organization and the consequent development of management styles using the limited criteria of the private sector results in the imposition of a certain form and set of expectations. Professionals bring with them into the public sector their own expectations of best practice, the best way to do things which have developed from their professional education. In particular, the dominance of calculability and rationalization in private sector firms provides a powerful model of legitimacy which undermines abstract notions of 'service' or 'the public good'. It becomes increasingly difficult for organizations to resist the demand for rationalization. In fact, the professionals who increasingly staff organizations embody through their own credentials a commitment to expertise and rationalization. Although these same professionals may in certain respects dislike and resist the implications of rationalization, e.g. doctors and their feelings about 'value for money' in the National Health Service, their general commitment to expertise makes a wholesale opposition to rationalization impossible.

All these processes create a significant pressure towards iso-morphism. The structure of rationalized relations in capitalist organizations are imposed on other money-based forms of organization. However, I wish now to argue that there remains a gap between the myth of 'institutional isomorphism' and the actual situation within these other organizations. This gap derives from two features. First, there is the power–knowledge dialectic identified by Foucault as a dynamic process where resistance/noncompliance continually arises. Thus whilst the organizational form legitimates itself in terms of rationalization, a gap develops between this and what actually happens. Second, there is the continued existence of alternative bases of organizational legitimation.

In considering the first of these I shall look at the argument developed by Meyer and Rowan (1977), namely that whilst organizations pretend that they have rational formal structures of control, in fact, because the work that they are doing is so different from the work done in the private sector, there is a gap between the myth and the reality. Meyer and Rowan state:

> Two very general problems face an organization if its success depends primarily on isomorphism with institutionalized rules. First, technical activities and demands for efficiency create conflicts and inconsistencies in an institutionalized organization's efforts to conform to the ceremonial rules of production. Second, because these ceremonial rules are transmitted by myths that may arise from different parts of the environment, the rules may conflict with one another. These inconsistencies make a concern for efficiency and tight coordination and control problematic. (Meyer and Rowan, 1977, p. 354)

Meyer and Rowan argue that institutionalized rules 'are couched at high levels of generalization, whereas technical activities vary with specific, unstandardized and possibly unique conditions' (p. 355). As a result, there is a loose coupling between the work that actually goes on within the organization and the face that is presented to the outside world:

> Institutionalized organizations protect their formal structures from evaluation on the basis of technical performance: inspection, evaluation and control of activities are minimized and coordination, interdependence and formal adjustments among structural units are handled informally . . . Because attempts to

> control and coordinate activities in institutionalized organiza-
> tions lead to conflicts and loss of legitimacy, elements of
> structure are decoupled from activities and from each other . . .
> The advantages of decoupling are clear. The assumption that
> formal structures are really working is buffered from the incon-
> sistencies and anomalies in technical activities. Also because
> integration is avoided disputes and conflicts are minimized and
> an organization can mobilize support from a broader range of
> external constituents. (p. 357)

The point that is being made here is that organizations borrow a
certain way of operating from other organizations. They are forced
to present a front to the outside world that is legitimate in terms of
the values of the outside world – a front that is rational and
embodies the norms of professionalism, credentialism and calculability. Within the organization, however, the techniques of rationalization, etc. continually run up against problems, especially the
recalcitrance of human beings and technology, which within the
state and civil society is magnified by competing non-calculable
ideals such as citizenship and formal equality. The idea that there is
an inescapable element in all labour processes that needs the active
co-operation of the worker and which cannot be totally calculated
for in advance, has been considered in Chapter 1. The notion that
within the state sector and in civil society there are other circumstances that resist the process of rationalization will be considered in
this chapter. It is worth noting here as it provides the raw material
for the continual dialectic of power and conflict between the
controllers/professionals whose job it is to calculate everything to
the nth degree, and the workers whose job it is to follow orders and
to get the job done (two things which are not always compatible).

Thus Meyer and Rowan argue that in certain organizations there
becomes an institutional separation between the task of rationalization, which becomes associated with its external legitimating
aspects, and the task of doing the job, which retains a relative
autonomy from this process. To avoid causing further problems,
the organization keeps the external husk of the form but does not
insist that the internal parts conform as well. This decoupling
works as long as the organization, in Meyer and Rowan's words,
'maintains elaborate displays of confidence, satisfaction, and good
faith, internally and externally' (p. 358). As long as the organization

presents to the outside world a view that everything is working well, and any complaints from the outside world can be dealt with or brushed aside, then decoupling is a viable option. It is easy, however, to see the sorts of pressures that can build up to threaten decoupling. To return to the example of education, it is clear that over the last ten years in Britain, there has been, for a variety of reasons, a gradual loss in confidence in the educational system. Whilst at one level teaching has become more professionalized – that is, more legitimate in societal terms through, for example, teaching becoming an all-graduate profession and through the expansion of examination and school-leaving qualifications to a wider percentage of the age cohort – at another level what is being taught within the classrooms has become more questioned. Increased professionalism has not been sufficient to allow teachers to beat off challenges to their work. The result has been a call for the increased accountability of teachers; this is reflected in a number of schemes, ranging from those concerned with teacher assessment to the increased role of parents in governing bodies, to plans for a national curriculum. Thus loose coupling between the institutionalized myth and what is actually occurring can be an unstable combination.

To summarize the argument, within our society organizations are expected to take a certain form. This form derives particularly from the role of rationalization in the structuring of organizations. Professionals within organizations seek to extend their role to give themselves a high level of control over activities within these boundaries. Sometimes this control derives from specific controls over the work which people do; most of the time it is a more generalized form of control operating through the monitoring of financial resources within the organizational setting. This process is adapted to the needs of operating in a market environment but it is carried and interpreted by certain professional groups, especially accountants, but also by other managers. Because of the central legitimacy of these institutions in our society, the model of organizational life that exists in them is perceived as *the* basic model of organizational life. It is carried over into other organizations, such as state organizations, which share a superficial similarity in so far as they are based on money. This carry-over is effected by coercion, mimesis and the professionals themselves. In non-capitalist organizations, the rationale of control becomes a mechanism for providing legitimacy to the operation of often ambiguous and unclear goals. It provides a mythical basis for legitimacy so long as no problems arise. However, where these organizations are no longer accepted as effective by the general public, the pressure for further changes increases, with the inevitable result that the model of capitalist industry is borrowed. Thus new mechanisms of control are introduced in an attempt to win back legitimacy. A continual dialectic is set up between professionals seeking to expand the sphere of rationalization and others within the organization who resist this process. (The institutional theory of organizations from which this argument is developed is reviewed in Zucker, 1987, and Scott, 1987; other studies which utilize and develop this framework include Tolbert and Zucker 1983; M. Meyer and Brown, 1977; M. Meyer, 1980, 1987; M. Meyer *et al.*, 1985; J. Meyer and Scott, 1983; J. Meyer, 1986.)

   This process needs to be located in a wider framework of social development in which values that can be the basis of opposition to rationality and calculation still survive. These values stem from the basic principles of modern Western states and the way in which they developed. Two are central: first, as has already been touched on, there is the belief in citizenship, i.e. that each individual member of the state has certain rights and obligations that are his/hers regardless of income or wealth. Whilst the extent of these rights and obligations is clearly a matter of negotiation, conflict and change, the framework of citizenship is not. Second, and associated with this, is the belief in the right to free and voluntary association; this is a value in its own right but is also essential to the operation of state and society. Individuals are free within the law to join with others for whatever purpose – economic, political or social. There is a fundamental sense in which these values stand in contradiction to the values of the market and efficiency (see Marshall, 1963, for the classic statement of this conflict). Citizenship rights belong to citizens by right; they are not purchasable, though in principle they could be (for example rights to education, health, etc.). Furthermore, because they are rights, the quality of them should reflect the dignity of the citizen and they should be provided in a proper manner without the commercial pressure of the private sector. This process in turn is subject to political accountability through democratic institutions.

   Figures 4.1 and 4.2 present an initial view of the difference between organizations in the capitalist sector and those in the state. (Organizations in the voluntary sector where the values of free association are central will be dealt with briefly later.) These differences can be spelled out as follows:

Figure 4.1

Figure 4.2

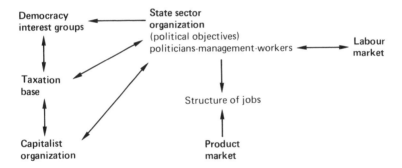

1. Within state sector organizations, political objectives have a central role in the structuring of the organization. The extent to which politicians are active in the formulation of organizational goals, structure and job design clearly varies; state sector organizations increasingly have a 'professional' management (a point to which I shall return) which may wish to set its own goals. However, so long as organizations remain within the state sector, there is a residual responsibility that the state and therefore politicians retain.
2. Political objectives in Western capitalist societies are derived in part at least from the calculation which political parties make regarding two factors: (a) the relationship between policies and electoral success; and (b) the relationship between powerful

interest groups and the potential for the implementation of policies in the light of possible resistance from such groups. Thus the activities of state sector organizations are carried out in a political environment in the sense that their actions have repercussions for the electoral survival of the incumbent party or parties. A central part in this process is increasingly played by the media, some of which may themselves be in the state sector, though most of which, in Western societies, are privately owned. These act as articulators if not creators of the public's perception of state sector organizations.

3. State sector organizations are dependent on a financial base for their operations. The state as a whole needs to raise taxes in order to pay for goods, services, labour, etc. Although there are other ways for governments to raise income, for example through loans from the private sector, taxation remains a central means of raising government revenue. There are limits, however, to how much tax can be raised and therefore to what level state services can be financed. First, taxation can affect voters' calculations about party support. If personal taxation is perceived as too high by electors, the electoral consequences can be disastrous for the ruling party; if it is perceived as reasonable, indeed falling, then the ruling party reaps the dividend, as the Conservatives did in the UK in 1987. (The concepts of high and low taxes are not givens; they derive from traditional expectations and political conflicts within particular countries – what is high in one country may be low in another. This is also related to the spread of direct vs. indirect taxation; as the name implies, direct taxation can affect the actions of capitalist organizations, causing them, for example, to redirect investment to areas of lower corporate taxation. This has a number of knock-on effects, the most pertinent of which is that a reduced corporate tax base necessitates an increasing level of personal taxation if state services are to remain at a standstill. Although states can seek to bridge this gap temporarily through increased borrowing, this tends simply to delay the onset of what O'Connor (1973) terms the 'fiscal crisis of the state'. (These themes are also discussed in detail in the work of Offe, 1984, and Gough, 1979.)

4. The actions of capitalist organizations have a direct impact on the state in a number of ways, for example through acting as an organized interest group and through the taxes they pay. They

are also relevant in two other ways. First, capitalist organizations can reject political demands deriving from the state. This is exemplified by the way in which, in the UK, the Labour government of 1974–9 was stymied in its attempts to introduce increased worker participation both through industrial democracy (as set out in the Bullock Committee report) and through trade union and shop steward involvement in planning (as developed by the National Enterprise Board and its planning agreements). Private sector organizations, led by the Confederation of British Industry (CBI) opposed these moves and effectively blocked their implementation. Only one planning agreement was ever signed (with Chrysler – the company was forced into it in return for a heavy government loan; the loan gave Chrysler the chance to stabilise their business so that they could sell it a little while later as a going concern to the French company Peugeot). As for industrial democracy, the recommendations of the Bullock Committee were quietly shelved.

Second, capitalist organizations affect state sector organizations by selling goods and services which either directly or indirectly compete with some of the goods and services provided by the state. For example, although the state has at present a monopoly over the mining of coal in the UK, capitalist organizations compete by providing the market with alternatives, e.g. through the importation of coal from other countries and through the production and distribution of other forms of fuel, the most important of which is oil. The capitalist sector can both seek to expand in areas where it is already in competition with the state and to open up to private sector penetration those areas which are at present state monopolies. Similarly, the state can seek to expand its monopolies, for instance by legislating out of existence private competitiors, by reducing relevant tax allowances, or by taking over companies/industries, as various Labour governments have done.

5. The final difference is product markets, which in relation to the state sector has two main meanings. On the one hand the product market can refer to a real market situation, as in the coal industry where British Coal competes almost as any other capitalist firm would in order to retain its markets, i.e. by rationalizing production, increasing productivity, etc. On the other hand, the product market can refer to the impact of state

services on clients who have nowhere else to go. For example, concerns about the state of the National Health Service in the UK can lead some of the more wealthy people in society to use market choice by buying private health insurance, but for the majority dissatisfaction with this state service can only be resolved, not by getting somebody else to provide the service, but by feeding complaints back through the democratic process.

All these factors make the structuring of jobs in the state sector a more highly complex and indeterminate task than in the capitalist sector. Crucially important in modern Western societies is the notion that the state embodies values of citizenship and democracy. The debate concerning the significance of citizenship has been wide-ranging; the essential point brought out by authors such as Marshall (1963) is that citizenship brings with it certain rights and duties. The main duty that forged the modern nation–state citizen was the duty of both men and women to fight and suffer in industrialized warfare. In return, the state, under political and social pressure to provide a return for the duty, developed ideas of citizenship rights, including in the First World War the rights of women to vote, and of 'a land fit for heroes'. In the aftermath of the Second World War in Britain, as Marshall argued, a more wide-ranging notion of the rights of the citizen, ranging from political through social to economic rights, was developed and embodied in institutions like the National Health Service, the education system and the social security system, and in the notion of full employment, etc. The conditions under which these rights were won and what they meant in practice are not my major concern here (though for discussions of this see Mann, 1986b, 1987; Hall, 1985, 1988; Giddens, 1985). What is more important is the idea of universal rights that citizens command. Although the element of calculability cannot be lost from this, nevertheless the notion that there are sets of values that transcend short-term economic considerations is crucial. State institutions, by their nature, embody such values; this gives them a degree of insulation from the forces of rational calculation and the capitalist market, which in turn means that the nature and dynamics of these organizations is significantly different from those located directly in the economic sector. In the next two sections I shall develop this point in relation to two areas of state organization in the UK: the nationalized coal-mining industry and the National Health Service.

The coal industry in Britain

The coal-mining industry was nationalized by the post-war Labour government for a number of reasons. Two of these reasons are of particular importance here. First, it was argued that coal was vital to the well-being of British society because it was the major source of energy. In the interwar years private coal companies had been unable to plan production and investment to fulfil the needs of society. Second, and associated with this, a great many people were employed in the coal industry. They had had to suffer long periods of unemployment as well as dangerous working conditions because of the failure of private capital. They needed and deserved a proper coal industry where production requirements were properly planned, investment in new mines and machinery was properly carried out, and a commitment to the health and safety of the workforce was properly maintained. Such goals outweighted the protestations of private mine owners. There was a clear recognition that coal production was too important to be left solely to the market. At first ambiguities in the goals of nationalization were overlooked; in the longer term, however, they left the industry open to pressure from forms of coercive and mimetic as well as professional isomorphism.

Could nationalization live up to the miners' expectations? There was one major reason why it might not:

> Nationalization ended the competition between coal owners for greater shares of coal markets but it did not touch the coal markets themselves. It removed competition in the production of coal but left the use of coal and, therefore, the primary determinant of the production of coal, to be determined by market forces. The coal industry, in consequence, continued to be shaped by market forces over which the administrators of its unified organization exercised no control. There were no means within the industry of insulating coal from the ravages of fluctuations in the level of trade generally, of displacement by other sources of energy. The coal industry under nationalization was as sensitive, responsive and malleable to market fluctuations as it had been under private ownership. (Allen, 1981, p. 32)

This was crucial to the forces shaping the work of the miners. It meant that the management of the industry, although no longer in the hands of private owners (though many individuals from the old companies remained in important managerial positions), was under similar market pressures to increase the efficiency of the industry to compete with other energy suppliers. Until the 1950s there was a shortage of energy and so coal could be sold almost at any price. However, once oil, as well as the nationalized electricity and gas industries, had rebuilt after the war and these were starting to increase capacity, market competition between them started in earnest. The alternative which involved central planning of energy production and consumption (although discussed in some Labour Party circles) never became a serious political option. It was market competition between energy sources that prevailed.

From the mid 1950s the impact of other energy sources, particularly oil, began to make major inroads into the market for coal. From 1957, the coal industry began to contract: miners found the job security they hoped for under nationalization to be illusory. Nearly three out of ten miners left the industry between 1957 and 1963, and 264 pits were closed (Allen, 1981, p. 41). The fact that employment opportunities were increasing elsewhere in the economy and that the miners' leadership accepted these cutbacks meant that resistance to the closures was minimal.

As well as reducing overall employment levels, the National Coal Board (NCB) sought to respond to competition in ways typical of capitalist organizations. In particular, it sought to increase the productivity of miners by mechanization and by increasing the intensity and pace of work. Up until this period, working at the face was still mainly done by hand; now, however, the NCB began to introduce mechanized face work, which had an impact on wage structures and supervision in the industry. Under the old system, miners had been paid on a piecework basis, according to how much coal they mined. Now, the Board argued, since it was the machinery that was primarily responsible for digging the coal, piecework payments were irrelevant. Miners themselves accepted this because piecework had been the cause of many industrial relations problems in the mines; stoppages and other interruptions which were no fault of the miners had led to loss of earnings for the miners. Also, the variability of coal seams meant that there were inequalities between miners' earnings as between regions, between pits in the same region, between different faces in the same pit, even between different shifts on the same face. Miners therefore initially welcomed the equality which Measured Day Work as an occupation gave them, though as the level of their fixed wage began to deteriorate relative to other manual workers, the temptation to look for new ways of restoring 'productivity bonuses' grew, particularly in the more productive pits. The abolition of piecework was interpreted by management as necessitating increased supervision. Miners, they felt, would no longer have a direct monetary incentive to work to their maximum. They therefore needed to be controlled more closely by management.

> The work situation for miners changed in essentially disturbing ways. Managers started to manage by directing, supervising in a manner so different from before . . . The functions of the underofficials altered first with the intensification of mechanization which gave them the facility to control the pace of work. They changed even more once the direct monetary incentive was taken out of work and the efforts of the miners were regulated by direct supervision. As the underofficials assumed important supervisory functions, they increased both in number and as a proportion of the number of face workers. Face workers began to feel they were breathing down their neck. (Allen, 1981, p. 92)

Alongside this process of mechanization and intensification, there were increasing dangers of injury. Mining had always been a dangerous occupation and, contrary to the hopes of the miners, remained so under nationalization. Although fewer of the great mine disasters of previous years occurred, the advent of the new machinery increased the possibility of individual injury.

By the end of the 1960s, the hopes for nationalization that the miners had held had not been realized. Jobs had been lost, the labour process significantly intensified, and miners had slipped down the earnings table for male manual workers. In certain parts of the industry, particularly Yorkshire, Scotland and South Wales, the reaction against this decline began to throw up a new, more militant set of leaders supported by miners determined to arrest the decline in their position. In 1971 this resulted in a major pay claim which was rejected by the NCB, who in turn were supported by Edward Heath's Conservative government, which by this stage was operating a pay policy in the public sector. The strike which followed rapidly brought power cuts to the country and the government felt forced to intervene by setting up a Court of Inquiry which recommended a substantial increase for the miners. The strike was important for a number of reasons. It showed that the miners and the NCB management had overestimated the decline in coal's product market. The withdrawal of coal supplies rapidly brought industry to a halt. The strike also showed the power of united trade union action, particularly where mass pickets and 'flying pickets' could count on support from other trade unions. Third, it showed that the government was unable to leave decisions to the NCB.

In 1973 a fourth crucial factor intervened which further tilted the balance of power towards the miners. This was the massive increase in oil prices consequent on the Middle East crisis of 1973. The price rise decisively improved the competitive position of coal, and the miners used this to argue again for an improvement in their wages and further expansion of the industry. Following an over-time ban and then a strike in support of their claim, they once again caused major power cuts. This was exacerbated by the actions of the Heath government, which intervened from the start and ordered a three-day working week in an attempt to conserve energy. When this failed, Heath called a general election on the issue of 'who governs – the miners or the government?' The electorate could not quite make up its mind, though Labour were the largest party in the new Parliament and immediately set about settling the strike. Although this was a period when government intervened directly in far more industrial disputes than it does in the 1980s, leading to characterizations of the period as the age of corporatism (for an extended discussion of these themes see the articles in Crouch, 1979), the fact that the mining industry was nationalized almost inevitably meant that any national dispute would become political. By the way in which it acted, the Conservative government increased the political impact of the miners' action. From a situation in which the industry had been managed within the public sector along lines which were similar to the private sector, by the mid 1970s mining was again a highly political issue.

In the period from the mid 1970s to the early 1980s management tried to win back some of the control which it had lost in the disputes of 1972 and 1974. Clearly, the worsening employment situation of the country as a whole and the mining regions in particular had an impact in reducing the power of the miners. The NCB worked on this in two ways. First, it sought to re-introduce forms of productivity bargaining. This had two purposes. It would re-establish a link between effort and reward which the NCB now felt had been prematurely cut; in doing so it would add a further weapon to management's control techniques. Just as important, productivity bargaining would reduce the solidarity of miners. The fact that wage claims in the early 1970s meant exactly the same across the country had considerably enhanced the unity of the miners. Productivity bargaining would begin to reduce this. Miners in more prosperous areas such as Nottinghamshire, where higher bonuses could be earned, would be less likely to unite with workers in other parts of the country.

Second, the NCB began a further stage of mechanization, involving the computerized control of mining systems. By the early 1980s, the product market conditions for energy fuels had again moved against coal. Oil was once again in plentiful supply and the price differential had altered in favour of oil. Furthermore, imports of foreign coal (from countries as far apart as South Africa and Poland) were beginning to enter the UK at prices which for political as much as economic reasons were well below the prices of UK-produced coal. The NCB interpreted these changes as necessitating increased productivity from British miners. As the Board's plans began to crystallize, they seemed to centre around two interlinked strategies – a technological one and a locational one.

Technologically, the so-called MINOS system was developed which aimed to computerize coal production and simultaneously reduce manpower (see Burns *et al.*, 1983, 1985, for an account of this). MINOS, however, was only effective in large, deep mines and could not therefore be introduced into many existing collieries. The NCB linked its expansion to the creation of so-called 'super-pits' in areas of newly discovered coal, in particular in the Selby area of Yorkshire, the Belvoir area of Leicestershire, and Margan in South Wales. The output from these and other 'super-pits' would be much cheaper in the long run than those of many existing mines. (The question of the economics of coal is obviously highly controversial; see, for example, Hopper *et al.*, 1986.) The NCB expected that demand for coal could not grow sufficiently to justify maintaining output from both the super-pits and the ordinary pits

(even though the ordinary pits had received recent capital investment and might in some cases even be working profitably).
Furthermore, the cost of coal from the older pits raised the overall
price of coal and thus reduced its competitive position against
imported coal and oil. The logic of the Board's position, therefore,
was towards substantial pit closures and a significant restructuring
of work underground.

These plans were endorsed by the incoming Conservative government, which also began to make contingency plans in the event
of another miners' strike. In the early years of the Thatcher
government there was an uneasy truce in the industry with the
closure plans looming in the background. The NCB at this time
was led by managers who had been long-serving in the industry
such as Derek Ezra and Norman Siddall, who believed that it might
be possible to manage the closures in the consensual way that had
been achieved in the 1960s. However, when the Conservative
government appointed Ian McGregor as Chairman of the NCB
(instead of Roy Mason, former miner and former Labour Cabinet
minister whom it had previously been strongly rumoured around
the House of Commons would be the next chairman), it was clear
that this was not to be the case. McGregor was a Canadian Scot
with substantial experience of industrial relations and strike-
breaking in both the USA and in the UK (during his time in charge
of the British Steel Corporation). He was keen to get on with the
pit closure programme and soon announced closures. When these
were resisted by miners, an uneven pattern of support spread across
the industry for strike action. Miners in Nottinghamshire in
particular resisted demands that they join the strike, and this split in
the NUM reduced their power in comparison to 1972 and 1974.
The preparations of the government and the NCB meant that
picketing was far less effective in stopping supplies, and that there
were stockpiles of coal, thus ensuring that there were no power
cuts.

After twelve months of struggle, the miners returned to work.
Many pits were closed, many miners left (and are still leaving) the
industry, whilst in the mines, managers sought to re-establish their
control with a vengeance, introducing a new disciplinary code and
restructuring working practices with only sporadic resistance from
the remaining miners. (See Beynon, 1985, for a contemporary
account of the issues involved from the miners' side and an attempt

to re-establish a socialist rationale for the management and control of the industry.)

The coal industry, like other nationalized industries, has been on the extreme end of state services in the sense that it has been most clearly subjected to market considerations, both in labour and product market terms. This was not inevitable. The Labour government of 1945–51 decided to institute a particular style of nationalization based very much on the model of private organizations. It rejected the idea that there should somehow be workers' control of the industry, which was argued for by a minority of miners and Labour Party members. (The debate about workers' control of industry in general and the mines in particular has had a long history in the British Labour Party – see, for example, Coates and Topham, 1970). Furthermore the Labour government did not build into the nationalization programme any form of co-operation with other competing energy sources such as gas and electricity, even though they were also nationalized. Thus it failed to provide for either a properly planned energy industry or a workers' controlled coal industry. Instead the coal industry was forced by successive governments to think in terms of markets and cost efficiency. When the miners in 1984–5 began to make an argument for coal based on social need, both to protect the country's access to home-produced 'clean' fuel – they rejected outright alternative dependencies on home-produced nuclear power and imported coal and oil – and to protect the lives and culture of the coalfield communities, they were forty years too late. Forty years of developing an alternative logic, maintaining management control and competing with other fuels on costs, could not be swept away in such a short time, no matter how powerful the emotional arguments presented and the examples of human suffering demonstrated. Labour governments had failed to provide a satisfactory rationale for nationalized industries that could convince the management, the workforce and the electorate. If the nationalized industries were to all intents and purposes being managed and financed like private sector organizations, why not put them in the private sector? This seems likely to be the fate of the surviving coal-mining industry as it has been the fate of more profitable nationalized industries such as British Telecom and British Gas.

The National Health Service

Not all state organizations are so directly threatened by market
relations; others have a more indirect relation to the market,
allowing for greater interplay between market and electoral considerations. In this section I shall look at the National Health Service in
the UK, and in particular, for reasons of space, on the work
situation of nurses. The argument is that while financial pressures
have resulted in a changing division of labour in nursing, the nature
of the nursing task itself and its location in a wider ideological
consensus of the citizen's right to health reduces the extent to which
these pressures can penetrate totally into the nursing labour process.

In order to demonstrate this argument, and which could in my
view be applied to other areas of state services such as teaching and
social work), I will use the concept of 'sentimental work' as
developed by Strauss *et al.* (1982). Strauss and his colleagues first of
all introduce the concept of 'sentimental work' as an ingredient of
work in general:

> Sentimental work is an ingredient in any kind of work where the
> object being worked on is alive, sentient, reacting – an ingredient
> either because deemed necessary to get the work done effectively
> or because of humanistic considerations. Sentimental work has
> its source in the elementary fact that any work done with or on
> human beings may have to take into account their response to
> that instrumental work (as with medical work); indeed their
> responses may be a central feature of that work. (Strauss *et al.*,
> 1982, 254)

Strauss *et al.* explain that people in hospitals are likely to have social
and psychological feelings of weakness, as well as suffering direct
physical problems. Thus patients are fearful of what is happening
to them, of its possible impact on the future for themselves and
their family. A crucial part of the hospital environment is the task
of calming the fears of the patient; this can be as crucial as the
medical work involved in trying to cure or heal the patient. Indeed,
it may be the *sine qua non* of treatment. It is this task which Strauss
et al. label as 'sentimental work'. The authors distinguish a number
of forms:

1. Interactional work and moral rules: these refer to the care which

nursing staff need to take to treat patients as individuals, not simply objects of medical work. Patients are likely to object if they feel that they are not being treated in a dignified, humane way.

2. Trust work: by this the authors refer to the special effort that nursing staff have to put in so that certain tasks can be done quickly and efficiently.

3. Composure work: patients in hospital are under great stress; they may be frightened either of the specific nature of their condition and diagnosis or of the unknown. This fear can undermine the carrying out of medical work. Strauss *et al.* say:

The great number of procedures and machine related tasks done to and for patients exposes them to potential loss of composure, whether poise, 'face', self-control. During these sessions, much of the sentimental work done amounts to the staff, usually the nurses, helping or enjoining patients to keep their composure. This is done not merely for reasons of compassion but to ensure that the tasks get done with the maximum dispatch and efficiency. Hand-holding or a touch on the brow, or soothing sounds of empathy or 'hang on it will soon be over' will often help to pull someone through a painful or frightening procedure. Failure to make these reassuring or helpful gestures can be consequential for completion of tasks since patients may cry, scream, change bodily position, collapse in panic, refuse to go on. (p. 262)

4. Biographical work: this refers to the need of the nursing staff to get to know something about the personal background of the patient. This may be necessary for undertaking both diagnostic and curative work.

5. Identity work: this refers to the work nursing staff do to help patients through the crises of their illness and maintain their sense of identity in the face of the debilitating effects of disease and injury.

6. Awareness of context work: this refers in particular to the way in which nurses either reveal or conceal aspects of the patient's illness, a particularly painful decision in cases of terminal illness.

7. Rectification work: this refers to the work that staff may have to do when patients express annoyance and anger at what they regard as bad treatment by doctors or nurses. Smoothing over the patient's feelings may be necessary to enable the healing process to continue.

In the UK this work is embedded in a wider set of relationships which stem from the foundation of the National Health Service by the Labour government in the immediate post-war years. The NHS played a central role in the creation of the social democratic consensus that dominated British society through to the 1970s. Although this consensus has broken down in the period since, there is still a sense in which the right of citizens to health care remains accepted by most people. Thus there is an integration of the micro-social task of nursing with the macro-political ideology of citizenship; this contrasts markedly with the USA, where health care is still predominantly based on market criteria and the ability to pay. (The nature of this integration in the UK can be critically examined for the way in which it distributes power between the citizen/consumer of health services and the professionals – see Stacey, 1984 – but this is outside the remit of my particular argument.)

Some types of sentimental work can also be said to appear in different forms in other state organizations, e.g. teaching and social work. Similarly, it has been argued that certain types of work in the private sector require such work. Hochschild, for example, refers to 'emotional labour' and defines it as follows:

> This labour requires one to induce or suppress feeling in order to sustain the outward countenance that produces the proper state of mind in others . . . This kind of labour calls for a coordination of mind and feeling, and it sometimes draws on a source of self that we honour as deep and integral to our individuality . . . I use the term 'emotional labour' to mean the management of feeling to create a publicly observable facial and bodily display; emotional labour is sold for a wage and therefore has an exchange value. (Hochschild, 1983, p. 7)

Hochschild's work concentrates particularly on flight attendants and the way in which they are trained to produce appropriate feelings that reduce anxiety and increase contentment among airline passengers, though there is an underlying argument that as the provision of services increases in importance relative to the production of goods, emotional labour is replacing physical labour in importance. Hochschild refers to this process overall as 'the commercialization of human feeling'. The combination of sen-

timental work with wider political ideologies and social relationships can therefore vary.

Whilst the work of nurses in the NHS has been subject to
scientific management-type rationalizing processes as the state has
sought to reduce overall costs, there has nevertheless been a core of
tasks centred around 'sentimental work' that both resists further
deskilling and provides the basis for a claim to wider job control for
nurses. Thus, unlike the private sector where it is possible to argue,
as Hochschild does, that 'emotional labour' can be designed into
the task in order to increase profitability, in certain public sector
organizations, emotional labour or sentimental work is necessarily
built in and management has to work around that. It cannot do
away with it (though it may try to reduce its importance) in the
way that management in the private sector can. The task would no
longer be the same, and the resistance to such changes both by
nurses and patients (in their role as consumers of the service and
electors) would be great.

How did sentimental work become so important in the first
place, and how did it become an essential part of the nursing as
opposed to any other occupation in the medical division of labour?
In order to answer this question it is necessary to look briefly at the
historical emergence of the occupation.

Nursing in the form it takes now was essentially developed in the
mid-nineteenth century under the leadership of women like Flor-
ence Nightingale. Whereas previously it was seen as a generally
disreputable occupation undertaken by ill-trained working-class
women, Nightingale and others sought to transform it into an
occupation worthy of middle-class 'ladies'. According to Gamarnikow, this necessitated two major reforms:

> The first was to establish a single stratified occupation with
> responsibility for patient care and the organization and manage-
> ment of nursing; and the other was to introduce this occupation
> into existing health care institutions or to reform existing
> arrangements to accord with the Nightingale blueprint. (Gamar-
> nikow, 1978, p. 103)

The first aim was accomplished through the emphasis on hygiene
and the sanitary idea. Nursing was to be concerned with the
physical, social and mental environment of care. This strictly
demarcated it from decisions over treatment, which were the

province of the 'male' doctor. The second aim was carried out through accepting a particular form of the sexual division of labour within the hospital setting. As Beechey and Perkins (1987, p. 81) say, 'This division between medicine and nursing, cure and care, embodied a strict form of sexual division of labour, with doctors being almost exclusively male and nurses almost exclusively female.' Gamarnikow also emphasizes this point:

> Nursing was set up and defined as women's work and a good nurse was seen as primarily a good woman. This 'deprofessionalized' the relations between nursing and medicine, and situated the nurse–doctor relation, characterized by the subordination of nursing to medicine, within a patriarchal structure. The occupational ideology of nursing thus genderised the division of labour; it associated science and authority with doctors and caring – putting science into practice – with women. In this way, health care based itself on allegedly sex-specific personal qualities. (Gamarnikow, 1978, p. 114)

There were, however, elements of this definition that allowed for an increased division of labour, as certain tasks could be passed on to non-nursing ancillary workers:

> Domestic tasks in nursing became gradually limited to the sanitary aspects of patient care ... As nursing developed, hygiene remained part of its practice only to the extent that it related to patient care. All other household chores were to be performed by maids under the supervision of nurses trained in the scientific principles of hygiene. (Gamarnikow, 1978, p. 120)

It was the separation out of these domestic tasks from 'sentimental work' that embodied the potential for a rationalization of the nursing task. From early on nurses were located in a division of labour between, on the one hand, doctors and on the other ancillary workers. (See Witz, 1986 for an account of the medical division of labour.)

Before the setting up of the National Health Service in Britain, hospitals were financed from a variety of sources including charities, voluntary subscriptions, insurance and the payment of fees. Following their move into the state sector, there was almost immediately a financing problem. In theory, the state would meet the costs of hospitals and their services as they were needed by patients, the money coming both from national insurance contributions and the general Exchequer fund. However, from early on, there were worries about the consequences of this. Carpenter (1976) argues that 'criteria of economic rationality' soon began to be applied. Manson (1976, p. 201) notes that 'From its inception, the National Health Service has been bedevilled by charges that money is being wasted.'

Specifically with regard to the nursing task, the pressure on costs eventually led to a complex reorganization first advocated in the Salmon Report on Nursing Management, published in 1966:

> The Salmon Report was part of the attempts by the state in the 1960s to increase labour productivity in the public services, directing scientific management techniques to the largest occupational groups, nurses and ancillary workers. The application of a 'foreign' rationality to nursing structures created however the preconditions for increased trade union membership and organization . . . For nurses the implementation of the Salmon Report imposed hierarchic, bureaucratic controls on nursing structures. Nursing work was further divided by the hiving off of management roles above ward level and the removal of unskilled work to auxiliary workers, leaving ward level staff with a loss of control over previous work practices. (Cousins, 1987, p. 111; see also Cousins, 1986)

The Salmon Report was a response to the emerging fiscal crisis of the state. Costs in the National Health Service drifted upwards for three main reasons. First, there was increased demand both as the age structure of the population changed (e.g. more old people who needed medical care) and as people as a whole became more used to the idea of a 'free' health service to which they had a right. Second, the technology of the health service increased both in the sense of new machines and operating techniques that could be used and in the sense of the new drugs that were being developed. Third, there was 'wages drift' in the NHS, in particular among nurses and ancillaries. Wage drift refers to the process whereby wages in the economy as a whole move roughly in step, even though productivity increases in one sector might be far ahead of those in another. Thus hospital staff might seek wage increases similar to those in manufacturing industry on the grounds of the maintenance of their relativities. However, whereas in manufacturing industries wage increases would usually be paid by the company out of productivity increases in the NHS it was difficult both to measure productivity increases and to achieve them. Wage increases in the NHS therefore almost inevitably meant higher wage bills with little compensating increase in productivity. Although governments sought to reduce the pressure on wages by recruiting nurses and ancillaries from overseas who 'provided both a supply of cheap labour whilst in training, as well as a permanent reserve of skilled workers' (Doyal *et al.*, 1981, p. 64), wage drift still existed and added to cost pressures on the NHS.

The Salmon Report was based on two principles derived from the practice of capitalist organizations: deskilling and scientific management. In relation to the first, Manson says:

A major objective was to ensure that trained nurses only did work that their training had fitted them for. Under all the principles of rational organization, it is wasteful to use skilled labour on work that can be carried out by unskilled workers and therefore it saves money to split work into skilled and unskilled components, with trained staff doing the former. This clearly has been the intention in nursing; ancillaries now are supposed to perform many of the menial tasks once carried out by nurses, whilst an increasing proportion of nursing auxiliaries take many of the more routine duties. (Manson, 1976, p. 206)

This reorganization, however, did not simply leave nurses with a more skilled job overall:

Whilst the skill content of the work performed by the trained nurse has increased, paradoxically this has meant that the span of discretion allowed the nurse has decreased. The intensity of work has increased, while the control over others has decreased. (Manson, 1976, p. 207)

As for scientific management, Salmon attacked the matron system of nursing management with its concentration of women in senior positions. Carpenter describes the tenor of the report as follows:

First, traditional nursing and modern business administration are contrasted and the former pronounced inferior to the latter. Second, the established methods of business administration are said to form a separate body of knowledge, managerial science, which are entirely suitable to nursing as they are to any other form of administration. (Carpenter, 1976, p. 176)

In a remarkably prescient passage about changes that have since begun with the introduction of the general manager (usually male) into the health service, Carpenter says:

> The logic of such changes is that, especially at highest levels, there is no particular reason why management of nurses need be carried out by nurses. The further one travels from the ward the less one can talk of 'nursing' or even 'nursing management', but rather management which applies the teachings derived from aspects of capitalist rationality to an area which just happens to be in nursing. In the future the new managerial elites may increasingly feel themselves to be managers first and nurses second or simply managers who are ex-nurses. By contrast under traditional definitions, the matrons of the traditional elite were always nurses first. (Carpenter, 1976, p. 184)

It is worth noting that the move towards managerialism has also resulted in changes in the sexual division of labour, since men have been encouraged to enter nursing in the more likely event now of reaching higher managerial levels. As Hearn (1982, p. 195) says, the outcome of Salmon in this sense was to create more posts in nursing management that were 'ripe for male capture'. Recently this process has gone further. The Conservative government has instituted a system of general management in the NHS. Managers are made responsible for the finance and running of their region or district within budgets set down by the government. Managers from the private sector have been encouraged to apply and become managers in the NHS. Moreover, a number of services have been put out to tender, resulting in private companies taking over certain functions such as cleaning and catering. (See D. Thompson, 1987, for an account of the managerial conflicts this is generating.)

The changes brought about by Salmon have had an increasing impact on nursing. From above, new styles of management have increased pressures on nurses, whilst from below rationalization of the tasks of ancillaries (leading in the 1980s to forms of privatization which further reduce the extent to which nurses can interact and control the work of others on the ward) has reduced the area of control of nurses (see Coyle, 1985). These processes have led to periodic outbursts of industrial-type militancy among nurses, culminating in the first-ever strike actions by serving nurses in January and February 1988 and continuing in late 1988 in response to the implementation of the government's pay deal.

To summarize, then, nursing developed as a gender-specific occupation to serve doctors and to provide an environment of physical and social caring for the patients. When the UK National Health Service was formed, the latent conflict between the domestic cleaning type tasks of nurses and the more caring, 'sentimental' type of work was resolved in a way that reduced costs. The more unskilled tasks of cleaning, etc. were separated off from the core tasks of nursing, thus reducing the overall wages bill. This was accompanied by increasing the professional management control of both nursing and ancillary work. Nevertheless, it is necessary to acknowledge the limits of the control process. Unlike many nationalized industries where there are forms of market competition acting as a direct pressure on management to change work relations, in the NHS the pressure is more indirect. Although private health insurance schemes and private hospitals have grown in recent years, competition between the private and public sectors in health care is minimal and non-existent in many areas such as geriatrics and mental illness. The facilities of private health care in the UK seem limited to a few main areas, involving a cost that remains beyond most people. Thus changes in the division of labour and management of the nursing task may arise from the fiscal crisis of the state, but the nature of the task remains resistant to wholesale reorganization and privatisation in the way that has recently faced previously nationalized services such as British Telecom and British Gas. Furthermore, the NHS remains highly political; there is every reason to believe that people in the UK at least associate the quality of health care with their rights as citizens. They do not wish to see it become a market service, no matter how much this is wrapped up in the jargon of 'insurance'. Whilst the public appreciate the funding difficulties of the NHS arising from the fiscal crisis of the state, they do not see this as giving management a *carte blanche* to rationalize hospitals in general or the nursing task in particular. Unlike nationalized industries such as mining, where the political value of 'nationalization' is now scarcely understood outside the mining communities themselves and where market forces are now allowed full reign, the caring tasks within health, education and social services still retain wider political legitimacy. This political legitimacy counterbalances arguments regarding the 'efficiency' of the services and makes for organizational difficulties in management and work. Whilst, at the moment, the argument for efficiency has the upper hand, the notion of service retains its importance and provides the basis for opposition to governmental and managerial rationalization policies in this sector. (See Davies, 1987, for a good account of the tensions in the NHS.)

Military and police organization

Other state sector organizations exist which use the ideology of citizenship to reduce their dependence on the market in rather a different way. The most obvious example is the armed forces; in the UK the Conservative government has committed billions of pounds to purchase Trident nuclear warheads, so that, according to the government, they need never be used (i.e. because of their deterrent effect)! The task of the military is to maintain the existence of the state itself as the embodiment of national identity; it is a task that is not constrained by normal considerations of economic efficiency. In times of military crisis, the economy and civil society can be subjected to wholesale restructuring in order to improve the state's war-fighting ability (for a discussion of the impact of the world wars in the UK see Marwick, 1970; for an analysis of war's theoretical significance for social cohesion and state formation see Mann, 1986b, and Giddens, 1985). Thus the military stands furthest away from the impact of the capitalist market. This is not to suggest that the military exists as an isolated enclave in capitalist societies. The labour it uses is labour that could go elsewhere; much of the weaponry it uses has been created by private companies looking for profit; the techniques of financial and manpower control it uses are increasingly borrowed from the capitalist sector. The goals it is seeking to achieve, however, are political – they are concerned with the survival of a certain definition of 'national values'. It can therefore appeal to the government on behalf of the 'national' interest to provide resources and material – financial and physical – that go beyond anything that any other state sector organization could claim.

Similar arguments could be made about certain other state organizations, for example the police and the secret service. So long as the public can be made to believe that these organizations are acting in the 'national' interest, they retain a secure financial basis upon which they can construct their own professional ideologies and organizational forms, relatively free from outside interference. Though the legitimation of these organizations may be challenged as a result of various incidents, such as police violence or secret service 'dirty tricks', these incidents are treated by most people as exceptions, not undermining the legitimacy of the organization as a whole. Like the military, these organizations cannot escape processes of rationalization, the scrutiny of their accounts, the need to show 'value for money', but they all retain a large area of autonomy to define their own needs and to have them served by government, indeed sometimes in spite of government (as Peter Wright, 1987, has described). At times of crisis, that power becomes even greater. Thus, in organizational terms, it is necessary to think of these organizations within the state sector as having a particular sort of autonomy and freedom both from market forces and from immediate governmental demands.

This relationship between state and economy, markets and citizenship, is one that ebbs and flows. State organizations are based on the rights of citizenship – they embody the idea that all persons, by virtue of being citizens, deserve certain rights – to health, education, law and order, defence. It is possible to imagine these principles being extended further – the right to a job, the right to housing, the right to decent income, the right to electricity, gas or some other form of fuel, the right to public transport, etc. In other words, we can conceive of an extension of the state and the idea of citizenship which potentially reduces the sphere of the market to a smaller and smaller part of society overall. The state increasingly becomes the planner of the society. This, of course, was the basis of the old socialist vision: to each according to his/her needs, from each according to ability. It may, in the 1980s, seem a long way away, but it remains part of the argument about the relationship between the state and the economy. It may be that at the moment capitalist values of efficiency have more impact on state sector organizations, than political ideas of service have on capitalist organizations. However, the present trend towards privatization and the subjection of the state to the market should not blind us to the power of the alternative idea – that the market should serve social values, not shape them.

Organizations in civil society

This notion is also relevant to organizations in civil society, where the pressure to conform to norms of rationality and calculation also exists in opposition to values based on free association, consensus and co-operation. The characteristic feature of such organizations is that whilst there is likely to be a permanent paid staff of some sort, the organization's character is defined significantly by its non-paid members who have joined out of a belief in its goals, and not out of a desire for material reward in the form of wages or salaries. Although the goals of the organization may seek the material advancement of its members, this is not necessarily the case. Thus the sorts of organizations to which I am referring are at one end of the spectrum – the more immediately materialistic organizations such as trade unions, through organizations which embody both material and social aspirations such as political parties, social clubs and masonic lodges, through to organizations which are predominantly altruistic and other-directed, such as charitable institutions and churches. In all of these organizations, there is characteristically a small permanent paid staff who keep things going on a day-to-day basis, and a wider group of people who are, or consider themselves to be, members. The relationship between these two groups is highly complex and variable. For instance, it was in relation to one of these types of organization, political parties, that Michels (1921) formulated his 'iron law of oligarchy'. The nature of the relationships within these organizations, based as they are on the predominantly voluntary coming together of people, differentiates them from both those in the capitalist economy and in the state sector. Once again, this is not to say that there is an insulation from the other sectors: dependence and interdependence exist here also. Aspects of 'scientific management' and bureaucracy may be transferred into this sector. As in the state sector, however, there are bases of resistance to the wholesale incorporation of such techniques.

For example, in religious organizations rationalization has not destroyed religious belief, though it may have reshaped it. Thus the inner core of religious belief cannot be done away with; it is central to the organization of religion. Whilst there might be a pressure on the one side to rationalize aspects of the organization, i.e. from those concerned with finance, presentation, etc., on the other side there will be resistance on the grounds that certain things are essential and cannot be done away with. Where these conflicts arise within different organizations in civil society cannot be deduced in advance. However, the crucial point is that they are there.

Three features in particular illustrate the way religious organizations have been penetrated by processes of rationalization (these arguments are derived from my reading of Wilson, 1961, 1969; Wallis, 1984).

1. The rationalization of the economic aspects of the organizations – the increased attention to rational money-making ventures and the need to control costs within the organization. This is particularly noticeable in the USA, where television evangelism involves both a major commitment to modern forms of communication and an overt appeal to the pockets of the believers.
2. The reduction in the importance of the specifically religious element in the church and the acceptance of a large amount of rational scientific thinking in the formulation of the Church's attitudes, policy and structure.
3. The rationalization of religious belief itself, reflected in certain sects as well as in the attempt to incorporate contemporary scientific and philosophical thought into statements of doctrine.

On the other hand there are certain inbuilt resistances in religion to its wholesale rationalization, particularly in relation to the belief process itself. These include:

1. The essential element of religiosity, i.e. God, eternity, etc. defies rational proof and calculation.
2. There is a powerful tendency for people to reject the overwhelming emphasis on rationality in the modern world and to look to churches and religion as a means of escape from such an emphasis.
3. The fact that commitment to such organizations is in an important sense voluntary. Thus there is an expectation, to put it crudely, that churches are different from factories. Whilst churches, like factories, may be said to have a job to do, were

they to institute controls of a similar nature at the heart of religious practice, they would be likely to experience a mass exodus.

The institutionalization of rational controls over the work and organization of churches therefore remains limited. The process of secularization has promoted such institutionalization, but how much further it will go in the spiritual domain (as opposed to the social and economic domain of religion) is unclear. A number of these issues arise in other organizations in civil society. Political parties, for example, have processes of rationalization in terms of the employment of professional staff to present policy in an electorally appealing manner and to run the party in an efficient 'managerial' way; this may include taking decisions, for instance, on redundancies, which may offend the ideology of the party. There are then tensions between these processes of rationalization and attempts to preserve in pristine condition aged structures and ideas to which the party faithful feel a real commitment. The modernization of political parties is almost as, if not more, complicated than the modernization of religion! Voluntary charity organizations are also pulled between the need to raise money through the efficient use of existing resources and their dependence on a pool of voluntary workers with a normative commitment to the organization's goals but an antipathy towards certain forms of professional fund-raising and management. These examples could be multiplied and developed to suggest that whilst there are powerful forces within the organizations pushing them towards the institutionalization of rational controls, the process is by no means complete.

Organizations in civil society are theoretically more independent of the state and the economy than the latter two are of each other. So long as there is money involved, there is bound to be a tendency for the accounting procedures and 'scientific management' techniques of capitalist organizations to transfer across, even into the organizations of civil society. Indeed, the state may give this process a boost by making a certain structure of monitoring accounts a *sine qua non* for the receipt of certain funds. However, organizations in civil society have resources to resist these pressures. They are based on voluntary co-operation aided by a paid bureaucracy. Because the organization is held together by some sort of consensus on values, the loyalty of its members may be severely tested if attempts are made to restructure them along lines characteristic of state or capitalist organizations. Conflicts necessarily arise within such organizations between those who want to rationalize (the modernizers) and those who want to stick by old values (the traditionalists). Political parties, trade unions, churches, etc. continually show evidence of this. This is not to say that similar conflicts do not arise in other organizations; they do, but in capitalist and state organizations power relations are much more clear-cut and the ability of the managerial group to force through its view is much less constrained by the need to find a consensus that is characteristic of organizations with a predominantly volunteer membership. The conflict between modernizers and traditionalists in such organizations embodies a serious choice that people and organizations must make; so long as that choice is still there, Weber's vision of the 'iron cage of bureaucracy' will not be completed. Organizations in civil society still embody a sphere of relative freedom from the dictates of capitalist rationality and bureaucratic structure. How long and the degree to which they can retain this is another question.

5 Organizations and Environments

Introduction

In this chapter I consider in more detail the influence of the environment on organizations. In particular, I concentrate on the impact of the market on organizations. The environment as a whole is a major source of uncertainty for managements trying to maintain processes of control and co-ordination within organizational boundaries. It is not surprising, therefore, that we find organizations coming together in order to manage that uncertainty, trying to supplement their power over the internal environment with power over the external environment. At this level, however, we are no longer looking just at the 'service class', the managers and professionals; we are now looking at the capitalist class as it co-ordinates its activities not just within capitalist organizations but through its position in the organizations of the state and civil society. Thus the rationalization process produced by the service class is complemented by the intra-class co-ordination maintained by the capitalist class.

In examining these issues I look first at the clearest theoretical exposition of the disruptive effects of the market: the population ecology approach to organizations. I argue that whilst this approach is valuable in its emphasis on the difficulties of controlling market forces, it overestimated these difficulties and sees 'automatic' economic processes ('the hidden hand') where in fact there are social forces at work. It underestimates the power of organizations to shape their environment. I then consider the 'markets and hierarchies' approach to organizations, which looks at the way in which organizations seek to reduce the importance of the market by incorporating elements of it into the organization. Once again, this provides valuable insights but is limited by its economic focus. Finally, I consider those approaches that take seriously the ways in which organizations link themselves together to avoid environmental uncertainty. This approach, known in general as the 'interorganizational networks' approach, provides the basis for a discussion of the significance of these networks. The argument which I follow from authors such as Useem (1984) and Mintz and Schwartz (1985) is that these networks are not simply the result of pragmatic adjustments by managers to environmental pressure; rather they reflect and reproduce the underlying basis of power in our society.

The population ecology approach to organizations

The primary level of analysis in this perspective is that of groups of organizations or, in the terms of the theory, 'populations'. This is linked also to a major interest in information and the way in which the organization acts upon information. The emphasis is on the inability of the organization to obtain accurate information about the environment and, more importantly, its inability to act effectively on any information that is gathered. Population ecology thus proposes a radical alternative to the approach taken in this book, which emphasizes the role of control and co-ordination in organizational life. In doing so, it performs a useful function by reminding us again not to take an over-rational or over-optimistic view of how organizations can operate. The argument here will be that population ecology can be a useful adjunct to organizational analysis so long as its aims are kept modest, but it cannot replace analysis which emphasizes the purposive nature of organizations and the role of individual and group power relations in organizational outcomes. Population ecology assumes that the market is all-powerful; unlike contingency theories, which I looked at earlier, population ecology argues that organizations cannot make a 'rational' adaptation to the market. This is to overemphasize the market and underestimate the extent to which co-ordinated activities can reduce uncertainty.

The population ecology approach, as its title implies, draws extensively from the natural sciences for some of its central concepts and more particularly its underlying rationale. (For a discussion of the reliance of organizational analysis on metaphors and analogies drawn from other disciplines, see Morgan, 1981, 1986.) The population ecology approach conceives of the world of organizations as divided up into populations. (For an early formulation of the perspective which builds on resource dependency see Aldrich, 1979; for a much more rigorously 'biologistic' approach see McKelvey, 1982.) Populations are defined as groups of organizations which share an environment. Within any particular population there are particular forms of organization which occupy specific parts of the wider environment, known as niches. The analogy is with the natural world: the animal population of the African jungle can be divided into different species, so that although elephants and giraffes share the same environment, they do no compete against each other for food supplies; they occupy different niches. However, there is not a comfortable state where every species/form of organization which wants a niche, has one. On the contrary, there is competition between species/forms to find niches that will enable them to survive. Thus the environment is in a continual state of flux as populations and species struggle to survive. Central to the perspective, then, is a view of competition between organizations and a view of the organizational life-cycle. Since survivability is so precarious and unpredictable, the birth, maturation and death of organizations become a central topic. (See Kimberly, 1980, for a series of papers using the life-cycle metaphor as their basis.)

Population ecology also adopts a selection view of change. In Darwinian evolutionary theory, species do not adapt to the environment. Rather what happens is that there is random mutation of individuals, caused by random genetic change. These random changes may or may not throw up individuals who are better suited to the environment and are therefore selected for survival by the environment. Thus the evolution of species cannot be interpreted in terms of the increased adaptation of individuals to the environment; rather it represents one possible evolution based on a series of random mutations which were suited to particular environments at particular times. Selection, rather than adaptation, is a central element in the population ecology approach.

Whilst there are certain differences of emphasis between the proponents of the approach, there is a heavy borrowing from Darwinian natural selection theory, emphasizing competition and selection. The forces of the environment and competition are all-powerful. The significance of this becomes clear if we look at the work of two of its main proponents, Hannan and Freeman (1977, 1983, 1984, 1987). Hannan and Freeman argue that organizations are very like animal species in that they cannot adapt to an environment. They have a certain form which is given at birth and which cannot be fundamentally reshaped. Hannan and Freeman argue that what they call structural inertia derives from a number of factors:

1. An organization's investment in plant, equipment and specialized personnel constitutes assets that are not easily transferable to other tasks and functions.
2 Decision-makers in organizations do not obtain anything like full information on activities within the organization or on environmental contingencies facing the sub-units.
3. There are severe political constraints against change in the sense that change may well serve to diminish the power of some groups in the organization and increase the power of others. The resulting conflict may often convince top decision-makers that inertia is preferable to the problems caused by change.
4. Organizations face constraints generated by their own history. Once standards of procedure and the allocation of tasks and authority have become the subject of normative agreement, the costs of change are greatly increased.

There are also a number of external pressures towards inertia:

1. Legal and fiscal barriers to entry and exit from markets are numerous. Usually barriers to entry are emphasized, e.g. market domination by large firms, but barriers to exit can also exist, e.g. where governments refuse to let large companies close down plants in vulnerable areas, as has happened in the British steel and car industries over the past decades.
2. Getting information about the external environment can be costly.
3. An organization's previous role may have become so entrenched in the minds of the public that any major adaptation may be seen as out of character and result in a loss of legitimacy.

4. Finally, there is the collective rationality problem: it may be rational for one organization to adapt in a certain way but if all organizations adapt in the same way there may be no overall gain, just a large cost in terms of internal politicking. Therefore it may be more in the organization's interest not to change.

For all these reasons, according to Hannan and Freeman, organizations have great difficulty in adapting to environmental changes. Instead, they argue, what is crucial is the form that the organization takes in its earliest stages of formation and how this relates to the environment in which it is located. This then raises the question of the organizational life-cycle.

The organizational life-cycle

For population ecology theorists, organizational sociology has committed a fundamental error. It has based its conclusions regarding organizations on those organizations which survive in a stable form for a long time. This group, it is argued, constitute merely the tip of the iceberg in terms of all the organizations that have existed. There are new organizations, both public and private, coming into existence every day; similarly there are many going out of existence. To draw general conclusions about organizations from those organizations which survive is like seeing history from the point of view of the victors. It is just as important to include all those who lost! Thus any particular population at any one time is but a snapshot of an evolution in process, where some organizations have just died, others are just beginning, whilst still others are in a stage of maturity or senile decay! In this view most studies of organizations are only looking at a small group; it is like studying human biology by looking at mature adult males rather than considering the whole process of birth, maturation and decline in both sexes. Organizations which survive for any length of time survive because, in their early stages, they fit an available environmental niche, not because they have been consciously adapted.

The formation of new organizations is therefore a crucial area of interest to this approach, because it is from these organizations that the environment selects the survivors. According to Hannan and Freeman, all new organizations are a gamble: no matter how much planning has gone into it, the survival of the new-born cannot be guaranteed. Indeed, it suffers from what is termed the 'liability of newness'. This involves certain immediate disadvantages:

1. Organizational newness often implies new roles for the organization as a social actor as well as for the individual participants in its. The new form operates blindly, and major blunders are easily committed. In the case of new firms in new industries, the problems are magnified even further.
2. The amount of time and effort required to learn and co-ordinate organizational roles is likely to be significant. During this learning period, behaviour is decidely non-routine and initiative is very important.
3. Because new firms are comprised mainly of strangers, trust may not be readily forthcoming, and organizational survival may be threatened by internal conflict.
4. New forms usually compete with existing firms that have well-established clienteles who are familiar with the existing firms' operating procedures and who are possibly resistant to change. New firms that cannot attract clients from existing firms are threatened by a lack of business. New organizations in new industries are spared the obligation of winning clients from established competitors; instead they have to create clienteles from scratch.

A number of research studies have begun to consider organizations from this perspective (see, for example, Pennings, 1982; Carroll and Delacroix, 1982; Aldrich and Auster, 1986; Singh *et al.*, 1986a, 1986b; see also the review by Carroll, 1984). These empirical studies have led to a more sophisticated use of the basic metaphor. For example, the relationship between adaptation and selection has been explored in various ways by the population ecologists. The environment, they argue, can be conceived of as either 'coarse-grained' or 'fine-grained'. A fine-grained environment is one in which changes are fairly common; in coarse-grained environments, on the other hand, changes are less frequent but more fundamental. So, for example, market demand for a product is frequently fine-grained; the number of packets of cereals sold over a year will vary, but within rather small limits. On the other hand, the legal environment for organizations is coarse-grained in the sense that there are rarely significant changes, but when they come, they can make a profound impact. Any particular organization operates within a niche where it will be subject to both fine-grained and coarse-grained changes. It is important, however, that organizations decide whether they are going to adapt to the coarse-grained elements of their environment or the fine-grained elements. In other words, are they going to be an organization capable of surviving major changes in the environment or are they going to build on the assumption that for all practical purposes their environment is going to remain much as it is for the foreseeable future? Choosing either of these strategies involves a high degree of risk and luck, and can only be rationally planned at the edges. According to Hannan and Freeman.

> The problem of ecological adaptation can be considered a game of change in which the population chooses a strategy and then the environment chooses an outcome (by, say, flipping a coin). If the environment 'comes up' in a state favourable to the organizational form, it prospers; otherwise it declines. (1977)

In particular, then, Hannan and Freeman argue that organizations can choose to specialize or generalize, and these strategies involve different risks. In the car industry, for example, there are some firms that could be said to specialize. Jaguar concentrates on producing a very specific type of car: high status, high price, a top of the market model. Rover cars, on the other hand, have produced a wide range of cars, from small ones to large family saloons. Jaguar is able to concentrate all its efforts – production, marketing, advertising, etc. – on the one specific market it is aiming for. Rover has had to spread itself across a variety of different markets. The specialist can successfully exploit the existing market as long as the environment remains stable. The problems for the specialist comes if there is major environmental change. For example, Jaguar would be severely hit by a major fall in the dollar, since this would increase Jaguar's prices relative to similar American makes and would almost certainly reduce its market share. The generalist, on the other hand, tends to have a degree of slack, so that major environmental change in one market can be compensated by concentrating more on another market.

Another way to look at this is through the concept of 'density dependence'. Brittain and Freeman (1980) develop this concept in the context of their analysis of the semiconductor industry in the USA. They distinguish between what they call r-strategists and

K-strategists. The former are organizations which move quickly to exploit resources as they first became available. Their structure makes them relatively inexpensive to set up: they concentrate on activities that require low levels of capital investment and simple structures. Their success depends heavily on first-mover advantages, which makes them high-risk and high-pay-off organizations which gain maximally from temporarily rich environments. Such organizations persist only where the pattern of resource availability is highly uncertain and resources are dispersed over time and space. K-strategists, on the other hand, are organizations that are structured to compete successfully in densely settled environments. K-strategist organizations generally expand into new resource spaces more slowly than r-strategists; they derive their advantages not from being the first into the market, but by being the most efficient once in it. Thus, in the long run, K-strategists are likely to outcompete r-strategists, unless r-strategists become K-strategists or alternatively move to a new niche. Thus as the population of a particular niche increases, i.e. becomes more dense, so K-strategists will outcompete r-strategists in the long run.

Events in the computer firm Sinclair Research provide an instructive illustration. Sinclair won first-mover advantages with its early home computers. Seeing that others were likely to move into the market and reduce the firm's profit level, Clive Sinclair (the firm's owner) sought to move into new niches. The pocket television was his first attempt, but unfortunately there was no great market awaiting two-inch televisions. He then went into the production of electric cars and brought out the Sinclair C5, which was an electric scooter for a single person. Again, though more emphatically, this found no market, and production was rapidly cut back and then wound up. In population ecology terms, Sinclair was following an r-strategy, seeing first mover advantages in new niches before they got crowded out with K-strategist competitors capable of out-competing him in the long run. Neither niche, however, provided him with the sort of massive boost that home computers had. On the contrary, the environment 'de-selected' Sinclair, and within a year of the C5 fiasco, Sinclair Research was taken over by Amstrad, a classic K-strategist.

McKelvey and Aldrich have examined this issue further. They argue that:

People in organizations are intentional or purposeful, but conditions are such that a particular organizational form cannot be attributed to any particular, identifiable, intentional act or set of acts . . . Since environments are diverse, uncertain and imperfectly perceived, we think it improbable that a particular individual will both have the correct view and *know* it. Since organizations are composed of people limited by bounded rationality suffering from limited or biased information and poor communication and subject to processes of social influence and constrictions of reality, we also think it improbable that a person with the 'correct' variation will be in a position to implement it. (McKelvey and Aldrich, 1983, p. 345)

However, according to these authors, there are ways in which organizations can avoid some of these consequences. Once again the Darwinian analogy is prominent. Survival depends on random changes which have a better fit with the environment than the existing organism. Translate that to organizations and the answer is basically to ensure that there is plenty of change in the organization, since with a bit of luck one of the states into which the organization or a part of it changes will fit the environment. McKelvey and Aldrich propose four principles:

1. *Variation*: organizations should (a) experiment frequently; (b) experiment inexpensively; (c) learn rapidly. The more effective and adapted an organization becomes to present conditions, the more it will reduce its ability to maintain the requisite variety necessary to adapt to the future.
2. *Selection*: variations need to be selected for or against by managers; people in organizations need to be encouraged to make experiments, and they need to know that these will be seriously considered by managers who will take action on clear criteria. People need to be aware of how internal selection processes are operating and what kinds of variations managers are selecting for or against.
3. *Retention*: organizations often fail to retain personnel holding key skills and generating new market niches. Thus, for example, new companies are often founded by individuals moving out of an existing company where their idea is not properly taken up. Brittain and Freeman (1980) found that this was

characteristic of the semi-conductor industry in the USA, where the group of firms dominant in the production of valves failed to take up transistor technology even though it was developed in their own laboratories. As a result, the individuals concerned moved out and set up their own companies. In turn, these companies fell victim to structural inertia when integrated circuit technology was developed. Thus a third set of firms were set up.

4. *Struggle*: complacency and satisfaction reduce the struggle for survival in some industries; people become fixed into a certain way of looking at things. McKelvey and Aldrich argue that 'The best practical message we have is to do anything possible to bring shake-out pressure to bear on organizational units and to place them in competitive postures against other organizational units.'

In conclusion, they argue, managers should attempt a balanced emphasis on all four principles as the best way of increasing the chances of survival of their organization. They conclude:

Such an even emphasis will not guarantee favourable selection but at least it will keep a manager from inadvertently helping the organization more quickly towards failure. The theory of natural selection explains the effects of a force that cannot be anticipated or countered in its effect but that can be understood. Organizations have more ability to adapt than organisms, we think; they have more ability to alter their niche space than organisms and they have the possibility of gaining a vision capable of steering them away from failure-enhancing mistakes.

It is worth noting that population ecologists do not reduce the competitive forces simply to the workings of the capitalist economy. They argue that the key concepts of niche, survival and density can be applied in other areas. For any particular organizational functioning there is a limit to the number of people who want it; thus, for example, there are only a limited number of trade unions that will survive, although many more may be founded in the early days of the emergence of this particular organizational form. The form which becomes successful is that which best fits the niche. Once again, the approach is both stimulating and at the same time frustrating. It is stimulating because it gets us to think in terms of populations of organizations and how they change and not be myopically attentive to what happens in a single organization. It is frustrating because it ignores so many other possible explanations. For example, it once again fails to take seriously the way in which large organizations can use their powers in and over the environment to destroy potential competitors. (Astley in particular has tried to rectify this weakness by developing the notion of community ecology and with it the idea of collective strategy; see Astley, 1984, 1985; Astley and Fombrun, 1983; Carney, 1987.) Nor does it consider the process of institutionalization and the way in which organizational forms become legitimate and unchallengable even where they may not 'fit' any particular niche. Nevertheless, it is important to remember that the population ecologists do not confine their analysis to capitalist companies, though in many ways they fit the model more closely than any other types of organization.

Population ecology: some concluding remarks

The theory of population ecology has boomed in recent years, particularly the USA. It has generated a new series of questions about the nature of organizations and their relationship to the environment. In doing this, it has raised in stark form the issue of agency and structure. For population ecology, the central facts of organizations – their survivability and durability – cannot be explained from the perspective of social actors. Rather, explanation must be in terms of how the environment selects particular organizations. The environment is seen to have a power that cannot be reduced to the action of other organizations. There are so many uncertainties in the environment according to this model that organizations are ineffective in changing it and thus ensuring their own conditions of existence. One might as well ask why the dinosaurs died out. It had to do with environmental changes that were not only beyond their control but also beyond their understanding. Population ecology is as much about deflating the egos of managers and planners as Darwinism was about deflating the egos of those who believed that human beings were distinctively God's creatures. The population of organizations we see around us is not the highest achievement of a great directing intelligence – in this case, management – but the haphazard creation of random organizational mutations best suited to particular environmental niches. As the environment changes, so will the population of organizations; particular organizations can no more ensure their own survival than particular dinosaurs could! Can one abandon intentionality and purposive rationality with such grand disdain as exhibited by the population ecologists?

The argument in this book has been that one cannot do so. Intentionality is always a central part of organizational life. The strategies which organizations develop and seek to pursue cannot be understood without understanding the intentions of those who developed them. Nevertheless, it is not sufficient to assume that because something is intended it will actually be achieved. On the contrary, I have already shown how within organizational boundaries there are many barriers to the achievement of goals. This is much more the case when organizations are considered in relation to their environments. As the population ecologists emphasize, environments are highly complex and, in certain circumstances (though not all – a point they seem to ignore), highly competitive, making the achievement of intentions very difficult. Nevertheless, organizations seek to reduce uncertainty in the environment, as has already been illustrated. To ignore all the processes whereby organizations do this would seem to be rather extreme.

Population ecology is undoubtedly a theory for the 1980s. Issues like start-ups, survival and decline resonated strongly with the problems of the recession-hit economies of Britain and the USA in the early 1980s. The fatalism of population ecology is in some ways little more than a reworked version of the hidden hand of the market philosophy first elaborated by Adam Smith and keenly espoused in the 1980s (at least in most spheres) by leaders like Ronald Reagan and Margaret Thatcher. However, it needs restating that concepts like 'environment' are really a form of shorthand for social processes that involve people. The naturalistic metaphor which is at the heart of population ecology is fundamentally flawed for the simple reason that people can reflect on their own behaviour and change it. Indeed, social behaviour is in a continuous process of construction and interpretation. We cannot afford to treat organizational events as though they just happen 'naturally' without anybody thinking or doing something.

Take as an example the concept of 'death'. There is an assumption that death is an unproblematic concept: we know when an organization has died, in the same way as we know when it was born. We can thus develop mortality tables which allow us to correlate births and deaths with other features of the environment. This, though, is to commit a naturalistic fallacy, which can be demonstrated by considering the notion of biological death. The biological death of the individual may seem relatively unproblematic, but its social dimensions must not be ignored. To take the most obvious example in the hi-tech medical world at the moment, it it clearly possible to keep people alive for long periods even when they remain in a state of deep coma. In order to resolve this, doctors have come up with the notion of 'brain-death'; but even this is subject to debate, and there remains equivocation about when people are actually dead. In other ways, death is socially constructed. In order that a person can be considered dead in our society, there must be a death certificate. Even then, death is not immediately recognized. In some areas, people stay on the electoral register until their death is proved by the Registration Officer actually seeing the death certificate. Most societies have a set of '*rites de passage*' (van Gennep, 1977) associated with people moving from a state of life to a state of death. Death itself, however, is considered by many religions as a form of life: the dead are not gone away; they remain present amongst the living in a different form and the living must take account of this in their everday actions, whether it be in the form of ancestor worship or simply respect for the dead.

If all this is the case for what at first sight seems as unproblematic as the death of an individual person, how much more problematic is the death of an organization? We may consider that for a business organization, bankruptcy is an unproblematic form of death, but the point at which receivers are brought in is not when some clear and objective state of financial ruin has been reached. Rather it depends on a host of interpretations and projections about the present and future health of the company, which are subject, as are any interpretations, to argument and conflict. (See Aris, 1985, for some examples of this; also Tinker, 1985, for a wider discussion of the manipulation of accounts; for an interesting discussion of the concept of organizational death in the context of an educational institution see Wilson, 1985; other recent attempts to tackle the issue include Whetten, 1987; Cameron, Kim and Whetten, 1987; McKinlay, 1987; Sutton, 1987.) Bankruptcy statistics can no more provide us with an unambiguous set of facts about the death of organizations than can suicide statistics about a particular sub-set of deaths among persons (see, for example, Douglas's classic critique of Durkheim's use of statistics about suicide: Durkheim, 1951; Douglas, 1967). To seek to correlate these statistics with another set and produce a set of determining relationships is to fall into the same methodological error as Durkheim.

The emphasis on newness, whilst undoubtedly drawing attention to an under-researched phenomenon, has the danger of neglecting the large organizations in both the state and the private sector, which do retain a stability over long periods of time. Multinationals like Ford, General Motors, Shell, ICI, etc. may have moved up and down slightly in some chart of total value produced, but they have remained important for many years now, and their power shows few signs of diminishing. The same could be said of the powerful organizations of the state and civil society. The reason for this is quite simple: once a certain size is reached, the power to control the environment increases and threats to the organization's survival can be reduced. The population ecologists, in their eagerness to emphasize competition and the market, neglect this. They ignore the way in which people within organizations will seek to shape the environment.

To the extent that population ecology becomes a way of thinking about organizations that neglects people, it is simply taking the study of organizations back to a mélange of systems theory and functionalism. On the other hand, if its insights are treated as new questions about how competition influences organizational survival, it can provide a stimulating new perspective in the study of organizations so long as it is supplemented by an understanding of the way in which these competitive forces can be controlled. It is to the analysis of this in the 'markets and hierarchies approach' that I shall now turn.

Markets and hierarchies

The markets and hierarchies approach, also sometimes known as either the 'market failures' or 'organizational failures' approach, is associated mainly with the American institutional economist, Oliver Williamson (1975), though the major historical studies by business historian Alfred Chandler (1962, 1977) are often seen as sharing the same basic framework. Williamson approached the study of organizations from the point of view of traditional market economics. In this view, the market is the optimal way in which individuals in pursuit of goods and services can interact. This is therefore the starting point, and the question is why do certain transactions get taken out of the market and instead take place in organizations (or, as Williamson continually calls them, 'hierarchies')? Williamson's is a radical approach to the analysis of organizations. It starts from the perspective of a world without organizations and, in a leap to a philosophical anthropology based on the myth of the world as naturally a market-place, asks how organizations ever could arise, since individuals in theory can best meet every need through market transactions. In order to make sociological sense of this, let me give an example from the real world rather than from Williamson's 'primeval market-place'.

Take the example of firms involved in the production of cars. Since the time of Henry Ford, car firms have become highly integrated. They will make their own car bodies, engines and trim; they will then assemble them and distribute the cars to their dealers. Williamson's point is that, according to the market model, it should be more advantageous for the individual firm to purchase each of these from the market. Thus the car firm would purchase bodies from a specialist body maker; it would purchase parts from specialist manufacturers; it would purchase distribution from a specialist transport firm, etc. The car firm would concentrate on just one of these processes itself – probably the assembly of the car. This would theoretically be more advantageous to the company because, to take the example of car bodies, there will be a number of firms competing to sell car bodies at the lowest price possible to car-assembly firms. Thus costs will be kept low whilst quality will be retained, because failure to achieve quality standards will result in the loss of the contract and the car assembly firm will switch its business to another manufacturer of car bodies.

This is not what has happened in reality; most modern car firms have become integrated (there are, of course, differences in the extent of integration – see Marsden *et al.*, 1985, and Altschuler *et al.*, 1985 – which the Williamson framework would seek to explain). In other words, what were previously market transactions are now transactions that occur within the organization; thus the car body plant passes the body over to the paint shop which passes it over to the assembly plant, etc. All this occurs within one organization and the transactions are internal to the hierarchy. The market model might be expected to predict that because the transactions are not disciplined by the market, they will become inefficient. Firms continuing to rely on the market could expect to out-compete firms utilizing internal transaction procedures. Why does this not happen? Williamson proposes two main answers to this question.

Bounded rationality and uncertainty/complexity

The first limit on the market is the fact that human behaviour involves bounded rationality. Williamson says:

> Bounded rationality refers to human behaviour that is 'intendedly rational but only limitedly so' (Simon). Although it is widely appreciated that human decision makers are not lightning calculators . . . the implications for economic organization have only been scratched . . . Bounded rationality involves neurophysiological limits on the one hand and language limits on the other. The physical limits take the form of rate and storage limits on the power of individuals to receive, store, retrieve and process information without error . . . Language limits refer to the inability of individuals to articulate their knowledge or feelings by the use of words, numbers or graphics in ways which permit them to be understood by others. (Williamson, 1975, pp. 21–2)

The consequence of this is starkly spelled out by Williamson when he says: 'But for bounded rationality, all economic exchange could be efficiently organized by contract' (1981, p. 553). In other words, a full market system founders on the inability of individuals to cost transactions in a rational way. Nevertheless, this is not an insuperable obstacle to the dominance of the market. Only where other conditions also exist do market transactions become 'inefficient'. These other conditions are complexity and uncertainty; under these conditions the consequences of conducting any particular transaction through the market become that much more difficult to predict. Thus where a firm requires a particularly complex piece of equipment to be made that may require continual modification in the design and production process, a market-based relationship may be inefficient. Where suppliers in the market are not able to guarantee certain standards of production or production by certain deadlines, the firm may not want to continue to rely on the market. In Williamson's terms, the market 'fails'.

Opportunism and small numbers

The second condition Williamson identifies as generating market failure derives from the opportunism that actors in a market transaction may exhibit:

> Opportunistic behaviour involves making 'false or empty, that is, self-disbelieved threats and promises' in the expectation that individual advantage will thereby be realized . . . The strategic manipulation of information or misrepresentation of intentions, however, are to be regarded as opportunistic. (1975, p. 26)

Opportunism, however, is only relevant if combined with a second characteristic – that of small numbers: Williamson is saying if this condition is not present then

> rivalry among large numbers of bidders will render opportunistic inclinations ineffectual. Parties who attempt to secure gains by strategic posturing will find at the contract renewal interval, that such behaviour is non-viable. Opposite parties will arrange alternative trades in which competitive terms are satisfied. (1975, p. 27)

Thus where there are only a small number of possible suppliers on the market, opportunism can flourish and the market will 'fail' in the sense that inefficiencies will arise.

Where markets 'fail', according to Williamson, hierarchies can succeed. In other words, transactions that were previously taking place in the market now take place in the organization. Thus a set of rules and procedures controls the relationship between individuals in the organization, thereby minimizing the problems of bounded rationality, complexity, opportunism and small numbers. To go back to the previous example of the car manufacturer, processes get taken into the organization where the market is failing. The strength of hierarchy is that it can partially control the dysfunctions that arise in the market under certain conditions. Pugh *et al.*, summarize the advantages of hierarchy according to Williamson as follows

First it extends the bounds on rationality . . . specialization enables each to deal with a part of the overall problem that is small enough to be comprehended . . . Second, sub-sections of an organization can attend to a given aspect of the uncertainty-complexity of a situation, so making manageable a problem which would in total be too uncertain-complex. Third, a hierarchy curbs opportunism. Pay, promotion and control techniques ensure that the parties work in some degree towards common goals. Fourth, where there are small numbers . . . the hierarchy can overrule bargaining. (Pugh *et al.*, 1987, p. 58)

Nevertheless, there are considerable problems with hierarchies. Perrow, in fact, goes so far as to argue that 'virtually all the advantages of hierarchy for reducing transaction costs and opportunism are repealed' (1981, p. 373). Williamson recognizes that within hierarchies, bureaucratic rigidities emerge, as does cheating, opportunism, alienation, etc. (1975, ch. 7). However, for him, this does not alter the central point that under certain circumstances, hierarchies are more efficient than markets. The fact that bureaucratic rigidities do emerge provides his model with a certain dynamism, because he links this with two crucial processes of change:

1. The boundaries between markets and hierarchies are not static; rather they can shift as firms consider whether to conduct transactions internally (through the hierarchy) or externally (through market transactions).
2. Those organizations will survive which are best able to build into their operation elements of both market and hierarchy.

This second point provides the vital link between Williamson and Chandler's business histories. Chandler's histories trace the growth of large-scale organizations in the United States in the period following 1870 (Chandler, 1962, 1977). Before this time, according to Chandler, there were very few large-scale organizations; in Williamson's terms, transactions were mainly market- and contract-based. Between 1870 and 1920, however, there was a massive expansion in the number of vertically integrated large enterprises in a number of US industries. Chandler traces the reasons for this to what he calls the 'revolution in transportation and communication' and the 'revolution in distribution and production'. Through the growth of railroads in the USA a huge new national market for goods was created. This market was catered for by the establishment of mass retailing outlets – department stores, mail-order companies and chain stores – selling commodities produced on a mass scale in the newly emergent consumer product industries. What Chandler argues (and this is part of what he shares with Williamson) is that market transactions between these separate organizations 'fail' and, as a consequence, a process of vertical integration occurs:

> Integration of mass production with mass distribution offered an opportunity for manufacturers to lower costs and increase productivity through more effective administration of the processes of production and distribution and coordination of the flow of goods through them. Yet the first industrialists to integrate these two basic sets of processes did not do so to exploit such economies. They did so because existing marketeers were unable to sell and distribute products in the volume they were produced. Once the inadequacies of existing marketeers became clear, manufacturers integrated forward into marketing. (1977, p. 287)

The new organizations that emerged had immediate problems of control. Putting together so many diverse activities under one umbrella necessitated a new structure. At first, however, the companies sought to proceed along the same lines as before, with power held centrally by one man or the central board of directors. Activities were divided up on a functional basis, i.e. sales, production, research, personnel, etc., with each 'function' responsible to the centre:

> The large majority became administered through centralized functionally departmentalized structures . . . the dominant centralized structure had one basic weakness. A very few men were still entrusted with a great number of complex decisions. (Chandler, 1962, p. 41)

According to Chandler, the consequence of this was that, particularly in the new industries of the time (the electrical, automobile and chemical industries), companies began to grow too unwieldy. They were too large for effective decision-making to be centralized. The result was that gradually a new form of organization emerged which separated strategic decision-making from operational decision-making; this new form was known as the multidivisional organization. In the multidivisional form, the organization is not divided by functions but rather by product or geographical area; each division of the company is responsible for all the operational issues. Top management at the centre is concerned with overall corporate strategy. Divisions report to the centre in terms of their profits and operating performance. Top management decides how to distribute profits and where to make major new investments. Top management are therefore not burdened with operational decisions, and divisional managers are not burdened with strategic decisions.

Chandler's studies show through detailed case studies of individual companies how the multidivisional form (known in the literature as the M-form) has gradually become the dominant form for large-scale industry in the United States. In later work, he and his collaborators have examined the extent to which this process has occurred in other countries, too (see especially Chandler and Daems, 1980). These studies have indicated that the timing of the appearance of multidivisional forms has been different. In Britain, they emerged only gradually in the 1950s, partially under the impact of US multinationals operating in the UK. Before that, large organizations tended to be organized either along unitary lines or through a holding company (Channon, 1977; Hannah, 1976). Indeed, these forms were still common in the 1960s and 1970s. In the car industry in particular, the bringing together of the many separate car companies into the British Leyland company did not immediately result in a reorganization along M-form lines. The separate companies retained their separate existence under the one umbrella, thus creating major problems of product range, wage relativities, economies of scale, etc. (see Loveridge, 1981). A crucial part of the reorganization of British Leyland has been the creation of an M-form organization with appropriate divisions. During the 1970s, more and more sectors of British industry began to take on this form, with consequences for their workforce both in terms of the accompanying rationalization of production (involving large-scale redundancies) and the new-style corporate policies for industrial relations which were involved, the most dramatic example again being British Leyland (see Marsden *et al.*, 1985; Willmann and Winch, 1985), though similar trends are apparent elsewhere. (For a consideration of the multidivisional form concentrating particularly on its implications for industrial relations and personnel management see Purcell, 1985; Purcell and Gray, 1984, 1986; Marginson *et al.*, 1988.)

The reason why the multidivisional form is so popular is because of the way in which it incorporates the advantages of both markets and hierarchies. According to Williamson and Ouchi:

> Removing top management from the operating affairs of the enterprise meant that, whereas bureaucratic control processes had governed previously, operating divisions were now governed in a quasi-market fashion. Thus divisions were assigned the status of quasi-firms and the central office assumed fuctions of review and resource allocation ordinarily associated with the capital market. As a consequence of these changes, the goal confusion (or incongruence) that had previously reigned was supplanted by subgoal clarity that was meaningfully related to enterprise objectives. The self-interest seeking that had once drained the energies of the enterprise was now turned to productive purposes. (Williamson and Ouchi, 1983, p. 60)

In this perspective, the best way to organize large-scale enterprises is through adopting a multidivisional form along these lines.

Unlike population ecology, therefore, this approach does not assume that organizations are inevitable victims of the environment. Instead, organizations make choices about their relationship to the environment. They can seek to incorporate aspects of the environment into their hierarchy or they can remain dependent on the market. According to this approach, under certain specific conditions, transactions occurring outside the time-space boundaries of the organization will be positively beneficial to the organization. In other conditions, however, they will not, and instead the organization will seek to bring the transactions inside its boundaries, which, however, would result in certain tensions of reproduction between the tendency of the hierarchy to become economically inefficient and the need for the transaction to occur within the hierarchy. One way of partially resolving this under specific conditions is to set up a multidivisional structure (though see Ouchi, 1980, and Wilkins and Ouchi, 1983, for another related way through the creation of a 'clan' culture within the organization).

A critical analysis of markets and hierarchy

There are a number of problems with this framework for organizational analysis. The main problem surrounds the causes of the transition from market to hierarchy and vice versa. Williamson and Chandler see this exclusively in 'efficiency' terms – that is, the costs of the transaction are reduced by shifting them from the market into the organization. However, alternative explanations of this can be made: Perrow, for example, says:

> If it is profitable, a firm integrates backward or forward for at least 3 reasons. First, a firm might find an adjacent area to be highly profitable but composed of small firms that could not match the capital of an acquiring firm. Second, they might see that the firms could be made profitable, because the acquiring firm could rig the market. In neither of these cases can any efficiencies be demonstrated by Williamson and Chandler. Third, acquiring related firms or setting up their own divisions might bring labour problems under control . . . these are not the efficiencies Williamson and Chandler would like us to have in mind . . . The explanations I have offered deal with power or control, not the efficiencies Williamson and Chandler would like us to have in mind. (Perrow, 1983, p. 381)

Similar points have been made by Francis:

> In many cases, markets are replaced by hierarchies as a result of domination by one party over the other rather than by mutual agreement on the basis of an expectation of mutual benefit. In a number of cases, the major benefits accruing from the switch arise from the resulting domination within the hierarchical relationship rather than because of a reduction in transaction costs. (Francis *et al.*, 1983, p. 113: see also Du Boff and Herman, 1980)

Perrow and Francis then draw our attention back to the wider social processes of domination within which decisions about efficiency are located. As Francis says,

> While Williamson's organizational failures framework offers much insight into the process whereby hierarchies replace markets . . . it understates the exercise of domination in the process.

A necessary refinement of the organizational failures framework is to drop the notion of system interests and substitute a thorough-going analysis of the interests of the various parties to the transaction. In addition, further analysis should be done of the various power resources each party has at its disposal. (Francis *et al.*, 1983, p. 115)

On a related point, it is possible to question the points Williamson and Chandler make with regard to the emergence of the multidivisional form. Once again, there is emphasis given to the efficiency criteria, making the move towards the M-form almost a natural corollary of large organizations. Although Chandler and his colleagues have investigated the differences between countries in terms of the take-up of the M-form, they do not seem to have incorporated the implications of this into their analysis. Fligstein, for example, has argued:

It is clear that Chandler underestimated the role of actors who were committed to a certain view of how large organizations should have grown. The power perspective suggests that key actors with certain interests who have the resources to implement their point of view on appropriate corporate strategy and hence structure, would choose to implement the multi-divisional form (MDF) net of strategy and to use the MDF as a structure which would enhance and extend their power. (Fligstein, 1985, p. 388)

Rather than assuming that the reason for the rise of the multidivisional form lies with the efficiency benefits that accrue, it is necessary to consider the point of view of those involved in the decision-making process.

These criticisms raise the necessity of redefining the useful elements of the markets and hierarchies approach. This can be done by returning to the social reproduction analysis presented earlier. Central to Williamson and Chandler's arguments is the role of information. Decisions regarding the relative merits of markets and hierarchies are seen as being based on information about relative efficiencies. Without information about competitor's levels of performance, about the nature of the market, about the possible consequences of changes in the market, there can be no rational process of decision-making, and yet the sociological nature of these information processes is totally ignored. It is possible to raise a number of intervening institutional variables that present themselves between markets and hierarchies and mediate the information-gathering process.

Probably the most crucial and until recently least explored mediating institutional practices are those of the accounting profession. It is the generation of socially legitimated and accepted information about relative profit rates and efficiency criteria that provides the basis for decisions regarding the relative merits of markets and hierarchies and these in turn are socially constructed. (In addition to the references previously cited, Thompson, 1977, 1978, 1982, addresses this issue critically; for more general discussions of this see Tomlinson, 1982; Cutler *et al.*, 1978; Tinker, 1985.) Thus the impetus within organizations either to bring more of the market into the hierarchy or alternatively to move elements of the hierarchy back into the market is socially produced through the accounting system.

This process of systematizing information within the firms on the basis of agreed criteria is supplemented by a second phenomenon that has been ignored. This is the creation of a whole set of intermediary information-gatherers outside the firms, whose role is to provide public (at least for those who can pay) information about markets and company developments. A plethora of organizations and professionals have emerged over the last fifty years whose role is to collect information on company activities and the state of the market. These include stockbrokers, management consultants, merchant banks and other institutions. The particular nature of these organizations needs to be located in the wider structure of relations between different fractions of capital (see Ingham, 1985; Moran, 1983; Longstreth, 1979; Scott, 1982). These intermediaries are also important in the bringing together of resources to allow firms to raise the capital to allow expansion. Much expansion may be self-financed, but we are now in an era of takeovers and mergers when huge companies can be threatened by companies that in terms of their overall value are smaller but which finance their takeovers via high levels of borrowing (so-called 'high leveraged bids'). It is the ability of intermediaries such as merchant banks to raise loans and other funds to finance expansion that is crucial, as well as their ability to mobilize shareholders either for or against bids. Once again, this area is unexplored in the market and hierarchies approach.

Finally, and connected to the previous point, there is the question of the supply of funds for growth. In Williamson and Chandler, this is seen as relatively unproblematic. However, unless expansion is internally funded, which is increasingly unlikely to be the case, organizations need to raise funds for growth. This in turn necessitates entering the money markets of the world, which in turn are linked through various capillaries to various sources of funds, as well as having their own dynamic of development, connected to currency exchange movements and government borrowing requirements. Once again, a relatively unexplored area here is the question of how these markets draw savings from the wider population of wage earners, through, for example, pension schemes, life insurance, etc. (For an initial attempt to examine this see Knights, 1985; Knights (with Tinker), 1988; see also Minns, 1980, 1982.)

There is not the space here to elaborate on these processes or to consider the very real differences between capitalist societies in regard to these processes. Nevertheless, even allowing for the critique of this approach by authors such as Francis and Perrow, we still have only half the story. If this approach is to have any value, it must not simply answer why transactions are then transferred from the market to a hierarchy, but how this occurs. What are the institutional supports for this process? How are such decisions taken? How are their consequences realized? This is the essence of what Foucault calls the micro-physics of power: it is through these conduits of institutional power and information that decision-making processes are channelled. The origins of these institutional complexes and the manner in which they reproduce and are reproduced is an issue which the market and hierarchies approach and in fact the study of organizations in general has not yet begun to analyse in any depth.

Markets and hierarchies thus places at the heart of its concern the relationship between the 'unplanned' nature of market relations and the 'planned' nature of organizational life. It suggests in typical economists' terms that the market will work to the benefit of all concerned except under certain specific circumstances. Under these circumstances, organizations should intervene, not in the sense of tinkering or disrupting ongoing market relations, but in the sense of completely taking out of the market certain transactions and planning and executing them within the organizational hierarchy. In this view, rationalization occurs through the expansion of calculation in a way which allows organizations to distinguish which transaction should remain based on market relations and which transactions can be undertaken most efficiently within the organization. This is a totally unsociological perspective on the organization. It fails to locate the organization as a power source in a network of other organizations, using its power to improve its position by taking over potential competitors. It fails to problematize the economic notion of 'transaction cost', neglecting the fact that any notions of costs have to be socially produced and that the process of social production brings with it the idea of social interests involved in the production of such ideas. It proposes a view of the state which amounts to little more than a social contract role – that is, individuals give up certain rights to the state as the only way in which they can guarantee overall safety and security for themselves and their property.

Thus there must be an ultimate guarantor of the conditions under which market transactions occur; it is not sufficient to expect individuals to provide this for themselves. In so far as the state performs roles, it does so because the market cannot perform them efficiently. Such a view neglects the deep historical roots of states and the notion that increasingly they have come to embody alternative values to the market (as has already been described). The state is not simply the safety-net for market failure; it has an autonomous existence associated in the current period with notions such as citizenship and the rights and duties of citizenship which allow it to intervene in the market for other reasons besides the lack of efficiency in market transactions. To ignore this is to indulge in a naive economism.

Resource dependence and interorganizational networks

The markets and hierarchies approach indicates how organizations seek to solve transaction cost problems by bringing certain areas of the environment into the organization, where they can be more tightly controlled. In the rest of this chapter, I argue that this process takes more complex forms than the markets and hierarchies approach suggest. Organizations seek to control their environment through making links with each other which allow a co-ordination of their activity. At this stage we see again the pressures on organizations to move in a similar direction. However, these pressures, rather than arising from the activities of the 'service class', as in the last chapter, can now be seen as arising from the desire of top decision-makers to retain control over their environment. In the final part of the chapter, the extent to which these processes can be considered part of a wider process of class co-ordination is briefly considered.

All organizations enter into exchanges with their environment. This is partly a necessity but it is also to do with choice and strategy. By reaching agreements with other organizations, by gaining knowledge of the environment, by creating coalitions of interest with other organizations, organizations are able to reduce their 'vulnerability' to environmental changes. (For a detailed review of many of these mechanisms see Pennings, 1981.) These types of transactions, which fall between Williamson's 'markets' and 'hierarchies', create innumerable interorganizational networks in modern societies. (The concept of social network has been subjected to considerable analysis; networks have properties such as density, centrality and reachability which can be statistically analysed and compared; in what follows I shall avoid these more technical issues and proceed using examples; for readers interested in more detail on social network analysis in general, see Scott, 1988; for network analysis as applied to the study of organizations see the following mainly methodological analyses: Aldrich and Whetten, 1981; Alba, 1982; Lincoln, 1982.) Is it possible to abstract a pattern from these organizational networks, to give them a theoretical meaning?

This is what the resource dependency approach attempts to do. This approach, drawing substantially from social exchange theory (see Blau, 1964, and Heath, 1976, for a discussion of this theory in general terms), argues that in an exchange relationship, each of the two partners to the exchange (the dyadic exchange is the basic building block of the theory) will seek to reduce their dependence on the other, whilst increasing the dependence of the other on them. This interaction and its successful resolution is the basis of power differentials between the two. Cook argues:

> Power derives from resource dependencies. To the extent that alternative sources are available to an organization in an exchange network, dependence is less and the organization has more bargaining power in terms of influencing the exchange ratio. (Cook, 1977, p. 68)

Expanding these ideas from simple dyadic relations into networks of organizations, it is possible to conceive of networks as structures of power, where the dependence and autonomy of particular organizations is reflected in the nature of their linkages to other organizations. In other words, the links represented in networks are attempts by organizations to increase their power over the environment through reducing their dependence on certain organizations whilst at the same time increasing the dependence of those organizations on them. (See Pfeffer and Salancik, 1978, for the most extensive working out of this perspective.) Thus the environment is controlled and co-ordinated through bringing relevant organizations into a co-ordinated relationship. In this view, then, the concept of environment can be reconceptualized and considered in terms of other organizations.

What is the nature of the environment when considered from this perspective? Clearly, organizations can be linked in all sorts of different ways. For the purposes of this discussion, I will distinguish two types of linkage. The first derives from linkages between organizations related to their ultimate product or service. The second type will be concerned with linkages on the basis of personnel, in particular the phenomenon of interlocking directorates.

Product/service networks

Organizations are centrally concerned with the provision of a service or a product. This necessitates the purchase or acquisition of inputs as well as the provision of outputs. Take the case of a small clothing company which manufactures shirts for the UK market. This company is a subcontractor of one of the large multiple retail chains that dominate the UK clothing industry (see Rainnie, 1984, for details of this domination). The large retailer purchases from many other such companies. It is the centre of their network. Should the retailer decide that the subcontractor is no longer needed or no longer produces work of the required quality, then the subcontractor is in an extremely difficult position. As Rainnie shows, this means that the clothing manufacturer will do everything within its power to meet the demands of the retailer, even where this means cutting margins to the bone and keeping wages low. Thus the clothing industry can be represented as a series of major centres which collect smaller organizations around themselves. The chances of survival outside these networks are exceedingly slim; similarly, the chances of moving between them are difficult. (A similar sort of phenomenon is found on a much larger scale in Japanese industry, where companies are linked through loose ties into 'families'; see Dore, 1983, and the next chapter). Analysing these relationships in terms of a network provides the background for understanding the power of the central organization.

Personnel linkages

It is also possible to produce interorganizational networks according to the extent to which the same people hold positions in more than one organization. The most popular example here is that of interlocking directorships. In most countries it is common for the top executives in large companies to hold non-executive directorships in other companies (see Stokman *et al.*, 1985; Scott and Griff, 1985; Mizruchi, 1982; Ornstein, 1984; Mizruchi and Schwartz, 1988). Most countries also seem to possess a group of people who by virtue of their previous positions, for example in government, the civil service or industry, are sought after by companies to be directors on their boards and who thus collect multiple non-executive directorships.

In recent years, extensive research efforts have gone into the analysis of these interlocking directorships from the point of view of social network theory. The methodology is simple in theory, though in practice, because of the huge numbers involved, it can become highly complex, as can the process of interpreting significance in the resulting patterns. In a population of organizations, there are certain people who are on the boards of more than one company. (The population can be extended to include positions not just in private sector companies but also within other major public institutions such as the boards of nationalized companies, the governors of major educational institutions, charities and voluntary bodies, employers' organizations and political parties, or interest groups.) Where somebody appears on two such bodies, they create a link between the two organizations. The empirical question then arises as to which organizations are connected in this network. Once the network has been mapped, we can then address its significance. The most comprehensive recent work in the British context has been by Scott and Griff (1984). This study was based upon a selection of the 200 largest non-financial enterprises and 50 large financial enterprises for 1904, 1938 and 1976. They concluded that there was a pattern to the interlocks, with certain people in certain key organizations more likely to be involved in multiple directorships than others. They argue that those people who sat on the board of more than one company (whom they called 'multiple directors') formed an 'inner circle' within the corporate directorate of business leaders. Because of their position on so many central organizations, and because of the frequency of their social interaction both within boardrooms and in other institutions, stretching back to similar educational experiences at school and university, this group were in a position to form a cohesive outlook about business and society which in turn enabled them to exercise leadership over business as a whole. According to Scott and Griff, this group had formed gradually as the nature of British society had changed:

> In the earliest period studies, the inner circle consisted mainly of entrepreneurial capitalists, a City of London core and provincial entrepreneurs, and formed part of a wider 'establishment' which headed the stratification system. Based in London and county 'Society', this establishment had gradually incorporated provincial business leaders. By the 1930s the City core had become all pervasive through the emerging fusion of banks and industry, and the inner circle, still part of an establishment, comprised a group of proto-finance capitalists. By 1976 an extensive national network had emerged within which the inner circle consisted almost exclusively of finance capitalists (co-ordinating controllers) . . . The finance capital model seems to be the most useful for grasping the structure of the network. The primary interlocks produced a network which was structured into recognisable cliques and clusters in which banks held central positions . . .

There is a group of finance capitalists, the inner circle of business leaders, who are simultaneously involved in both banking and industry. (Scott and Griff, 1985, pp. 180–1)

Scott and Griff, then, argue that in the UK, the pattern of interlocking directorships between organizations is one in which the banks are at the centre, sending to and receiving directors from the main industrial companies. As one moves out of this inner circle, there are fewer multiple directorships and connections are less significant. (Extensive work has also been done on this subject in the USA; see especially Mintz and Schwartz, 1985; Burt, 1983; Useem, 1984; Mizruchi, 1982.)

There are a number of other types of links between organizations besides product/service links and personnel links. The most important is probably that where organizations involve themselves in joint ventures for particular purposes. For example, since 1946, four of the Seven Sisters (i.e. the major oil companies in the world) – Socal (Standard Oil of California), Texaco, Mobil and Exxon – have run a joint oil-producing company in Saudi Arabia known as ARAMCO. This has been a major source of crude oil for the American oil companies, and although it is now substantially under the control of the Saudi government in terms of its output level, it remains owned by the American companies (Sampson, 1975). In an era when many products are the result of high capital investment spread over many years, it is becoming increasingly common for companies to join together, particularly in hi-tech areas, to pool expertise and spread risks – for example, the European Airbus project, which involves companies from France, Germany, Britain and Spain.

Interorganizational linkages can also build up when companies agree not to compete with each other. For example, in 1910 the two largest tobacco companies in the world, Imperial Tobacco of Britain and American Tobacco of the USA agreed, after a fierce price war, not to compete against each other in each other's home markets. They further agreed to form a third company – to be known as British American Tobacco and owned one-third by Imperial and two-thirds by American Tobacco – which was to have free run at the rest of the world (Corina, 1973). (For other examples of interorganizational linkages of this kind, see Edstrom *et al.*, 1984.)

Networks and power

So far I have discussed the nature of networks, their possible implications, and the different types of network linkages. I now want to return to the question which lies at the heart of this: what is the significance of interorganizational networks? As I suggested earlier, the hidden agenda behind the analysis of networks is that of power. Unlike the previous two approaches, population ecology, and markets and hierarchies, the linkages that arise between organizations are ways in which organizations try to control for the possible uncertainties of the environment. In particular, more powerful organizations (and within them more powerful people) seek to ensure the reproduction of their power by shaping and controlling the actions of other organizations in the environment.

However, consistent with the approach adopted in this text, this issue can only be properly addressed if we distinguish power as an enabler from power as a constraint. First I shall briefly review the two main approaches to the analysis of interorganizational networks and the significance of power within them. I will then suggest that these theories effectively embody the two distinctive views of power and that it is necessary to achieve some sort of synthesis along the lines previously suggested.

The first approach to linkages derives from the work of Pfeffer and Salancik (1978) but is used by many other authors (for example, Allen, 1974; Pennings, 1980, 1981; Pennings *et al.*, 1984; Dastmalchian, 1984; Burt, 1983). The argument here is that modern organizations increasingly make links to each other for the specific purpose of obtaining information about aspects of the environment which are of direct importance to their operations. So, for example, research within this perspective is concerned to show that through rational co-operation and linking together, organizations can gain more information about their environment, and thus act in a more effective manner (see, for example, Pfeffer and Salancik, 1978, chapters 5–8, where this approach is consistently applied to a wide variety of organizations from business through to voluntary and charitable organizations; see also Van de Ven and Walker, 1984, for an application of this perspective to child care and health organizations). This is not to say that these authors neglect the concept of power as a constraint; there is a recognition that organizations are potentially competing for scarce resources and thus power may be exerted in order to maintain the organization's position. However, the main point is that linkages are understood as rational responses to situations of environmental uncertainty. This is demonstrated particularly clearly in the analysis of interlocking directorships as it comes out of this perspective. In this view, interlocking directorships are a means whereby organizations which mutually depend on each other, for example, for customers, can share information about their past, present and future plans. It is no accident that this analysis of networks has a pluralistic ring. It is in fact little more than a reformulation of pluralistic models of power in modern society (see Lukes, 1974, for a review of this approach). In these views modern society is characterized by a competition between interest groups which rise and fall according to the importance accorded to particular issues. Power is not concentrated but dispersed among competing groups both within and between networks. Networks themselves are rational responses to this competitive situation; they are ways in which organizations seek to gain temporary advantage over others, but these advantages will not last. Networks are impermanent, and as interests change, so may the networks. So whilst power is a central consideration (see, for example, *Power in Organizations* by Pfeffer, 1981, one of the leading proponents of this perspective), it is the power involved in interest group conflict.

Resource dependency theory has been criticized for not distinguishing between types of networks and the depth and strength of links. It is certainly the case that there are many networks of organizations, but should we give them all the same weight? It is very difficult, for example, in the statistical analyses of networks to allow for either the 'strength' of a tie, i.e. how important it is and what influence it brings, or the 'duration' of a tie, i.e. how long has it existed. (See Palmer, 1983a, 1983b, on the methodological and theoretical issues regarding 'broken ties', i.e. where links are discontinued.)

Thus it can be argued that the resource dependency theorists fail to take note of the fact that there are different sorts of networks. There are those networks that arise, as they suggest, from problems of interdependence; these tend to be relatively small networks, of limited duration and usually of a co-operative nature. There are, however, other types of networks. First, there are those that arise from the influence of one powerful organization, which by virtue

of its stranglehold over certain resources can control other organizations, for example the clothing industry in the UK, where retail
distributors dominate over the manufacturing suppliers. Second,
there are those networks of influence, the significance of which is
wider than short-time interests. It is these types of network that
particularly interest Marxist analyses.

In the Marxist view, the significance of networks lies in the fact
that they constitute structures of domination both within the
capitalist class as well as over society as a whole. There are a
number of variants to this theme, each of which has its own
proponents. For example, there is the idea that modern capitalism
consists of a relatively small number of monopolies which are
connected to a larger number of small dependent companies. In this
view, the network consists of a series of hubs to which less
powerful organizations are connected. This perspective derives
from the writing of Sweezy (1939). In this view, banks are
incorporated into the power structure through their relationships
with the monopolies, and there is a fusion of banking and industrial
capital.

The second perspective gives a more independent influence to
financial institutions. In this view, there has been an increasing
tendency for financial institutions, and especially banks, to dominate industry. Thus the central points in the networks are represented particularly by banks, which have client organizations
linked to them. This perspective is frequently accompanied by the
idea that banks are highly integrated among themselves.

Both of these positions argue in terms of the emergence of a
stable set of relationships that reflect the increased power of finance.
Thus interorganizational networks are ways in which this central
group can control and co-ordinate activities across a wide range of
organizations in the interests of one particular group.

Marxist analyses point in particular to the failure of other
approaches to consider financial interlocks between organizations.
Two, in particular, are of significance: share ownership and loans.
In relation to the former, until fairly recently in both the UK and
the USA there has been a clear tendency for the extent of individual
shareholding to decline and be replaced by institutional share-
owning. Institutions such as pensions funds, insurance companies,
merchant banks, investment companies, etc. are likely to be the
major shareholders in British companies. These organizations

accumulate funds from individuals in many different ways – pensions, insurance, unit trusts, investment options, etc. They then manage these funds by spreading them across a portfolio of interests, including shareholding as well as loan stocks, commodities, land, etc. The concentration of share ownership in individual companies means that although a large company may have hundreds of thousands of small shareholders, the bulk of its shares are owned by a relatively small number of institutions. Scott (1985, 1986) argues that these institutions constitute a 'constellation of interests' which can exert a powerful influence over management, particularly at times of crisis (see Morgan and Hooper, 1987, for a detailed examination of these issues). These institutions themselves become interdependent and are almost forced to co-ordinate their activities. This results from the nature of the stock exchange; if one institution with a major shareholding in a company decides that it wants to sell its shares, the price will almost inevitably fall if it releases them all at one go. If more than one institution starts to sell, the price will definitely fall; the sellers find the price they are receiving for their shares declining, whilst those who hold on also find the value of their shares going down. There is then considerable pressure on institutions once they have bought into a company to stay there or only adjust their interests at the margin. If, however, a major crisis of management occurs and the institutions have to take action, they are again best advised to do so as a group. Thus in this view financial institutions have significant power which they can exercise over those organizations in which they hold shares.

This power can also be increased by the nature of company expansion and the need to take on loans. Banks and other institutions which arrange loans will seek to ensure that they are satisfied about the direction in which the company is going. Major loans or issues of new stock may only be agreed by the financial institutions where there is acceptance by the organization of certain guidelines (not just financial) laid down by the banks, etc.

Both the concentration of share ownership and the dependence of companies on loans, etc. leads Marxists to argue that the crucial interorganizational networks are those which link organizations into the financial sector. The financial sector, it is argued, plays a central role in ensuring that environmental risks are reduced; it becomes the arena for the restructuring of organizations. Only with the approval of the financial institutions can organizations set about taking over other firms or expanding their area of operations. This approval, moreover, is not a once-and-for-all phenomenon; it is constructed day by day, minute by minute on the stock exchanges of the world, where share price movements reflect in the main the perceptions of the managers of the financial institutions regarding the future of the organizations in which they are investing.

To return to the original argument, it seems that organizations, so far from being helpless in the face of market forces, do their best to control these forces. At the highest level, this process of co-ordination is achieved by the pivotal role of the financial institutions.

This argument has been taken further in the work of Useem (1984). Useem is interested in showing that the control of the financial institutions can be located in the hands of a small group of people. These people in turn are not simply interested in co-ordinating the economic needs of their organizations; they are interested in the more general process of the reproduction of the conditions of existence of capitalist society. This brings them into organizations in the state and civil society. This is what Useem calls the 'inner circle'. This 'inner circle' consists of those people who hold multiple directorships. Through their position on a number of boards, this group get to see the problems and interests of the capitalist class as whole. They hold multiple directorships not because of stategic considerations, as resource dependency argues, but because of the need for a form of class-wide co-ordination. Whereas in the past this class-wide co-ordination could be achieved through informal mechanisms, often resting on the basis of shared social and educational backgrounds, this is now no longer feasible. Instead, in the era of giant corporations, it is the people who head these corporations who come to articulate and formulate publicly the interests of the class as a whole. Through their top corporate position, they are invited on to other boards; as a result of this experience, they see the wider interests of the class, and finally they become the 'political' representatives of the class through their positions on government advisory boards, employers' federations, educational and charitable institutions, etc. So, Useem argues, this inner circle becomes the most powerful group within the class, forming a closely connected network of individuals who articulate the interests of business in public and form it in private. In this perspective, therefore, networks of influence and power spread far beyond companies into all spheres of social life; furthermore, these are not shifting, temporary networks but rather permanently established and self-regenerating structures of power and domination.

In Britain, as Scott (1985) has suggested, these individuals constitute what used to be referred to as the Establishment. Frequently they have a base in wealth that has been inherited. This has given them the springboard from which they have advanced into positions in the central industrial, financial and governmental institutions. This distinguishes them from the 'service class' analysed in Chapter 4. Whilst members of the inner circle are increasingly likely to have professional training, it is not this that provides them with accelerated mobility to the senior positions, but rather the monetary, social and cultural capital that they have inherited. This is not to say that members of the 'service class' cannot rise and enter this group, as can some of the recent successful entrepreneurs (whose family background might have been in the working class or lower middle class). The numbers from such groups, however, remain small in comparison to those who have inherited positions. In the UK this process of inheritance is aided considerably by the continued existence of private education, with its close links to the major prestigious universities. Such links help forge a continuing social framework for the formation of the inner circle; this is further cemented by the peculiar rituals of British upper-class life, revolving around the City of London and institutions such as gentlemen's clubs and the London season.

The inner circle in this sense constitute a group of individuals with shared interests in the maintenance of the existing system. It is not necessary to use any conspiracy theory to explain what occurs. Selection for positions of power in the City, the civil service and the key institutions of civil society such as the Church, occur on the basis of knowledge about an individual's background and reliability. This ensures an element of uniformity, since the nature of the valued characteristics has been learned at an early point and reinforced continually through adult life. Thus institutions like the BBC, the civil service, the Bank of England, the Church of England, as well as the major companies and financial institutions, are run by people who have learnt the same values in the same schools, universities, clubs, family circles and places of work. As a number of authors (e.g. Skopcol, 1979; Mann, 1987) have pointed out, social disorder is much more likely to occur when the elite is split than when the working class is discontented. The inner circle is a method of ensuring that the elite is not split but reproduces the existing order, although not without change (that would be reactionary conservatism). Indeed, part of the role of the inner circle, according to Useem, is to determine when and how sacrifices should be made that are in the interests of the class as a whole, even though it may involve the decline of a section of the class. Through reproducing the existing order of power, the inner circle is central in reducing uncertainty for organizations. Organizations are held off from ruthless competition and from antagonism through the role that the inner circle plays in mediating conflicts.

Within the Marxist framework, interorganizational networks are seen as important empirical demonstrations of the nature of the capitalist class. These networks are seen as showing the existence of certain cliques or clusters of power, located in central positions. These cliques consist of the major industrial and financial institutions, to which other organizations (including non-business organizations) are related in a dependent manner. Dependent organizations are controlled primarily through the activities of a small group of individuals at the heart of these financial and industrial giants. These individuals – the 'inner circle' – control power in such a way as to reproduce the network which results in the domination of other interests within the capitalist class and within society as a whole.

Networks and power: some preliminary conclusions

Resource dependency and Marxism are inevitably broad perspectives, and in this section it has not been possible to provide a full evaluation of them. Both of the perspectives emphasize the importance of information-gathering to modern organizations, as an aid to the control of the environment. In the same way that the markets and hierarchies approach drew attention to the factors influencing the 'internalization of the environment', so these perspectives show that it is not necessary to go that far. Rather organizations can monitor the environment through entering into relationships with other organizations. They can create coalitions of interest or structures of domination which reduce their vulnerability to the environment. Organizations reach outside their boundaries to reduce uncertainty and unpredictability. It is not this which differentiates these two theories, but rather their interpretation of its significance. This interpretation, in turn, relates to what sort of society we are now living in.

Resource dependency theory emphasizes that all organizations seek to control their environment to varying degrees. Any organization can be analysed in terms of its location within a network. Taking the argument further, resource dependency theorists argue that networks reflect power relations: when organizations try to control and predict the environment, they are in effect trying to constrain the activities of other organizations. Clearly not all organizations can be effective in what is partly a zero-sum game (though also partly a non-zero-sum game in that predictability can bring advantages to both sides). Thus, as part of the analysis, we would want to know which organizations within the network have the power and why; the answer presented by resource dependency is that those organizations with resources try to ration or reduce the access of other organizations to the resources they need. It is control over scarce resources that generates power within a network. Organizations can try to change the balance of power within networks by finding alternative sources; thus from this perspective power relations are dynamic and changing. Power is not permanently endowed in any particular part of the network, nor do all the different networks in society add up to one overall cohesive pattern in which a small group of organizations exercise ultimate power and influence. Rather power is dispersed through the creation of many different networks which grow and decline as organizations change.

The Marxist view, on the other hand, emphasizes the basic stability of the power relations in networks and their stable reproduction. The power of large organizations, both financial and industrial, is perpetuated through their control over the network. Although there may be a number of subsidiary networks, it makes sense to consider society as made up of one main network which has a centre made up of a particularly powerful set of organizations. The network keeps a large number of organizations bound together through ties of personnel, capital, lending, etc., which effectively serve the interests of the major organizations at the centre. The differences between these two perspectives cannot be resolved simply through network analysis with its rather limited positivistic methodology. A full answer can only rest on a wider understanding of the dynamics of organizations which incorporates not just external features such as networks but also the operation of management control within organizations. Nevertheless, network analysis provides an important intermediary level of understanding between individual organizations and wider social arrangements. For these reasons, it is an important and expanding area of organizational analysis.

For my own part, I believe that analyses built around the Marxist perspective provide the most satisfactory explanation of the interaction between organizations. Intentionality remains important; the controllers of organizations seek to expand their area of control and co-ordination into the environmment. The ways in which they do this may not always be rational and effective, as I showed in Chapter 2, but this does not affect the point that they are attempting it. The results of this can be clearly seen in countries like the UK and the USA, where the inner circle seeks to manage political, economic and social conflicts. Given the complexity of modern society and the multiplicity of interest groups, classes and sources of power, it is not surprising that these societies still exhibit high levels of disorder at certain times. It certainly would be surprising if such disorder were not massively increased if the inner circle failed to reproduce itself and thus carry out its task of co-ordination on a societal scale.

6 Organizations in and across Societies

Introduction

In the preface to the first German edition of *Capital*, Karl Marx defended himself against the charge made by his French and German critics that his analysis of capitalism was based solely on the English experience and was therefore irrelevant to other countries. Marx's simple answer was to quote the Latin phrase '*De te fabula narratur*' (*Capital*, vol. 1, p. 8), which roughly translated means 'This is going to happen to you as well'. It succinctly expresses an approach to the study of society that has in many ways dominated sociology until recently.

The worldwide impact of capitalism and industrialism is a truism; its power to sweep away old established ways of life in the Americas, Africa, Asia and Australia is well established. With this understanding, however, a basic error has often been made in believing that these processes are capable of wiping the 'social slate' clean so that societies and their component parts are rebuilt in the image of the heartlands of capitalism and industrialism. Such an approach and expectation has fed many powerful social and organizational theories. In this chapter, I argue that this approach is invalid, and that processes of state formation are more complex than this allows. The understanding of organizations needs to be located in the specific nature of the social formation of particular nation-states. The worldwide features and interaction of the emerging world system penetrate into these processes of social formation; they do not, however, destroy completely the endoge-

195

nous set of social relations except under specific circumstances. This combination of universalistic and particularistic features in turn needs to be historically contextualized as a feature of specific international market and inter-state relations. Organizational life in the early 1990s is more than ever penetrated by the international context of market and state relations. These processes of competition and the learning and diffusion of technological and organizational innovations are making the study of any particular society and its organizational forms inextricably intertwined with the evolution and development of organizations in other societies.

Theories of society and organizational universals

The idea that the forces changing nineteenth-century Europe were ushering in a new age for all of humankind was central to the social theories of the time. Whilst authors such as Marx, Weber, Durkheim, Spencer, Tonnies and others might have conceptualized the process differently, they all held to the notion of societies passing across a great divide from a pre-industrial system to an industrial one. If we consider this concept further, however, it is possible to realize the need for greater conceptual clarity. Model A illustrates one simple way of conceiving of the process of change:

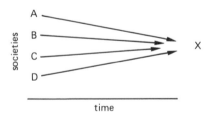

In this model, societies A–D converge over time to take the form of society X. Such a model has two basic assumptions: that societies A–D are independent and do not interact, and that they change at the same rate. There are also two problems with the model. First, it does not specify why societies are changing. Second, it is not clear whether societies A–D are subsumed into society X or remain independent but with X-like characteristics. These issues are basic to the study of societies and organizations. They can be rephrased in the following way:

1. To what extent do societies change as a result of endogenous or exogenous factors?
2. What determines the rate at which societies change?
3. To what extent are societies the most useful unit of analysis as opposed to, for example, world systems or interstate systems?
4. To what extent are societies converging on a common form?

Why do these questions matter for the study of organizations? The answer is simple and has already started to emerge in previous chapters. They matter because as societies become more vulnerable and open to international factors related both to the market and to the existence of international state systems and blocs, so the survival of any particular organization is related to its location in this international economic, political and military environment. The consequent widening of the perspectives of management and organizations that has resulted from this has made even more problematic the idea that there is one best way to organize that is universally valid.

In the next section, I look in more detail at the Japanese experience because it is undoubtedly this phenomenon that has contributed so much to recent debates in this area. I will commence by considering the Japanese employment system, locating this in its particular social and cultural context; from there I will go on to consider its potential for transferability to other contexts. My argument will be that whilst elements of the system may be transferable, it is firmly locked into a deep-rooted social context which is unique. The creation and reproduction of this context, however, should not be understood as simply an endogenous phenomenon. The impact of war and the consequent initial incorporation of Japan within the US sphere of influence was crucial to the formation of these social conditions in the post–war period. Taking this argument further, Japan's economic growth and its consequent rise in importance in world markets and in the interstate system may be generating further changes in Japanese society. The Japanese case illustrates the way in which endogenous and exogenous factors interpenetrate to form a particular social formation characterized by specific class relationships and state forms. I then go on to consider the form of these relationships in the USSR.

Here the fundamentally different relationships between state, economy and civil society make for a very different pattern of organizations.

The central point of these two examples is to show that differences and similarities between organizations in different societies should not be reduced to cultural phenomena; they are in fact the effect of complex interactions between classes, state and culture that need to be considered in their historical specificity. This is not to reduce the study of organizations to an idiographic approach to phenomena, precisely because there are forces that operate across societal and state boundaries which mean that one cannot study these social formations in isolation from each other. The final section of the chapter argues that these processes, although endemic in an era of international markets and interstate systems, are increasingly powerful at present due to the development of multinational organizations, the growth of worldwide trading in currencies, shares and commodities, and changes in the nature of the interstate system. Thus a complex process is at work changing the 'national' base of organizational life and creating ever tighter international links; the institutional and political framework for these changes, however, lags behind, creating a new set of conflicts and crises played out still within the old and now increasingly irrelevant institutional form of the nation-state.

Japan: culture and organizations

The Japanese employment system consists essentially of the following features: lifetime employment in return for company loyalty, education and training in return for commitment to production targets. (For details see, for example, Abegglen, 1958; Cole, 1979; Dore, 1974; Ouchi, 1981; McMillan, 1985; Sato and Hoshino, 1984.) Workers in large Japanese companies usually belong to a trade union, but the union works closely with management to ensure that production is maintained. The main role of the union is to bargain for its members during the annual wage round. Management is left in sole control of the labour process itself. Payment systems include a large component for seniority and length of service with the company. Most workers will have been recruited to the company straight from high school or university. It is practically unknown even at top levels of management for people to move from one company to another. Workers and managers are recruited into large companies with an expectation of life-time employment, during which time they will be trained according to the organization's view of their abilities. In return for lifetime employment and the range of social, educational and cultural facilities provided, employees are expected to reciprocate with loyalty and commitment to the company.

A number of points of clarification need to be made before considering in more detail the origins and causes of the Japanese system. First, the system I have described only applies to the large-firm sector of Japanese industry. There are many workers who are not employed by the large firms and who do not receive the same benefits as the workers for the big companies. However, they are not outside the system, but integral to it. The reason for this relates to the way in which the main Japanese firms seek to control variations in the market and to maximize their efficiency. Essentially the large Japanese companies are central nodes in networks of relationships with other large companies and a myriad of smaller ones. With regard to the former, the post-war break-up of the large Zaibetsu companies by the US occupying forces was primarily a legal device; it did not affect the personal, social and business ties that remained between companies previously united in one group. Although now legally separate, they retained links as suppliers of raw materials, machinery and capital to each other, e.g. Mitsubishi Steel, Mitsubishi Bank and Mitsubishi Electric. Large companies remain organized into loosely interlocked families of firms (Dore, 1983). These networks are in turn connected to particular groups of small firms. These allow the large companies to contract out for various parts of the production process to organizations which do not have the same overheads in terms of labour and material costs as they do. The small companies frequently employ many more women at lower rates of pay than the large companies; employees in the small companies lack the educational and welfare facilities of the large companies. Often, workers from large companies on retirement at 55 become employed in small firms linked in this way to the large company. The network of suppliers and contractors gives the large company a buffer in times of economic decline. It will be the associated companies that have to cut production first of all, and possibly, therefore, employment numbers. Large companies, however, are reluctant to be totally instrumental about their links with small suppliers and cut them loose completely at times of economic decline. The relationship with the suppliers is also one shaped by long-standing links and mutual obligation.

The reasons for this relate to the use of the 'kanban' or 'just-in-time' production system in Japan, which needs to be analysed in depth at this point. What is the 'kanban' system? This can be answered by comparing it with the traditional production system in Western car companies. (Much of this discussion relies on the excellent account in Cusumano, 1985.) Ford's initial development of car manufacturing assembly-line production involved the mass production of parts that were stored and then brought to the assembly line as required to be fitted to the cars. The cars were then stored until they could be sold. Alfred Sloan at General Motors soon challenged Ford's dominance by showing that Ford had gone too far in terms of standardization ('any colour so long as it's black', as the old joke had it). Sloan saw that the market for cars depended on a process of market differentiation; this meant not only providing different cars for different sorts of people, but also persuading those who could afford it to go in for an annual model change. Thus the production system required to serve this differentiated market became highly complex, with car firms stocking large inventories both of parts and of vehicles awaiting sale. These inventories tied up large amounts of capital between the time they were produced and the time their value was realized at point of sale. For long periods, companies could have millions of dollars simply sitting around in their car parks and warehouses, just rusting away. Fluctuations in demand tended to be dealt with by over-producing throughout the year in the expectation of sudden upturns in demand. When the price of oil rocketed in 1973–4, the problems of this production system were graphically illustrated. Demand for the so-called 'gas guzzlers' of the US companies plummeted, whilst the companies were left with large inventories of parts and vehicles that many fewer people wanted.

This production system was also difficult to control in terms of levels of quality. Some companies, for example, would utilize a large number of suppliers for the same part in order to guard against problems in any one supplier and to ensure that delivery could be guaranteed. However, when it came to using the parts, even supposing faults were discovered, it would be extremely difficult to trace exactly where the faulty parts had come from and who should replace them. They might have been sitting in the warehouse for weeks or even months. Thus the complex task of bringing parts together from different suppliers led to quality control problems at the end of the production process. When parts were finally checked at this point, many faulty ones may already have been fixed on vehicles. The difficulties and time involved in checking and replacing faulty parts were immense and tended therefore to discourage high levels of quality control.

The Japanese kanban system developed initially out of the particular situation of Japanese industry in the 1950s, but it proved a powerful weapon against large inventories and poor quality control. Toyota, according to Cusumano, were particularly keen to avoid large inventory costs. They did this through setting up a system of supply with their contractors whereby so many parts were delivered to a particular area of the factory where they were needed. These parts could be delivered daily or even more often if necessary. As parts were delivered they could be checked and inspected; faults identified could be reported immediately to the component company concerned and the necessary adjustment made within a few hours. This system operated all the way down the assembly line, even to the retail outlets themselves. Fluctuations or changes in demand could be responded to almost immediately. Suppliers, too, were expected to operate a similar system, keeping inventory costs as low as possible. Changes in the exact specification of models could be made relatively quickly using existing technology. Thus the Japanese production system was highly flexible and responsive to changing markets.

Thus whilst small firm suppliers and contractors in Japan are more vulnerable to economic fluctuations than the major firms, they are nevertheless closely interlocked with them. This is partially reflected in the location of the suppliers, the need for constant information, and delivery on a daily if not more frequent basis, bringing them into close geographical proximity to the large companies. There is therefore a link between the large firm and the supplier which is based on concepts of loyalty and trust similar to that evoked among the workforce. Clearly the large firm has the dominant position in any such relationship, but it is clear that unlike other countries where sub-contracting is a fiercely competitive business and there can be frequent changes in contractor relationships (see Rainnie, 1984), in Japan these are much more stable. This allows contractors and the main company to work much more closely together on the development of products and the further perfection of the kanban system.

The employment system, the use of small contractors, and the kanban system have given Japanese firms a strong competitive position in world markets over the last three decades. This position has been greatly enhanced by the nature and role of the Japanese state in this period. Most noticeable to foreign observers has been the role of the Ministry of International Trade and Industry (known as MITI) (see Ouchi, 1984, and McMillan, 1985, for a detailed analysis). MITI performs a number of functions mainly associated with the creation of detailed plans and strategies for particular industrial sectors. It brings managers from the various sectors together with government bureaucrats in order to consider in detail the future of particular sectors' of the economy. These detailed discussions then become the basis for generating an overall vision of future industrial development. MITI then aids companies in the co-ordination and development of areas identified as central to economic growth; for example, the development of so-called fifth-generation intelligent computers is being spearheaded in Japan by MITI. In this way, research and development costs in areas identified as essential to the country's future become shared among all the companies, thus aiding in the achievement of industry standard technologies. This in turn increases the economies of scale that companies and suppliers can achieve, thus cheapening the cost and increasing interchangeability. Whilst the companies compete in the final market, they co-operate in the earlier stages. In the video recorder industry, for example, Japanese companies came together to develop two formats, VHS and Beta; these two soon swept the board, rapidly displacing European competitors such as Video 2000 (see Rosenbloom and Cusumano, 1987, on the VCR industry in Japan). MITI also aids in the running down of declining sectors. According to McMillan:

> Japan's export strategy represents a realistic national strategy of continually shifting into high value added, high productivity sectors and, of course, exiting from industries which do not meet these criteria. (McMillan, 1985, p. 85)

The emphasis on growth sectors where production can rapidly reach high levels of output creates large economies of scale, so that often, as in the case of colour televisions, large plants can be created where the home demand is limited, the expectation being that the export market will take up most of the demand. The relationship between economies of scale and an export-oriented strategy was developed more in Japan than in any other country. Japanese companies saw early that if they could penetrate foreign markets, they could build large plants with significant economies of scale (though the degree of strategic foresight involved should not be over-exaggerated – see Pascale's 1984 account of Honda's takeover of the US motorcycle market, which is seen to owe as much to chance and luck as long-term planning).

In the USA, such was the size of the internal market that an export strategy seemed irrelevant to many companies. Similarly, for a long time producers in Britain were content to rely on the home market in the expectation that home consumers would always prefer home-produced goods. By the 1970s, however, these fallacies were beginning to be exposed. Japanese industry, with its high levels of quality and low level of costs, was gaining export markets around the world, thus undercutting the home markets of its competitors as well as beating them in new markets. Although by the 1970s all industrialized countries recognized the importance of exports and the role these played in lowering costs overall and strengthening an economy, it was by then almost too late. Whilst Western countries had exported their surplus, after the home market had been served, the Japanese had almost done the opposite. Their export-oriented growth strategy had given them a base in low-cost, high-quality products that the Western countries would find difficult to emulate.

The export-oriented strategy necessitated careful industrial planning and a willingness to be ruthless as changes occurred. Here MITI played a significant role in encouraging the gradual winding down of production capacity when it became obvious that lower-cost producers were now entering and outcompeting the Japanese, as happened in textiles. MITI allowed cartels and protectionism at this point, though it has also recently encouraged companies in declining areas to make use of cheaper sources of labour and relocate part of their operations to other countries in South East Asia, thus re-establishing a form of competitive advantage.

The ability of MITI to play this role in industrial development needs also to be linked to the specific nature of the post-1945 Japanese state. A key factor that still differentiates Japan from other major Western societies is that under Article IX of its American-imposed post-war constitution, it is pledged to 'forever renounce war' and never to 'maintain any war potential'. As a result, Japan maintains only a 'self-defence force' and not an army with attacking potential. Whatever the hyperbole associated with this concept of 'self-defence', figures show that Japan spends under 1 per cent of its GNP on military expenditure compared to 6.1 per cent in the USA, 4.3 per cent in Germany, 5.4 per cent in the UK and 4.1 per cent in France (according to McMillan, 1985 p. 314). The impact of defence spending on economic growth is an area fraught with difficulty and controversy. There are good reasons to believe that purely from an economic point of view, where defence spending involves spending on production and development within a country, it can act both to expand the economy (almost as a form of Keynesian deficit spending) and to generate technological advance, which has wider commercial spin-offs. However, where defence is heavily weighted towards salaries and wages, maintenance costs, and the importation of foreign-produced weapons systems, high defence spending has a less productive impact on the economy. Furthermore, defence spending on research and new development is frequently a chancey business and can lead to massive expenditure with few long-term advantages. There are many classic examples of what Staw (1976) calls getting further into 'the big muddy' in this area, for example, Britain's Blue Streak missile and now Reagan's Star Wars programme.

Spending on research and development is, nevertheless, critical. In Britain, the government's overall support for research and development is heavily skewed towards the military, although it still ends up purchasing or leasing from abroad, as in the forthcoming Trident programme for nuclear warheads. Japan, on the other hand, concentrates its research and development resources on commercial ventures which reap tangible benefits over the short and medium term, rather than promising pie-in-the-sky for the long term. Thus Japan, by concentrating its research and development expenditure on civilian industry/export-related projects, gives itself a major advantage.

This in turn has another spin-off effect which is related to the

Japanese government's macro-economic policy regarding the level of its currency. Military spending has had a large impact on the world's currency system. It was the USA's commitment to war in South-Est Asia during the 1960s, as well as its massive expenditure on its armed forces in Europe, that fundamentally weakened the dollar, overstretching the US economy beyond a level where it could maintain currency stability and high military expenditure, and eventually leading indirectly to the current monetary instability. Although US multinationals and the not insignificant sale of US military technology abroad managed to hide this gap for a long time, in the case of Japan, which in the main had no need to purchase US weaponry and rejected US consumer commodities, there grew a startling trade imbalance. Whilst the Japanese particularly over the last ten years have sold cars, televisions, videos and computers by the millions to the USA, the USA has failed to sell very much back to Japan. Japan has increasingly developed a dollar surplus as a result of this unequal balance of trade. Furthermore, the Japanese for a long time resisted what financial markets talk of as a 'readjustment of currencies', i.e. making the yen more valuable against the dollar, which would theoretically make Japanese goods more expensive to purchase in the US and American goods cheaper in Japan. In theory such an adjustment would lead to lower US imports and higher US exports, thus rebalancing the trade between the two countries. Even when the dollar/yen exchange rate has altered to the dollar's advantage, US companies have failed to penetrate Japanese markets, thus reaffirming Japanese views that the problem is not the exchange rate, which the Japanese have tried to keep to their own advantage through policies of protectionism and high interest rates.

It is necessary to avoid an over-simple cultural interpretation of Japanese success. The Japanese industrial system exists at a number of levels; at the shop-floor level, there is the permanent employment system; at the production system level, there is the kanban and associated companies system; at the strategic level, there is the MITI provision of information, research and co-ordinated planning; at the state level there is the low priority of military spending and the protection of the yen. It is important to recognize the complexity of these interrelationships because the question of what other countries can learn from Japan is so frequently considered in the limited context of shopfloor relations. Before I go on to consider this issue in more depth, it is necessary to tackle briefly the question of how this system came about.

The origins of the Japanese system

There is a frequent tendency in discussions of Japan to argue that what we now see is somehow an extension of pre-industrial 'samurai' philosophy into an industrial context. In its crudest form this type of theory argues that in the era of Japanese feudalism, strong bonds of loyalty and responsibility bound together the various strata of society – the peasants, the samurai and the royal family. As the threat from the West became obvious in the late nineteenth century, the samurai in particular saw that in order to survive Japan would have to modernize. As a result, under government sponsorship, industries were set up into which the values of the old Japan were inserted. Labour relations were built on pre-existing notions of loyalty, and the result was a successful state-directed industrialization drive, in which the social harmony of pre-industrial Japan was transferred into the twentieth century. Clearly, if this view is correct the chances of Western organizations learning from Japan are limited, since the Japanese system is dependent on these long-lasting and deeply held values that are peculiar to Japanese feudalism; they are certainly non-existent in the American context and long buried in Europe.

Japan's development is more complex than this type of account suggests, though elements are correct. What follows will be a selective account of its development which concentrates in particular on the interrelationship between the state, civil society and the economy.

In the feudal period Japanese society consisted of a rigid hierarchy of statuses from the Emperor at the top through the 'daimyo' (the feudal lords) to the samurai (the warrior class), to the farmers, artisans and merchants; below these groups were the peasants. In the 200 and more years up to the opening of Japan to Western influence in the 1850s and 1860s, the Emperor was no more than a figurehead. In this period (known as the Tokugawa Shogunate), ultimate power was theoretically in the hands of the Shogun, the dominant feudal lord, though in fact it was parcelled out amongst the daimyo:

> The Tokugawa Shogunate imposed unity on Japan without centralism. It in effect stabilized a kind of condominium between the suzerain shogunal regime, based on the Tokugawa capital of Edo and the autonomous Daimyo governments in the provincial fiefs . . . Within their domains . . . all the daimyo . . . commanded an untempered authority; the direct writ of the Shogunate stopped at the frontiers of their fiefs. They issued laws, administered justice, raised taxes and maintained troops. (Anderson, 1974, pp. 444–6)

The unity of Japan was enhanced by the emphasis placed on traditional valued embodied in the person of the Emperor and on total hostility to foreigners. From the 1630s onwards, Japan had been closed to foreigners except for a Dutch-Chinese enclave off Nagasaki. Similarly, no Japanese were allowed to leave the country. It was not until the 1850s that this edifice was shaken by the arrival of a squadron of US Navy ships led by Commodore Perry. These were followed soon after by Russian, British and French warships which the Japanese were unable militarily to resist. These foreign powers demanded the 'opening up' of Japan to foreign trade. Although the extent of foreign trade grew only slowly, the fact that Japan was forced to open up as a result of its military inferiority to the Western powers had an unsettling effect. The Shogunate seemed unable to respond and was blamed for the loss of Japanese honour. In 1867, a revolt was launched against the Shogunate in the name of the Emperor and with the aim of rebuilding Japan for the modern age. The Meiji restoration, as it is known, radically restructured Japanese society in the name of tradition:

> The Meiji state . . . promptly proceeded to a sweeping arc of measures to abolish feudalism from above – the most radical such programme ever to be enacted. The fief system was liquidated, the four-estate order destroyed, the equality of every citizen before the law proclaimed, calendar and dress reformed, a unified market and single currency created and industrialization and military expansion systematically promoted. A capitalist economy and polity emerged directly from the elimination of the Shogunate. (Anderson, 1974, p. 460)

Under the Meiji restoration, the ruling groups of Japan sought to effect a revolution from above. This was based partially on a commercialization of agricultural production in order to generate surpluses for investment in industry and food for the workers in the towns. The repressive powers of the state backed up the landlords in ensuring that higher levels of agricultural production were achieved by the peasantry. At the same time, measures such as the introduction of military conscription (1872–3) and universal compulsory education served to reinforce traditional Japanese ideology, especially loyalty to the Emperor. In this way the authorities ensured that any potential for peasant revolt remained unrealized.

The government ensured that the surpluses generated in the countryside were used to support the development of Japanese industry, particularly those associated with rebuilding the military power of the country such as arsenals and shipyards. This necessitated the rapid development of a skilled labour force, which was central to industry's success. Contrary to the myth of essential Japanese continuity, however, this period was characterized by high levels of conflict, as employers and workers competed with each other and entered into conflict. Skilled workers sought to maximize their earning power by moving around between employers and withdrawing their labour where necessary. Employers responded by lock-outs and labour repression. In these early stages Japan followed very much the Western pattern of early industrialization, with fierce industrial conflict threatening to spill over into social conflict (see Littler, 1980, 1982; Westney, 1980).

It was at this point that Japanese employers and the state took decisive steps to ensure a different direction to their social development. There was no smooth continuity between the values and structure of traditional Japan and those of the new society; they had to be adapted and redeveloped. The advantage that Japan had over other countries was as much its late development (and therefore its ability to see the lessons of other societies) as its particular pre-industrial structure: 'How to adapt traditional principles to large enterprise was something that had to be invented or learned' (Dore, 1973, p. 392). The state played a central part in this through, for example, restricting labour mobility. Employers responded by consciously setting out to develop 'family'-like relationships on a company scale, by offering internal training and permanent employment in return for company loyalty and industrial order.

Reinforced by the effects of education and conscription, the rebirth of Japanese military pride with the victory over Russia in 1905 and participation (of a limited sort) in the First World War on the side of the victorious powers, labour was increasingly incorporated into the new system. Although there were still strikes in the 1920s, dissent was gradually suppressed and trade unionism incorporated into the company. As the companies grew into what were known as Zaibetsu, they remained closely linked to the state, relying still on protection from foreign competition and also looking to the state to provide them with assured access to markets and raw materials. Thus they were integrally linked to Japanese expansionism in the 1930s into China and South-East Asia, and supported the development of the South-East Asia trading zone that was to consist of former European colonies in Asia as far west as India and as far east as the Philippines.

Thus, by the late 1930s there was a powerful combination of forces within Japan pushing it towards military conflict with the European powers and its major competitor for influence in the Pacific, the USA. One may speculate that a significant part of its economic aims could have been achieved by Japan if it had been more circumspect in the way it used its military power. This, however, is irrelevant to what actually happened, because in the event Japan's methods drew it into a fateful conflagration with the Allies, and the USA in particular.

It is important not to underestimate the significance of the Second World War. Perhaps the strongest element of continuity in Japan in the period 1860–1945 was militarism and loyalty to the Emperor. The development of Japan's industrial power went on beneath this shield of continuity. The war rent apart the shield of militarism, but by this time the industrial base was sufficiently established, though obviously battered from the war, that it could survive without the shield. Old values such as loyalty survived, but they were shorn of much of their militaristic connotations for most of the population by the traumatic experience of war, symbolized above all by the nuclear destruction of Hiroshima and Nagasaki. The occupying American forces played a significant role in these changes. Japan was forced to take on a new constitution, which, as pointed out above, allowed only for a 'self-defence force'.

The Americans, under their regent, General MacArthur, brought with them their twin notions of free trade unionism and opposition to trusts. MacArthur broke up the Zaibetsu as legal entities, insisting on higher levels of competition in the economy. He also encouraged the setting up of independent trade unions. This gave rise quickly to widespread industrial conflict as managers and employees battled over the spoils of austerity. This in turn was linked to the growth of socialist and communist ideas under the impact of military defeat. The Americans, however, increasingly conscious of the Cold War and the need to keep Japan within the Western orbit, gradually reined back on their reforming zeal, and allowed for the informal re-establishment of the Zaibetsu and company trade unionism (associated with the replacement of radicals in the trade unions by more accommodating individuals – see Cusumano, 1985, for a detailed account of this process in the Japanese automobile industry).

By the time of the Korean war and the economic expansion that it fuelled in Japan, Japanese society was rebuilding the elements of the employment system from the pre-war years, in conjunction with a state that was still closely linked to industry but now with less of a militaristic bent. Its characteristic features of lifetime employment, large-scale companies linked to a myriad of smaller suppliers, a state that provided support to industry in selective areas, and minimized military expenditure were well established. Some of these features were clearly developments from traditional Japan, others derived from conscious decisions taken in the early stages of the Meiji restoration, still others from the interventions of the MacArthur years. Together they made up a unique combination of forces.

To return to the central question: is it possible that any of the results of these circumstances could be successfully transferred to organizations in other societies?

The Japanese system abroad?

There are two possible ways of answering this question. The first way is to look at how Japanese companies go about organizing when they set up production facilities in other countries. The other way is to consider how far foreign companies have been able to borrow successfully from Japan.

White and Trevor (1983), in their major study of British workers in Japanese-owned factories in the UK, argue that the Japanese did not seek to set up the system of permanent employment characteristic of their home base. Nor indeed, they argued, was there any particular effort to increase welfare provision or training for British workers. The differences between Japanese-owned companies in the UK and other companies in the UK were essentially in the sphere of working practices:

> Workers in Japanese owned manufacturing companies in particular reported a highly distinctive profile of working practices . . . an organized or orderly approach, an emphasis on detail, an overriding priority attached to quality and a punctilious sense of discipline. (White and Trevor, 1983, pp. 127–8)

Why have Japanese companies been able to develop these working practices, whilst not providing the permanent employment system that accompanies them in Japan? The answer lies clearly in current labour market conditions in the UK. The decision of Japanese firms to locate in areas of high unemployment such as North-East England, South Wales and Central Scotland maximizes the employer's bargaining position *vis-à-vis* the workers. The development of greenfield sites where single union agreements with no strike deals can be negotiated at national level separate from existing local bargaining arrangements, further enhances the employer's power, without having to incur the high costs of lifetime employment. From the point of view of the workers in these areas, decent levels of wages with a firm that has a reputation for growth and stability of employment is more than adequate recompense, and surveys indicate a high level of job satisfaction in these companies. The relative paucity of Japanese managers willing and able to move around the world to manage a more fully fledged version of the home system may also play a part. However, it is important to note that it is not just the Japanese who can reap the 'advantages' for working practices of high unemployment and greenfield sites; other companies, both foreign and British, are also doing so. Even in older sites, company managements are confronting trade unions and work groups in such a way as to undermine old-style working practices and replace them in the manner outlined by Trevor and White. (For an important discussion of these issues see the special edition of the *Industrial Relations Journal*, 1988, on 'Japanization', especially the articles by Ackroyd *et al.*,

Crowther and Garrahan, Dickens and Savage, Graham, Morris, Smith, and Wilkinson and Oliver; see also Turnbull, 1986, 1988.) Explicitly incorporating Japanese practices into companies without a Japanese connection is now a topic widely considered. According to Ouchi (1981), for example, there are already firms in the USA which have these characteristics. These firms, such as IBM, Hewlett-Packard and other high-technology companies, he describes as operating with Theory Z, i.e. they do not fit into McGregor's classification of management practices either being based on Theory X (scientific management) or Theory Y (human relations). Rather they have parts of both: they are strong on control but also look after their employees. This theme is taken up in a slightly different way by Peters and Waterman (1982), who argue that American industry should not be so pessimistic about the Japanese challenge, since many companies already possess the characteristics that will enable them to meet this threat. The main difference these authors point to between the US 'excellent' companies and the Japanese companies is the continued dominance of individual ambition and striving in the US companies as opposed to the collectivism of the Japanese firms. These approaches, however, as has already been discussed, rely on a very impressionistic analysis of both Japan and the USA. They concentrate on fairly intangible phenomena such as style and leadership, whereas there are significant material advantages that Japan has developed through the interaction of its employment system, its production system, its system of economic organization and its system of state–economy interaction.

The translation of management practices around the globe has only just begun. The extent to which the Japanese system as a whole can be translated to other societies is likely to be limited because of its very specific conditions of existence. However, there are elements of the Japanese system that relate to very specific modes of organization production and employment which correspond to those that have developed in certain companies in the West. Rather than arguing that companies need to take on wholesale the cultural characteristics of Japan, a more limited and realistic objective would be for them to take on those practices which already exist in these societies. However, the key factor which sets Japanese companies apart is not their individual success but their location in a society which is able to reproduce this success and the conditions of success at a macro-level, i.e. with carefully directed research and development planning, stable, strong currencies and relative industrial and political harmony. Thus it is not the adoption of the practices of individual companies that will fundamentally alter the balance of power.

Organizations in Soviet-type societies

The importance of locating organizations within particular social contexts can also be usefully illustrated in relation to Soviet-type societies. The point was made in the Introduction that the model economy-civil society-state is not applicable to Soviet-type societies. The Russian Revolution destroyed the small amount of 'civil society' that had managed to emerge under Tsarist autocracy. Similarly, after various experiments with markets in the 1920s, the Bolsheviks rejected these as well. Instead they sought to construct a society which was controlled and directed by the state, led in turn by the party. There was to be no autonomous sphere for either market relations or civil society. Whilst there could be black markets in goods and religion might be tolerated so long as it did not threaten the state, it was only by sufferance of the state that either was allowed to exist. All organizations in society were basically to be run by the state. Their conditions of existence, their form, their membership, etc. were all laid down by the state. Any conflict with management by workers is simultaneously a conflict with the state; any attempt to develop genuinely independent organizations in civil society may also be seen as a challenge to the state. It is the state that licenses and controls organizations which in capitalist societies would have autonomy. This should not be interpreted, however, as meaning that every action and detail within organizations is controlled by the state, as various 'totalitarianist' theories of the USSR have argued. The fact that there is no constitutional separation of the spheres of economy-civil society-state does not mean that there is no autonomy of action at various levels within the system. Although the state is dominant and shapes the framework within which organizations exist, it cannot control all aspects of human activity. Thus in what follows I will try to show both how the lack of institutional separation politicizes organizations and how autonomy is possible within organizations.

I shall illustrate these themes briefly by reference to organizations that in the West would be in separate spheres – economic organizations (economy), psychiatric health services (state) and religion (civil society).

The essential feature of the Soviet system which flows from its socialist nature is state planning of economic production. In the Soviet Union, officially sanctioned markets are a very small proportion of total output. All output is planned centrally, and this necessitates determining many details about the 'needs of society' and ensuring that these are met in a co-ordinated fashion. The central plan attempts to do this by outlining needs at the social level; these are then taken down to the ministries for the particular industries, and these in their turn pass on targets for production to areas and factories. (The relationship between areas, industries and national plans is highly complex and changing: for detailed accounts see Lavigne, 1974; Nove, 1977; Littlejohn, 1985.) The difficulties of bureaucratically co-ordinating all the production of a society the size of the USSR are immense. Nove says:

> In the USSR at this time, there are 12 million identifiably different products (disaggregated down to specific types of ball-bearings, designs of cloth, size of brown shoes, etc., and so on.) There are close to 50,000 industrial establishments plus, of course, thousands of construction enterprises, transport under-takings, collective and state farms, wholesaling organs and retail outlets. None of them can produce or distribute anything without the coordinated cooperation of the activities of number-ous economic units which produce, transport or distribute . . . A doubtless sarcastic Soviet author remarked: 'Mathematicians have calculated that in order to draft an accurate and fully integrated plan for material supply just for the Ukraine for just one year requires the labour of the entire world's population for 10 million years.' (Nove, 1983, p. 33)

The huge difficulty of the task does not stop the Soviet hierarchy from trying. Indices of production are created for ministries (there are ministries for each of the main industries in the economy) by GOSPLAN (the State Planning Commission) on the basis of previous and projected needs. These indices in turn are passed on to the industrial associations and finally the enterprises themselves.

Any production target for any particular enterprise necessitates the adequate supply of materials (both machinery/raw materials and labour) from a host of other enterprises. If for any reason these supplies are not forthcoming, there are (at least formally) within the plan system, unlike the market system, no alternative suppliers. The result is that production delays occur, which causes further delays elsewhere in the system. Enterprise management can try to get around this by utilizing the 'black market'; often this involves building up personalized ties with the managers of other factories who can supply things which might be needed, and in return you supply them with things they may need. Alternatively managers of enterprises can try to 'cheat the plan' by skimping on the require-ments of production and thus producing items of a lower quality than is required. This low quality may not be revealed until the product is well out of the way of the enterprise; when it is discovered it causes further delays in the system and disrupts the plan yet again.

Targets seem to be incapable of including a qualitative dimen-sion; indeed, the quantitative dimensions themselves can often result in a skewing of production, depending upon which particular measure of production is used. Targets set in terms of weight encourage managers to produce large, bulky items; targets set in terms of value encourage managers to use high-value raw mate-rials. No index yet seems to have been devised which encourages managers to produce what people actually want to buy. Ellman summarizes all these problems in terms of three main weaknesses:

A major weakness of the Marxist-Leninist theory of planning (and of the institutions based on that theory) is that it fails to take any account of ignorance, despite its fundamental importance . . . It assumes a perfect knowledge, determinist world in which unique plans can be drawn up for the present and the future . . . the inadequacy of the techniques used to process such data as are available is the main reason for the instability of the plans . . . The planning techniques currently used (material balances and input-output) are such that the current plans are always inconsis-tent . . . One of the reasons for the inconsistency of the current plans which in turn is a major cause of their instability is precisely that the planning of production and supply for the entire national community is regarded as too complicated for any one organiza-tion and accordingly is split up among many organizations. This creates enormous coordination problems. (Ellman, 1979, pp. 66–7)

Thus ignorance, complexity and inadequate techniques intervene to disrupt the plan.

At the level of the workplace the contradiction between the central plan and the enterprise's ability to achieve the plan has a somewhat unexpected effect as regards how the work is done. In order to consider this it is necessary to look at the way the enterprises are managed. Since Lenin first praised Taylorism for generating massive increases in productivity, the USSR and Soviet-type societies have seen scientific management techniques as a central part of the process of economic development. (The major exception to this, of course, is China in the era of the cultural revolution; for reasons of space I am unable to consider this, but see Warner, 1987, for extended discussions of the cultural revolution and the succeeding period.)

Management in the USSR is unhindered by trade unions. Trade unions, unlike in the West, are essentially integrated into the state apparatus. Their role is not to defend workers against management, but to aid managers in the achievement of production quotas. They may negotiate with enterprise management about the safety or social club benefits, but management is left to look after the work situation. Managers use this unhindered power mainly to follow classic Taylorist injuctions (which fit into the socialist idea of 'from each according to his worth, to each according to his work') regarding the need to link productivity and pay. Thus the few existing accounts of work in Soviet-type societies tend to emphasize the importance of piecework (e.g. Harazti, 1977; Burawoy, 1985; Littler, 1984). Piecework can be a two-edged weapon for management, as capitalist managers learnt in the nineteenth century. On the one hand, management can continually try to tighten up on rates (this is what Harazti in particular emphasizes); on the other hand this induces game-playing (or what Taylor called 'soldiering') among shopfloor workers. Thus we can see at least two areas of indeterminancy emerging in the economic system, contrary to the idea of the plan. First there is the problem of achieving plan targets and the need to make informal arrangements between enterprises, and second there is the problem of control over workers.

One way in which the Soviet system differs from the West and which derives partially from ideology and partially from a pragmatic response to the situation, is in the collective nature of productivity agreements in some factories. The scientific management of work (abbreviated after its Russian language form to NOT) is an adaptation of Taylorism arising from the need not just to raise productivity but also to maintain conformity between the ideology of socialism and the demands of productivity. In the USSR, NOT is achieved through the use of a brigade system:

> The brigade system is intended not only to improve productivity . . . but also to motivate workers, to constrain the labour policy of managers and to reconcile the interests of individual workers with those of the industrial enterprise and society as a whole . . . The objectives of the brigade system are (a) to encourage maximum effort by individual members, (b) to provide an incentive to economize on labour employed, (c) to stabilize labour mobility and enhance labour discipline, (d) to involve workers in management, to increase their personal responsibility for state affairs in the collective, and (e) to make the labour collective not only a unit of production but also a social unit. (Lane, 1987, p. 186)

Under the brigade system an element of autonomy is given to the shopfloor workers. Whilst Taylorist techniques of work design and rates for jobs are developed and implemented by management, managerial control over the labour process is constrained by two features, namely the ideology of Soviet society and the shortcomings of the planning system itself. With regard to the former, Lane says:

> The Soviet ideology of labour provides greater constraints on the political leadership than is found under capitalism; not only is there an expectation that paid work will be provided for all, but that such work is required to be 'satisfying'. (p. 16)

Thus Soviet authors have advocated participation at the level of the workplace for these reasons:

> The objective of reform on the shopfloor should be to create a subjective feeling on the part of the worker of being an owner of the enterprises. The brigade system is advocated as a means to this end. (Lane, p. 191)

Another feature of the Soviet economy that encourages relative autonomy is the looseness of the plan. The scarcities resulting from the plan lead to a situation where the work available can vary dramatically.   Thus managers need to be able to call on the co-operation of their workforce to work hard at particular times and at other times to work slowly.   A number of authors have looked at this in Hungary.   Burawoy and Lukacs say:

> The socialist firm must continually adapt to the exigencies of supply uncertainty, that is, to the continually changing form and flow of materials, labour and machinery into the enterprise.   This requires continual improvisation and readjustment of the labour process and therefore mandates a flexible managerial organization.   To be effective, shopfloor organization must be allowed a certain autonomy to respond to changing supplies; it cannot be controlled from above. (Burawoy and Lukacs, 1985, p. 726)

Stark has shown how this leads to a high level of informal bargaining between workers and managers:

> The ability to exploit uncertainties facing managers gives workers the opportunity to engage in transactive bargaining . . . market relations are cultivated inside the socialist firm as a means to reduce or surmount uncertainties from its environment. (Stark, 1986, p. 496; see also Sabel and Stark, 1982)

Stark shows how in Hungary this problem has led to the development of subcontracting units (abbreviated from the Hungarian form to VGMs) within firms.   VGMs comprise up to thirty members, which 'negotiate contracts to produce goods or services in their "off" hours using the firm's equipment' (Stark, 1986, p. 496).   VGMs allow the firms to meet the irregular demands of the planning system by giving flexibility out of hours.   Brigades, on the other hand, as they operate in the USSR, try to generate flexibility within working hours by heightening workgroup solidarity.   Both involve giving a degree of autonomy to the workforce, which accords well with the ideology of socialism.

To what extent are these features essential to the operation of the system as opposed to peripheral reforms?   It is commonplace in the West to note the formal commitment of Soviet management to Taylorism and bureaucracy and assume that this represents the system as a whole.   In my view, however, this is too simple.   Writing of the USSR, Lane says:

While forms of worker participation in the USSR have been criticized as being inadequate by Western writers, they in practice involve very much more control over the job situation than do Western experiments. In the West workers resist management. All schemes for worker participation (Western and Soviet) are advocated within the context of production goals set by management. The brigade system combines job enrichment, job rotation, control of the work setting and participation in the design of the job process. (Lane, 1987, pp. 205–6)

What is important is that in the USSR, there are systemic forces causing this, unlike the West, where reforms are piecemeal and limited to specific cases. In the Soviet-style economies, the ideology of socialism and the manner in which central planning works, pushes organizations in this direction. Undoubtedly workers may respond with a display of apathy and resistance to what they see as further incorporation; such feelings may be reinforced by the general political and social environment in which they are located. Furthermore, managers may resent having to grant autonomy and simply respond by increasing production rates (as seems to have been the case in the factory in which Harazti, 1977, worked). However, it would be wrong to dismiss work organization in Soviet-type societies as Taylorist. It may not be socialist but at the level of the enterprise and the labour process, there is evidence that it differs significantly from that in Western societies. Furthermore, as recent reforms loosen the control of the plan still further, they will increase the need for flexibility in the workplace.

Turning briefly to other aspects of state organization in the USSR, it is possible to show the direct penetration of political objectives into organizational arenas which in Western capitalist societies possess an autonomy. One of the most disturbing and dramatic to Western eyes relates to the way in which the state in the USSR has controlled the development and use of scientific knowledge for political purposes. During the 1970s for example, it became commonplace to use psychiatric institutions to stifle political dissent. A number of Soviet psychiatrists became well-known for the ease with which they equated political dissent with mental illness. Hosking (1985, p. 426) writes: 'Such men have been willing to return diagnoses of "creeping schizophrenia", characterized by such features as "poor adaptation" to the social environment, "moralizing" and "paranoid reformist delusions".' Using psychiatric labelling in this way was better for the authorities than using the criminal courts:

> Once the necessary diagnosis has been obtained, no further 'evidence' is needed, such as might be contested in court, the sentence is indefinite, and the certified insane do not enjoy even the meagre civil rights (correspondence, visits) that remain to prisoners. If it seems desirable, furthermore, the 'patient' can be treated with drugs that make him ill or depressed or cause great pain. (Hosking, 1985, p. 426)

Although it would be naive to assume that the use of psychiatry to control dissent is confined to the Soviet Union (see, for example, the rash of anti-psychiatry books that appeared in the West in the 1960s and early 1970s emphasizing the use of psychiatry as a form of social control), the dominance of political objectives and the lack of alternative institutional spheres means that organizations are more likely to be affected by direct political interference than in the West.

Another example of how political objectives penetrated the process of production of scientific knowledge is the Lysenko affair in the USSR. Lysenko was a Soviet scientist working at the height of Stalinism and he claimed that biological characteristics derived from the environment could be passed on generationally. Lysenko's ideas involved a rejection of Darwin's notion that genetic change derived from random mutation and returned to Lamarckian ideas of the influence of the environment. This suited the regime for two reasons. First, Lysenko argued that it was possible to produce plant species able to survive Russian winters by using his techniques. Second, at a more general level, Lysenko's ideas held out the hope that the personality type necessary for socialism ('socialist man and woman') could be produced rapidly. For almost twenty years, Lysenko's ideas dominated Soviet biology; they were pronounced as genuinely 'socialist' science and contrasted with the 'bourgeois science' of the West:

> The Weissmanist-Mendelist-Morganist current in biology is an anti-popular, pseudo-scientific, pernicious tendency. It disarms practice and orientates man towards resignation to the allegedly

eternal laws of nature, towards passivity, and an aimless search for hidden treasure and expectation of lucky accidents (Lysenko, quoted in Hosking, 1985, p. 312)

Such examples have been repeated in other areas of knowledge both in the natural sciences and the social sciences (where the rewriting of history has been particularly noticeable). The doctrine was expressed in the slogan that 'there are no fortresses the Bolsheviks cannot storm'. Hosking (1985, p. 312) refers to this as the belief that everything can yield to 'willpower'. In my terms, political ideology implemented by the state can penetrate deep into any organizational formation. It would clearly be necessary to note that these processes are no longer as noticeable under Gorbachev and *glasnost* as they were in the heyday of Stalinism. The point is, however, that there is no systemic reason why such things could not happen again, since Soviet societies in their present form lack the constitutional separation necessary to provide for autonomy both from the state and within the state, though Gorbachev's reforms seem to be partially about developing this separation.

The final area I wish to consider is that of religion. The development of religion as an institutionally separate sphere from the state or the economy was part of a long process of social development in the West. Nevertheless, it was a central part of the process whereby the sphere of civil society was created. Religious organization provided a place separate from work and politics where people could develop their own identities and come to grips with the cycle of human experience. In certain European societies, such as pre-revolutionary Russia, the separation between the state and religious organization had barely occurred by the start of the twentieth century. In these societies the state and the Church were closely intertwined; there had not been the opening up of civil society to allow a space in which a plurality of religious organizations could exist and allow for the independent development of individual identity. Thus although religion was powerful in pre-revolutionary Russia, its integral relationship with the Tsarist state, as well as the inbuilt Marxist materialist rejection of religion, meant that the Bolsheviks never countenanced the idea of religious organizations being allowed free rein. Hosking says:

> The Soviet state with its all-embracing ideology rapidly took on itself . . . many of the claims and attributes of an established

church. It was prone therefore to regard religious movements and particularly the formerly established Russian Orthodox Church as its rivals. (Hosking, p. 227)

In the early days of the Soviet state, churches were deprived of all their wealth and property. Although religious worship was not banned completely, its conditions of existence were closely monitored. Congregations had to register with the state; they were then allowed to employ a priest. They had to hire church buildings back from the state. From 1929 they were not allowed to proselytize for new supporters outside the churches. Although there was a rapprochement between the Church and the state as a result of the German invasion and the fight to save the 'Russian motherland', 'the subordination of church to state remained in force' (Hosking, 1985; p. 237).

In the Kruschev years, there was a further intensification of the drive against the Russian Orthodox Church. Ten thousand churches were closed and the authority of parish priests reduced even further than previously. There was a State Council for the Affairs of the Russian Orthodox Church:

> No ordination or transfer takes place without careful monitoring by senior Council officials. Clergy are classified according to the degree to which they are 'loyal' to socialist society, or, on the contrary, try to activate the religious life and strengthen the influence of the Church among the population. What the council values in priests and bishops is inactivity, a purely formal attitude to divine service, readiness to preach Soviet patriotism, the party's social policy and participation in the international peace movement. The Soviet state, in other words, is no longer trying to destroy the Church but to use it as a pliant instrument. (Hosking, p. 442)

There are, of course, other religious organizations in the USSR, especially Jews, Baptists, Catholics and Muslims. They face similar pressure. The state tries to incorporate part of the leadership and set clear conditions for the nature of religious worship – in particular that it supports the existing regime. This creates a two-fold pressure among those who reject this interference. First, many have ceased to participate in religious activities, preferring to avoid all the problems associated with worship in the Soviet system.

Second, others have taken up a militant stance against incorporation, refusing to bend to the state's demands and setting up, often in secret, their own places of orthodox worship, free from state interference. It is also necessary to note that there are differences in other Soviet-style societies. In particular, in Poland, where the Catholic Church had a strong existence separate from the Polish state, which has only existed as an independent entity intermittently over the last thousand years, religious worship is much more widespread. This is not unrelated to a more general struggle in Poland to establish a space for civil society, reflected in the struggle for independent trade unions carried on under the banner of Solidarity in the early 1980s. Nevertheless, in general terms it is possible to say that religious organizations in Soviet-type societies lack the independence that is characteristic of them in Western societies. This is explicable in terms of the lack of an institutional separation of state, economy and civil society in these countries.

In conclusion, I have shown that in Soviet-type societies there is a dominance over all organizations of the state. All organizations are involved in the reproduction of the state and are therefore expected to fit in with the ideology of the state in a way that does not occur in Western societies. This is not to say that there is state control over everything that goes on within organizations. This is just as unlikely as the prospect that a central plan could determine all aspects of economic production. There are areas of autonomy even within the economic sector, and it is possible to see in certain of the Soviet bloc countries efforts to create a space for independent organizations that could constitute the beginnings of the formation of civil society. At present, these possibilities remain in the future. Nevertheless, a truly comparative sociology of organizations would do well to take notice of events in these countries.

Organizations and societies: some general considerations

The previous discussion about Japan and the USSR has aimed to bring out the way in which organizational forms are shaped by the social and political environment in which they are located. Organizational forms draw on social resources from many different levels; they need to be understood in terms of the societies in which they are located, as producing and being reproduced within a particular set of social relations. Such a view avoids the more crass notions in which organizations are seen as expressions of certain cultural essences that have somehow developed in particular societies. There are no cultural essences, only the real material processes through which people have organized their lives. These processes embody culture, in the sense of 'sense-making categories' but these are not fixed; they change as the conditions of social relations change.

The concept of society itself needs contextualizing, however. The term 'society' is often used to denote the set of social relationships geographically bounded and circumscribed by the state. This interrelation between state and society is a relatively recent phenomenon. Even in Europe, previous to the sixteenth or seventeenth centuries, territorial boundaries were badly defined and frequently interchangeable according to family marriages and military expeditions. Political powers were parcelled up between various levels of the feudal hierarchy. For the great majority of people, concepts of nation and state had no meaning. Only with the growth and development of European nation-states did these conditions change and through the military might of these states eventually come to impact on the whole world. (For accounts of these processes, see Anderson, 1983; Mann, 1986a; Hall, 1985; Wallerstein, 1974, 1980.) In current conditions, however, the link between the state and society is beginning to decline as social relationships are affected as much by forces beyond the boundaries of any one nation-state (see Lash and Urry, 1987, for an account of these processes.)

Two linked factors are of major importance here: the growth of multinational enterprises and the growth of international finance. Both of these factors mean that the nation state no longer has the same capability of controlling its economic destiny; without this control, it does not have the power and resources to mediate between the competing interests of capital and labour. Thus the institutions of corporatism break down, resulting in a further fragmentation of interests between different types of employer and employee. This process in turn is fundamentally altering the nature of organizations and participation in them in the 1980s and will continue to do so into the foreseeable future. Essentially, it could be argued that as membership of nation states *per se* decreases in saliency for people (as it can no longer deliver social and economic well-being), membership of organizations becomes more important. Thus wealth, income and social standing are increasingly derived from being a member of, for example, IBM rather than being British or American. Clearly this opens up a disjuncture between social and cultural expectations and feelings (which still remain nation-based) and economic expectations (that are organization-based). It is to these changes that I shall turn now.

The growth of multinationals has occurred in a number of phases. Only in their latest stages of development have they begun to constitute a major force undermining rather than reinforcing nation states (or at least the nation states of the developed Western European and US economies). Forms of multinational organization have existed throughout the history of capitalism, but until the post-war period, multinationals were based chiefly on the extraction of raw materials from areas outside the main industrialized world. Thus from the late nineteenth century oil companies had developed production sites across the world from where they shipped oil back to the industrialized countries. Similarly, many raw materials crucial to the industrial and personal consumption of the West were delivered via multinationals. Some of the multinationals acted essentially as agents between small-scale peasant producers and the purchasers located in the West. These multinationals, known as 'factors' in the Far East, later diversified into larger-scale merchanting, banking and shipping, creating groups such as Jardine Mathieson and Swires. Other multinationals set up production facilities consisting of plantations, mines, and oil wells, usually run by whites, with native populations coerced and dispossessed of land, forced into acting as an unskilled labour force. Multinationals of this sort were closely tied in with the development and maintenance of Empire. The protection of their investment was seen as requiring a stable government, preferably itself composed of whites from the home state of the multinational. Although the organizations themselves were multinational in scope, they were integrally and closely tied to their home state.

The early post-war period is characterized by the development of new forms of multinational organization. (Much of this section is informed by Armstrong *et al.*, 1984, and Lash and Urry, 1987.) In this period, the key feature is the growth of direct US investment in the European economies. Companies like Ford and General Motors which already had plants in Britain began to expand their operations both in the UK and in Europe. Other American firms followed suit, setting up production facilities in Western Europe. Whereas the multinationals based on raw materials were of necessity forced to go to where they could get the raw materials from, the American multinationals consciously decided to produce in the countries where their new markets were. This had a number of advantages for them: it reduced any threat from tariff barriers that might be erected to direct US exports; it reduced costs of transportation and labour; and got the organization into new expanding markets. On the disadvantage side, it increased the problems of co-ordinating the organization once it had plants spread around the world. However, the development of the multi-divisional form could be readily adapted to the internationalization of production. Also problematic was the style of management and industrial relations that was operated by Americans in European countries. In the main this was resolved by a two-fold response. On the one hand, the Americans brought over all their highly developed techniques of management control, ranging from controls over budgets through to controls over the pace and quality of work. This in turn in the short term gave them a considerable advantage over indigenous European firms which in general lacked this level of sophistication. In the long run these countries would start to catch up, though the process took longer in some countries than others (compare, for example, Britain and Germany). On the other hand, when it came to industrial relations, the Americans were cautious, preferring in the main (although Ford were an exception) to work with European institutions as they were rather than try to alter them radically (though this has since changed). American companies in Europe in the main recruited locally except for top managers, though even these positions were gradually filled by Europeans once the company was satisfied that it had the right people in place and the reporting and monitoring system for the US head office was adequately installed.

As the Japanese and European economies started to develop, the competitive advantage of US multinationals decreased. A number of things started to happen. First, European companies started to develop on a multinational basis both within Europe and in the rest of the world. Second, and related to this, was the growing competition for market share that became increasingly severe from the mid 1960s onwards. These changes impacted on firms in two distinct ways, via costs and product market innovation. With regard to the latter, firms increasingly had to decide whether they were going for a mass market or a particular specialist niche within a market. Whichever of these was chosen, it was increasingly clear that markets would be changing rapidly, and firms needed to be in a position to respond in terms of new products. With regard to costs, it was clear that there was much greater pressure to reduce costs than there had been previously. Multinationals were in a position to do this by changing their internal organization; they also had one very important weapon: they could move or at least threaten to move their production facilities if they were not getting the cost reductions they wanted. It is at this point that 'organized capitalism' starts to disintegrate.

Once multinationals' location policies are determined not just by market considerations but also by cost factors (which in turn can be shaped, manipulated and selectively presented through transfer pricing and skilful accounting), national governments find their power severely weakened. In order to attract or keep multinational investment, they may introduce forms of subsidy – the provision of rent or rate free accommodations, selective tax concessions, grants towards costs, etc. These in turn, however, become part of the competitive process as different countries vie with each other to provide the most generous incentives to multinationals. Even incentives are not enough. Just as important is a labour force with the right characteristics – willing to take work at the right level of wages and not to disrupt industrial relations.

In the late 1960s and 1970s, multinationals began to expand their investment into parts of the Third World in order to take advantage of cheaper wage costs. In areas like Hong Kong, the Philippines, Singapore, India and Brazil, the multinationals found governments that were willing to ensure a docile and quiescent labour force at very low wages, as well as various forms of subsidy for locating plants there (see Harris, 1986). Relocation necessitated a form of reorganization; since the labour force was not highly skilled, only the low-skill parts of the production process could be relocated. However, first in textiles and clothing, and later in the electrical and computing components industries, firms separated these low-level skills from the more complex tasks of design and relocated them around the world. The revolution in transport costs deriving from container shipping, together with the reduction of labour costs, made this a competitive option for companies in certain industries. The growth of information technology in computers and satellites meant that costs and problems in production across the world could be monitored from a head office in the USA, Europe or Japan. Whilst setting up plants across the world had some human costs for the top management who were expected to travel around and run them, its greatest impact has been on the power of national governments. Multinationals decide where to invest on the basis of a wealth of information regarding different sites across the world. Whilst governments can try to use various incentives to obtain a result favourable to them, there are too many factors to predict a simple outcome. Multinationals will move in and out of regions and countries according to factors which go beyond the power of any one state to influence, and in which the social impact of relocation is very low on the agenda.

The second major force for disorganization derives from instability and change in the sphere of international finance (for a useful discussion see Strange, 1986). In addition to production becoming supranational, so the funds and surpluses generated in production are being distributed increasingly at supranational level, with states having only a limited amount of control over the process. It is possible to distinguish four main phases in this development:

1. The growth of the Eurodollar market.
2. The abolition of fixed exchange rates.
3. The impact of the oil price rises in the mid 1970s.
4. The development of round-the-world trading in currency and shares.

The growth of the Eurodollar market developed out of the expansion of US multinationals and the economic policies of the US government in the post-war years. World monetary stability derived from the fact that the value of the dollar was fixed; thus all international exchange could occur in dollars without anybody fearing that the dollar's value might fall. Europeans and others willingly accepted dollars in payment for commodities and services; the dollar was 'as good as gold'. US companies and the government financed their expansion through the use of dollars. As a result, dollars flowed into the European banking system, particularly into the City of London. The Eurodollar market refers to the process whereby the banks in which these dollars were deposited proceeded to lend these dollars to other clients in Europe. Thus European companies financed their expansion with dollars. The key advantage of the Eurodollar market was that it was not directly controlled by any central bank; thus whereas there was a Bank of England that could reduce or increase the flow of pounds sterling into the economy and as a result reduce or increase credit provision in Britain, Eurodollars lacked any form of self-regulation. The Eurodollar market could act contrary to governmental wishes without fear of sanction.

The problem with the Eurodollar market at this stage, was that it depended on the dollar holding its value. By the early 1970s, however, pressure was beginning to build for an effective devaluation of the dollar. For nearly twenty years the outflow of dollars from the USA had not been matched by an inflow of funds from other countries. The USA was buying more than it could afford on world markets, and it was only a matter of time until a currency adjustment occurred. This had a destablizing impact not just on banks but also on multinational companies, which now held large amounts of dollars as well as other foreign currencies. With currencies set at fixed rates, the pressure put on central banks by commercial banks and others worried that a devaluation was about to occur was causing a lurch from one crisis to another as first one currency and then another became the target. Because currencies could not change their value gradually but rather had to do it overnight, there was considerable advantage to be had from making the right bet. Once the dollar came under the microscope of the currency speculators, instability became endemic.

The solution that was devised was to let currencies float 'naturally' according to market perceptions of their value. The system of fixed exchange rates was abolished. Whilst national governments and central banks would watch over the process and in most cases operate a policy of keeping their currency within a certain range of values through a policy of selective purchasing, they were no longer committed to defending one particular rate. Whilst certain immediate consequences were foreseen, such as the potential instability in markets and prices arising from continuous exchange rate movements, one of the most far-reaching effects became obvious only gradually. If exchange rates were continually changing, then guessing which way a rate would move would be extremely profitable if large enough sums of money were involved. Of course, currency speculation had occurred during the era of fixed exchange rates, but it was only in the relatively unusual circumstances of an actual de- or revaluation that large profits and/or losses could be made. With floating exchange rates, profits could be made by the minute.

Adding to the trading possibilities was the growth in a market for futures, a market which first developed in Chicago, where futures trading on commodities was already well-established. Eventually this had reached London. In currency futures, banks and institutions could make contracts for an option to buy a currency at a certain value in the future. If the currency's value deviated from the one on which they had an option, they would either exercise the option (if the currency was now more valuable) or let the option lapse (in which case they had only lost the price of the option). Speculation on currency, then, once fixed rates were abolished, had both a short-term and a medium-term side to it: one could gamble on the way currencies would move in the next twenty-four hours, or one could move into the futures market and gamble on three-monthly trends.

What really expanded this process out of all expectations, however, was the oil price rise of the mid 1970s. The massive expansion of industrial production in the 1950s and 1960s had been built on the supply of cheap raw materials from around the world, and in particular the supply of oil. When, in the wake of the Yom Kippur war between Egypt and Israel in 1973, the Arab states decided to impose restrictions on the export of oil and later set increased prices for oil, it became clear that an irrevocable change in the system was taking place. Although the ability of the oil producers in OPEC to maintain a common front has not been sustained under the impact of the different interests involved and the development of oil conservation and alternative supplies, there has nevertheless been a major increase in the cost of oil. The major beneficiaries of this have been the Arab states, where the increase of wealth far outstrips their ability to put it to any useful investment purpose. As a result, the wealth became 'recycled'. The Arabs left it with the Western banking system for them to invest it. The result was two-fold. First, there was suddenly a great influx of capital available for currency speculation, thus vastly magnifying previous trends. Second, there was a further change in the international division of labour. Non-oil-producing countries in Asia, Africa and South America suddenly had to find a lot more money to pay for their more expensive oil imports. Simultaneously, however, the chance opened up for them to further their own industrial development by borrowing the recycled money and seeking to tempt into their countries multinationals looking for new locations by providing a superior economic infrastructure. Both of these factors precipitated a huge expansion of lending facilities to the poorer countries of the world, but particularly those which looked as if they could be on the verge of a take-off into self-propelled industrialization. The temptation to invest in these areas was increased by the severe deflationary impact of the oil price rise on the West and a consequent shrinking of markets and increasing of competition. Thus, in the mid-1970s, countries in the Third World soon found the Western banking system willing and able to lend vast sums of money to fund large-scale projects.

The weakness of all this was that the projects in the Third World were based on the belief that there could be world economic expansion which would result in Third World locations and manufacturing plants being used. Although in some areas the new investments were used in this way, in many more cases they became highly expensive white elephants that were of no use. The debtor country, however, was lumbered with interest and capital repayments, which by the early 1980s were severely distorting their economies. Thus a large proportion of all their export earnings went on servicing debt repayments. In order to do this, they had to constrict home consumption severely and at the same time expand their exports, leading to acute social tension and massive inflation. In countries like Mexico, Brazil and Argentina, the governments were forced into considering defaulting on the entire debt that they had built up during the mid 1970s (see the accounts of Harris, 1983, and George, 1988).

From the point of view of the Western banking system, the debt crisis in these countries was also a crisis for them. Such was the investment of the American and British banks in particular that if a major nation defaulted on its debts, the banks themselves would be in severe trouble. The impact of the effective bankruptcy of a major British clearing bank such as the Midland, which was heavily involved both on its own account and through the Californian subsidiary Crocker Bank, would have been devastating both socially and politically. Thus the government and the Bank of England have been heavily involved in planning a response to the problem. The banks themselves have taken two measures. First, they have agreed periodically to a rescheduling of debts; in effect, this involves writing off part of the value of a debt by allowing its costs to be spread out over a longer period of time. This means that the banks no longer have the earnings in current years which they projected when they originally made the loans. Second, banks have had to increase their contingency reserves in order to ensure that they do not collapse should there be a major default.

In order to increase their contingency reserves, banks in the 1980s have been forced to become more highly competitive. Only through earning more in traditional or new areas of business could they protect themselves. This has led to the fourth factor identified earlier, increased competition in the financial sector. Banks have sought to enter areas previously closed to them. In order to do this, they have pressured government into deregulating areas of financial services such as the Stock Exchange in the UK. Thus there are now many more 'players' in this area than previously – companies competing to invest people's money or to lend them money. Similarly, there is much more money available for 'playing' with. Changing pressures on pensions and insurances have given both the old players in these sectors and the new financial conglomerates more to go after.

The increased number of players and the increased number of stakes for playing with have in turn necessitated the need for an increased number of places to play in. Financial institutions in London saw no reason why their investment should be confined to the trading hours of the London exchange. The technology and marketing arrangement are now in place that can allow for twenty-four-hour trading across the world. This was how the players wanted to play. Huge institutions such as Nomura of Japan, Citicorp of New York, the Deutsch Bank of Germany, Credit Suisse of Switzerland and Barclays of London play the markets twenty-four hours a day from their different offices across the world.

From the point of view of governments, this process has necessitated a process of deregulation. In the UK, regulations on overseas investment and on trading in stocks and shares have been abolished, to be replaced by a new structure of regulation that fits in with the highly competitive international framework of twenty-four-hour markets. (For accounts of these changes see Hamilton, 1986, and Harris *et al.*, 1988.)

The result is a highly complex trading environment where institutions make choices about the time-scales, nature and risk level of their investments on the basis of a picture of worldwide economic developments. Furthermore, these choices are not simply relevant to financial institutions. Multinational producers and traders who deal in foreign currencies are also drawn into these markets. When large companies consider the raising of loans, the sale of shares or the purchase of currency, their perspective is not national; they search for the best deal they can get anywhere in the world. They are taken well beyond the bounds of their original home state.

Taking these two phenomena together, the growth of multinationals and the internationalization of the financial system, we have powerful forces that reduce the roles of nation states. It is not that the growth of organizational forms directly challenges state power, nor indeed that it is not at certain points integrated with it. Yet in the final analysis, the power of these organizations and the changes they are making pass *through* states rather than being dependent on them.

Summary

This chapter has aimed to show that organizations can only be properly understood by locating them in their social context. For most of the past two centuries that context has been determined mainly by developments within the borders of nation states. Within these borders, social classes and political parties have formed which gave a basic shape to social life. This shape existed at a number of levels: at one level there were the expectations that social actors had about each other with regard to fundamental social roles, e.g. about being a manager, a worker, etc. At another level, there were the institutions that had accumulated over the prolonged period of industrialization; at a further level still, there was the state with its goal of directing and shaping social changes. Individual nation states developed their own shape according to many and varied contingencies. These shapes continually changed and developed. They were not fixed in concrete but rather produced and reproduced under a variety of circumstances which could lead to significant change. Most significant of all was the gradual bursting of the nation state framework itself. Although in many ways nation states retain their hold over people's consciousness and the structure of their political institutions, nevertheless the boundaries of nation states have been breached over the last twenty years. The growth of multinationals and changes in the world financial system have led to degrees of integration between states that make the independent economic actions of any individual state extremely difficult. (A similar process has occurred with regard to international foreign relations. States locate themselves in power blocs, particularly NATO and the Warsaw Pact. Whilst nuances of foreign policy may differ within pacts, the chances of the minor members within the pacts pursuing their own independent foreign policy are virtually nil.)

The decline of the nation state is having a profound impact. Because the political institutions of the nation state remain still the ones to which people look for political change, the gap between the expectations and the reality can only increase. The organizations which shape our lives are increasingly supranational, but our political understanding of them remains national. The next few decades will reveal the way in which social life adjusts its expectations and institutions to the reality of supranational power.

7 Conclusion: Organizational Futures, Organizational Dilemmas

Introduction

In this final chapter I consider a number of central dilemmas in organizational futures which have arisen from the analysis presented so far. Essential to this is the theory of structuration which I presented at the start of the book and have used since. In particular, I wish to reiterate the importance of both a diachronic and a synchronic view of organizational life, but with a priority given to the diachronic. There is still a powerful tendency in the study of organizations to look at them as though one could take a snapshot of a particular moment. That snapshot then becomes the basis for analysing relationships between the parts that are pictured together: structure, culture, labour process, etc. are considered as a unity bound together, as it were, by the parameters of the snapshot. In this view the better the snapshot, the more sophisticated the camera, the more we can explain about the organization. The content of the explanation, however, is a construct of the method of explanation, and whilst it may provide a powerful story about the snapshot, it is a limited story.

The above analogy makes sense in relation to the analysis of photographs in real life. Photographs are always constructs of a particular eye (or is it I?). In the hands of skilled practitioners and sometimes even the unskilled, a photograph can hint at underlying dynamics in natural and social environments. It is not completely static, but compare it to the art of the film-maker. A film is also a construction, but in film moments are placed in a sequence where causal relationships can be uncovered. Time can be given a substance that photography can only address indirectly. It would be irrelevant to prioritize one above the other, one as more true than the other. Both are constructs; both can reveal 'truths'. It follows from this that we need to consider combining the two in order to give a better picture, though it is difficult to know quite what such a combination would consist of. If we are to view organizations properly, we have to hold on to this duality between diachrony and synchrony, between stability and change, between reality and possibility, between present and future. This can be best done by locating organizational analysis firmly within the framework of structuration theory.

Organizations cannot survive unless at each particular moment of their existence they reproduce themselves in the relationships of their members and participants. This necessitates that individuals perform actions that reproduce these relationships. Such actions can never be guaranteed, though there are a number of reasons why they become 'predictable'. Many actions become almost reflex, learnt at an early age and deeply embedded in our character. Other actions we perform because of a form of rational calculation that it is in our best interests. Still other actions are based on traditional ways of doing things, deriving from this an emotional power over us. Predictability is different from a guarantee: we can break the hold of reflex actions; we can recalculate rationality; we can question tradition. Actions are but the tip of the iceberg of organizational life; beneath lie our personal expectations and hopes based on our individual circumstances and our membership in wider social groupings. These expectations change and so may our actions.

Actions are open-ended in the sense that most of the time they are, if not in detail then in outline, predictable and yet by their very nature unpredictable in the last analysis. Unless we accept this and begin to consider some of the ways in which actions do change, we end up with a static and sterile conception of organizations which fails adequately to capture their dynamism and sense of flux. The concept of action inevitably implies choice – the idea that I could act in another way. To choose an unexpected form of action implies certain consequences, usually harmful to the person who has so acted. To act otherwise, to act out of the ordinary, disrupts established patterns and therefore risks upsetting others; it may also risk bringing down moral or coercive sanctions on the one who has acted differently. Of course, acting unexpectedly can have a positive value; it can present reality in a new light, lead to new questions and to new, better ways of doing things. It can also have a novelty effect: jokes, humour, sudden displays of emotion, exasperation and temper may be temporary disruptions of the stability of organizational life, but they also provide a breathing space during which one can be distanced from the 'treadmill' effect of much social interaction (see Linstead, 1985, for a discussion of humour in organizations).

Actions are also made open-ended by their location in complex environments. Misunderstanding between people or the selective re-interpretation and manipulation of communication can lead to a gradual change in the basis of social interaction. This is particularly relevant when we distinguish between face-to-face interaction and the more distanced interaction characteristic of many relationships within organizations, where the people concerned may never actually meet each other 'in the flesh'. Where we are engaged in routine, face-to-face interaction, we develop and refine shared assumptions about the basis of interaction; there develops what Bernstein (1971) has called an 'indexicality' of speech and interaction. We know what the other means without the other having to make the whole thing explicit. However, once we move outside face-to-face interaction, the conditions for indexicality decline. Exact meanings become more difficult to interpret, and this is not resolved by simply increasing the word level. More words can lead to more errors or attempts at manipulation. So the basis of organizational relationships can change, sometimes without either or both parties noticing, sometimes because it is in the interests and power of one party to make the changes.

Similarly, the conditions of action may change. People/ organizations which we expected to act in a certain way no longer do so because of a change in their priorities. Thus the basis for predictability is no longer there. Our actions also have to change. New relationships need to be forged. In the intricately connected and interdependent way in which we live now, it is obvious that stability of action is precarious. Indeed, we live with uncertainty and prepare for contingencies. Our actions are loosely coupled to our conditions of existence in that we recognize the inevitability of change and are tolerant of it so long as it stays within certain limits and proceeds at a slow enough pace. When these limits of tolerance are passed, the responses of individuals and organizations become much more haphazard; the process of survival itself becomes much more problematic and there may have to be wholesale reorganization of expectations and actions.

The conditions of organizational and social stability are therefore precarious. Depending on our position within the organization, we may act in the expected way for most, if not all of our life. But there arise many opportunities to act otherwise, to act in a slightly different way, to act in a radically different way. At the top of the organization, planning for change is a central part of the role of top executives; anticipating and reacting to changes in the internal and external environments continually open up new directions for the future. Further down in the organization, the planning for change is less obvious, though the opportunities for change still exist. Indeed, the disruption of relationships, for example between managers and workers, can lead to strikes and wider conflicts that occasionally affect not only the organization but also the wider social fabric, for example when strikes take on a political meaning, as in the miners' strikes of 1972, 1974 and 1984–5 in the UK. Moments of crisis and choice are endemic in organizational life; there is no way in which they can be avoided. Whilst there are powerful forces maintaining stability and consensus, there are equally powerful forces opening organizations up to change. It is only the false certainty of the snapshot approach to organization studies that conceals this.

Once we move to the interorganizational, the societal and the international levels, processes of change can only be looked at in the long term. The patterns of change, which seem so far removed from the influence of most people, nevertheless have major impacts on the lives of all of us. It is not that these changes are made by some extra-human force. Whilst it is difficult to calculate the impact of particular decisions in such an interrelated and complex world, and thus events cannot be straightforwardly ascribed to the intentionality of particular actors, nevertheless there are central powerful groups in our society. These groups in particular are continually taking decisions which, taken in their entirety, contribute in a major way to the reproduction and change of our society.

The way in which those decisions are taken, the principles upon which they are based, the extent of participation in those decisions, the way in which they are implemented, as well as the decisions themselves, are all open to question in the sense that they could have been different. There are choices involved.

In the rest of this concluding chapter I wish to consider a number of choices or dilemmas in organizations that in my view are central to the future of our society. These dilemmas are:

1. Democracy versus autocracy in work.
2. Co-ordination versus anarchy.
3. Plan versus market.
4. National versus multinational forms.

Each of these in my view expresses a fundamental crisis within modern organizations and societies. Although for any particular organization the extent to which these either overlap or occur at the same time may differ, they nevertheless imply a series of choices that are being made. At many different points within organizations these issues arise and are temporarily resolved, but the choices remain firmly on the agenda for the future of post-industrial societies and organizations.

Democracy vs autocracy at work

The crises and choices that are opened up here have been central dilemmas in the organization of work since industrialization began. On the one side are those who believe that nobody in their right mind would voluntarily want to spend their life working; so when people go to work it is only because they are effectively forced to do so in order to survive. When people do work then they are out to ensure that they receive maximum reward for minimum effort. In this view the job of management is centrally concerned with making sure that people are working properly. It involves devising systems of job design that allow for control and supervision. The emphasis is on fragmentation and routinization, the breaking up of craft skills and high levels of authority vested in management and supervisors. Technology is to be used to reduce further the direct control of the workers; technology is used to replace people and/or their skills. The vision of scientific management is one of control in which all parts fit together and human beings are simply one type of part with no more expectation that they will actively contribute to the organization than there would be that a machine could talk. In this view the major contribution that work makes is to people's out-of-work styles of life. Thus industrialization, technology, scientific management, etc. may not be particularly nice in terms of the pressures they put on people at work, but out of work they provide a material consumer culture undreamt of and allow for the expression of individuality and uniqueness outside the workplace in a way that previous economic systems could not.

On the other hand are those who view work as something essential to human dignity, as an expression of an individual's identity. In this view, people thirst for the right sort of work where their contribution is valued. Work brings people together in a co-operative endeavour; it stretches their minds and their physical capacities in a way that potentially brings high levels of personal satisfaction. From this point of view, work systems should be developed in ways that allow these feelings to be used. Thus work groups should be encouraged to develop and take on responsibilities for the organization and design of tasks. The role of technology should not be to do away with people or their skills but to act as a supplemental addition to what people can already achieve. If we bring people together and give them responsibility, then according to this view they will produce more and better goods. There is an ambiguity in this view with regard to the material benefits of industrialization. On the one hand, there is the argument that if people work co-operatively they will produce more, so it makes sense from a purely materialist point of view to adopt more co-operative modes of organizing. On the other hand, there are those that argue that the material benefits of industrialization are illusory; they are based on the super-exploitation of the Third World and the destruction of the natural environment. Neither of these can continue indefinitely, and so it is necessary to turn back to smaller-scale co-operative endeavours.

Although the debate about the organization of work takes many forms, it is essential to understand its linkage to wider political issues. Whereas many recent authors in the organization behaviour tradition see this as a technical problem about the relationship between structure/leadership and efficiency, in fact the issue goes much deeper. At its heart is the old socialist argument which says that capitalism needs its system of hierarchical control in order to extract surplus value from workers. If work was really organized in a co-operative, democratic manner, then workers would see that it was irrational for the fruits of their labour to be distributed so unequally, with so much more going to the managerial hierarchy and shareholders than to the people who do the actual job. (This was the argument authors such as Mallet, 1975, and Gorz, 1976, made about France in the late 1960s and early 1970s to explain the rising militancy of the 'new working class', i.e. the technicians, supervisors and lower managers who participated in the May 1968 troubles in France.) If all the key decisions about work were taken by the workers, then where would be the justice in a hierarchical rewards system? Thus the argument about democracy at work is itself an ambiguous argument, because it raises not just the issue of control at the level of the job itself but control over the organization and society as a whole.

This tension between democracy and autocracy at work is particularly salient at the present time due to three phenomena:

1. *The success of more co-operative forms of shopfloor relations in countries like Japan*
Although it would clearly be wrong to view Japanese organizations as democratic, they do nevertheless seek to draw out of their workforce a much higher degree of commitment, co-operation and loyalty than is expected in the West. This commitment develops out of the way in which the organization is structured: management is concerned to achieve consensus both within itself and with the workforce through encouraging people to come up with new suggestions and to discuss possible changes. This is reinforced by the lack of strong visible status barriers within the company workforce, and the lifetime employment system, both allowing for a much clearer ideological message about the value the company puts on its employees. As has been pointed out previously, these features are not unique to Japan; certain American, British and European companies also have them, though not to the same extent. The powerful economic position of Japanese companies has forced firms in these other societies to reconsider their previous practices. Although there were previously many management-led experiments in forms of industrial democracy such as job participation, consultation, etc., these were frequently fairly blatant

attempts by management to restore their own control; they were usually brought in at time of growing shopfloor power in an attempt to incorporate workers and thus draw the sting out of the independent countervailing power of trade unions. It is arguable that the current round of interest in such issues as quality circles and consultation is qualitatively different precisely because it has come at a time when workers are in a weak bargaining position. Thus, for the first time, British and American management are to a limited extent introducing these experiments not to incorporate trade unions but to avoid them altogether. The creation of co-operative relations in these settings is therefore based not just on the inferior market position of the workers in times of high unemployment, but also on the lack of trade union/collective power within the workplace. It is thus a very limited, one-sided form of consensus that is created, and the extent to which it would survive changed economic and social conditions that restructured the fundamental power relations is unclear.

2. *Increased education and the changing nature of the work ethic*
(For a detailed discussion of this see Rose, 1985.) During the 1960s and 1970s it was argued that increased standards of education would lead to dissatisfaction with traditional work organizations. People who had learnt to express and value their own opinions and to think about issues in a rational and logical fashion would be less likely to accept what looked like the arbitrary diktats of managers. Thus shopfloor workers were seen as likely to become increasingly rebellious against routinized and degrading assembly-line conditions in factories. Also, higher-education-trained professionals would expect more authority to be granted them by virtue of their expertise. Similarly, both these groups, it was agreed, would be much more likely to have alternative values and aspirations to their work-centred existence. Hedonistic personal fulfilment away from work could be expected to reduce commitment at work. The idea was that the internalized work ethic that made people want to work and guilty when they did not, was increasingly being replaced by a new orientation to work where work was a secondary activity to leisure and outside-work lifestyle. The optimistic voices of the 1960s and early 1970s had hardly died down when by the late 1970s trends operating from a different direction were similarly seen to be threatening conventional ideas of work. The rise of mass unem-

ployment, particularly among young people it was argued, was also generating a rejection of the old-style work ethic. Where long-term 'real work' was an improbable prospect for many people, the idea that there were other means of expressing identity arose. Whilst these means clearly suffered from the material impoverishment of the conditions in which they were produced (unlike that other 1980s phenomenon, the Yuppies, who seemed to symbolize the unification of a hedonistic, narcissistic life-style with a highly rewarded work situation), they were nevertheless a reaction against the work ethic. People began to talk of a future without work: 'Farewell to the Working Class', (as Gorz, 1982, put it), as though a fundamental watershed had been reached which necessitated a reconsideration of the relationship between employment, work and economic well-being. If people rejected the current conditions of work, or if they had no work ethic, what would happen to organizations?

3. *Technological developments*
The new information technology of the 1980s has a number of possible effects:

(a) It can lead to labour-saving measures within organizations.
(b) It can lead to a polarization of skills – on the one side, the technology needs a highly skilled workforce to design, produce and maintain it; on the other side, it can be operated by people using only a fraction of their potential skill.
(c) It can lead to a spatial redistribution of work, within cities, regions, states and across the world. The potential for decentralizing tasks, to the extent of people working in their own homes and communicating to a central computer through networked terminals, is already being realized in certain areas.

These phenomena mean that the conditions under which work is organized are in a state of flux. At the heart of these changes is a conflict over how far work will be designed and organized to enhance people's commitment and identity or how far it will continue to be designed to maximize control over people. This conflict opens up moments of choice and decisions within organizational settings. The processes of production and reproduction are altered as conflicts and decisions regarding the nature of work organization occur. The direction of the changes that are occurring remains open; that alternative futures are open, however, is not in doubt.

Co-ordination vs anarchy

The second main dilemma can be simply expressed. The more things there are that need to go right, the more things there are to go wrong! The structuring of organizations has become increasingly complex as the complexity of internal and external environments has increased. There has been a massive expansion in the way organizations seek to control themselves and others. Professionals have developed systems of knowledge and operation to deal with areas like accountancy, law, health, personnel, etc. Managers in organizations have developed systems for monitoring and evaluating performance. Scientists and engineers have developed systems for producing new and cheaper commodities. Organizations consist of many different groups, each with their own solutions to their own problems. All groups may legitimate their activity by reference to overarching organizational goals; they will all claim the central importance of their way of seeing things to the survival and success of the organization. They will all be seeking to increase their own power. On the one hand, they will be seeking power over other groups – the power to impose their own definition of the problem and the appropriate solution on the organization as a whole. On the other hand, they will be seeking the power that is inserted into the very way the organization works – the power to define what is measured, what is thought about, what is acted upon. This power, as Foucault pointed out, is intricately bound up with the development of professional knowledge. It is not that power derives from knowledge or vice versa, but that the two move along in tandem. In Foucault's analysis, the construction of a power/knowledge discourse is a process whereby new areas of organizational life become opened up to processes of control. Definition of the phenomenon as abnormal, inefficient, etc. is simultaneously an invitation to intervene and reconstruct – to develop, in medical terms, a therapeutic technology; in organizational terms, a plan of control.

The consequences of this process are clear in modern organizations. There is a multitude of complex power discourses operating continually, sometimes on the same part, sometimes on different parts of the organization. Each power discourse potentially seeks to expand its sphere of operation by discovering new 'facts', new problems and new solutions specific to its mode of operation. Within the organization, then, this leads to a number of competing 'rationalities of action'. This has two effects:

1. The generation of conflict between the rationalities and the inability of any one to gain complete power within the organization. Whilst one may gain predominance at one level, another may gain equal predominance at another. Thus accounting rationality may predominate at top board level, whilst production rationality may predominate at other levels.
2. The generation of multiple sites of resistance, based upon other 'rationalities of action' which go beyond those based on managerial and professional power/knowledge discourses, e.g. trade unionism. Resistance is a further spur to the discourses, however, because it shows that knowledge and power have not reached their 'completion'. Every resistance is an invitation to further control. Resistance does not stop the development and expansion of power/knowledge discourses; rather it is inbuilt into the process. Without resistance there would be no propulsion to the expansion of power/knowledge.

Holding the organization together under these circumstances is clearly a highly complex task. Almost inevitably organizational choices open up as discourses compete for power and control. The resolution of these choices is seldom a complete victory for one discourse over the other; rather there is a temporary resolution where one rationality of action gains predominance at a particular level whilst the others are confined to their particular niches.

The problem of co-ordination and control goes further, however, because the more knowledge develops and seeks to control a wider range of phenomena, the more things can go wrong because of the unintended and unexpected interaction of totally separate factors. Perrow (1984), in his analysis of nuclear power, has illustrated how this occurs. As technology becomes more complex and ambitious in its scope, it simultaneously creates greater risks. Nuclear power demands a high level of technical expertise to plan, develop and operate. The conditions for making it work safely are highly complex, but how many possible contingencies must the designers take into account? There are internal and external contingencies which may damage a nuclear power plant and create a nuclear explosion, but how far can we or should we plan for such contingencies as earthquakes, operator error, etc.? Perrow suggests that what makes nuclear power so dangerous is that it consists of a series of tightly coupled and highly interdependent processes. Thus if any one thing goes wrong, no matter how small, it can have catastrophic effects. Perrow's argument is that technology and organizations should build slack into themselves, ensuring a loose coupling between parts that delays the interactive effects of factors going wrong and thus allows for intervention. Building in loose coupling, however, also has the effect of reducing the level of co-ordination between the parts and opens the organization up to the fragmenting tendencies noted earlier. How are organizations to resolve this: through more and tighter control, or looser links between parts?

The process of production and reproduction in organizations is continually being altered by the competition between competing rationalities. At moments of crisis and change, opportunities arise for different groups to attempt to lever their rationality, their power/knowledge discourse into a key position. In doing this, groups continually overreach themselves, claiming to achieve a co-ordination and rationality that is impossible. The competition generates potential anarchy as organizations continually expand their scope for control and, at the same time, expand their scope for mistakes.

Market vs plan

This theme develops very much out of the previous one. Organizations increasingly plan their operations both internally and externally. At what point can we expect 'plans' to outweigh in importance the market mechanism? Economists point to the virtues of the market in ensuring efficiency; in this view, competition between organizations drives the less efficient out of business, and the public interest is served in the long run. Others, however, point to the consequences of this: the decline of key industries and along with them the social areas in which they are located; the inequality between groups, classes, regions and states that is generated. Long ago Marx talked about the 'anarchy of the market' and the resulting human and social waste that accompanied the so-called adjustments of the 'hidden hand'. This model of the market, however, has never been more than a model. At societal level, governments have intervened to plan aspects of market relations; this has included providing a legal and fiscal framework for markets. Without some framework of trust, as Durkheim (1968) argued, it would be impossible to guarantee that free market contracts would be agreed. Thus behind market relations are non-market relations. Increasingly, after 1945, governments in the West have sought to plan aspects of the economic environment, providing forms of tax incentives and regional aid to encourage developments in certain areas, reflating and deflating the economy, developing forms of planning at industry and sector levels, and specifically subsidizing certain industries, where market pressures might otherwise result in companies going out of business.

At the organizational level, the market model has never been allowed to dominate. Where circumstances have been appropriate, organizations have entered into co-operative relations with each other, sharing information, research and development costs, and markets. These types of co-operation can be formalized at various levels, ranging from trade associations, through cartels to interlocking directorates. Each is a way of avoiding the worst consequences of the market; instead of anarchy, organizations look for predictability. They seek to extend into the environment the principles of co-ordination and control on which their internal structure is based. In this way, modern capitalist economies are simultaneously based on plans and markets.

Planning in its most clear-cut form is associated with Soviet-style economies and the attempt to develop targets of performance for all enterprises within the economy. Successful planning to this extent is far beyond the capabilities of social systems at the moment. Though it is possible to specify inputs and outputs in plans, it is impossible to take into account the differences that motivation, skill and innovation within the production process can make to output. There is little incentive in a planned economy to over-fulfil targets and therefore a tendency at enterprise level towards stagnation. As to the relationship between planned outputs and consumer demand, there is as yet no mechanism for a short-term feedback of consumer tastes into the plan. (Indeed, long-term plans have not given much priority to consumer demand, concentrating instead on heavy industry and military expenditure.) The result is that the plan and its targets dominate over the needs and wishes of both enterprises and consumers. Whilst enterprises and consumers may express dissatisfaction, the main moving force of the system remains the plan, which comes down to individuals as a series of separate directives lacking an overall logic or coherence.

Central planning also depends upon a co-ordination of production which remains beyond our capabilities at the moment. The sheer number of commodities and services that are produced in industrial societies far surpasses anything previously imaginable. How is it possible to plan not only how many of each item will be needed but also when, where and at what level of quality they will be needed? These difficulties are to a certain extent circumvented in the Soviet Union by hoarding (to avoid shortages), by black marketeering (including informal deals between nearby enterprises) and by cutting corners (producing to minimum quality standards and leaving end users to face the consequences). Nevertheless, each pragmatic adjustment further undermines the plan and its chances of even minimum success. It is these sorts of tensions that are forcing the Soviet Union under Gorbachev to consider ways of making the economy work which combine elements of planning with elements of markets.

It is possible to discern a movement towards a combination of plan and market in both the West and the Soviet bloc. In the West, planning within organizations is on the increase. Attempts to predict and control environmental contingencies increase as methods of collecting and analysing data are improved under the impact of information technologies. Market forces remain of significance, though their operation is no longer as predicted by traditional economists. The conditions under which markets work have been set by national governments, though, as will be discussed shortly, they are no longer controlled by national governments. In planned economies such as the USSR and China, the difficulties of planning centrally are resulting in increased experimentation with markets. It is important to note, however, that this combination of plan and market has, within it, an unending dialectic similar to that identified in the previous section. As products and demands emerge, organizations seek to plan to meet demand; in the process of planning, new aspects open up, encouraging other products to satisfy other demands, which in turn drives other organizations in other directions. Thus there is a continuous drive to control an environment that continually slips out of control. Planning mechanisms have expanded enormously both within public and private organizations over the last few decades. There is no reason to expect that this process is anywhere near completion. The complexity of information gathered is a function of the complexity of information sought.

Organizations and societies are therefore faced with the dilemma as to how far to plan the allocation of resources. The alternative of simply allowing markets to reign supreme has never really been relevant, as markets themselves are social constructions. Indeed, it would be an affront to the professional dignity of managers and their myriad advisers, researchers, etc. to think otherwise. Organizations are about planning, not just of the internal environment but also of the external environment. What remains to be decided and enters continuously into issues of the production and reproduction of organizations is the extent and level of planning that can exist. This leads to the final central organizational dilemma.

National vs multinational

The issue of control and power can be reconceptualized as a phenomenon existing at a number of levels. The first is that of immediate, face-to-face interaction. In such a situation, where there are two parties interacting, deviations from expected courses of action can be sanctioned in a number of ways, ranging from physical coercion through verbal rebuke to emotional punishment. I can exercise power over another to the extent that I can physically, verbally or emotionally dominate him/her. However, I may need to call on other outside forces to help punish the 'deviant'. For example, the law with all its attendant physical and moral power can be called on, or I may call on others informally linked together to use their moral and social powers of persuasion to sanction the offender. In both these cases I draw on expectations about the actions of others outside the face-to-face interaction. These 'others' exist as further sets of face-to-face relationships which institutionalize expectations – that is, they monitor and sanction adequate performance.

Human societies have, in very basic terms, evolved from a form whereby face-to-face interactions were backed up by the proximity in time and space of sanctioning institutions to a form whereby these institutions were located at a distance from the interactions themselves, and yet nevertheless were closely integrated with them. Essentially, this describes the transition from agricultural, village-based forms of social organization (which could be loosely integrated into empires based on military rule) to town- and city-based forms of social organization, located in and tied to the formation of nation states. In the former, social life predominantly took place within the limits of face-to-face interaction. Occasionally, new 'faces' arrived, usually driven on by dreams of military conquest and imperial grandeur. Such changes could destroy the old basis of face-to-face interaction, as sometimes occurred, or more likely could leave them relatively intact whilst installing a new 'face' (a landlord, a tax-gatherer, a bureaucrat) in the village.

As towns and cities developed, however, power became channelled in much more intricate ways. Military power was supplemented by legal and other social institutions which united people far beyond face-to-face interaction into what Anderson (1983) has called an 'imagined community'. This community was the nation state, which had territorial boundaries within which it held the monopoly of the legal use of armed force. The development of the nation state was a complex, many-sided process. The nation became the focus of people's hopes and expectations. It became the source of ultimate power within its own geographical borders. People gave their lives for their country in war; in return, they expected their country to provide them with something.

Although this process varies across the world, the advent of mass citizenship is linked in most areas to the development of notions of rights and duties accruing to the status of 'citizen'. Social welfare and economic well-being are the duties of the state; in return the citizen is duty-bound to loyalty and obedience to the state and its laws. The state penetrates deep into people's lives, shaping their individual subjectivity through its institutions of education and control.

This centrality, however, is a relatively recent phenomenon. Face-to-face interactions draw on the institutionalized power of the state. Power at this level is reinforced by the way in which the institutions of the state have shaped expectations. The power of doctors over patients, social workers over clients, managers over workers, are all in some sense dependent on the state, and yet the dominance of the state hides a basic instability, emerging from the growing gap between the nation state and the international economy. A number of authors (Hall, 1985; Mann, 1986a; Wallerstein, 1974, 1980; Anderson, 1974) have pointed to the interdependence of nation states and capitalism in the seventeenth and eighteenth centuries. Without nation states to provide stable frameworks for commercial and industrial activity, these authors argue, capitalist development could never have commenced. In fact, the nation state became the political form for people seeking to industrialize. By the 1960s the whole world was divided up into nation states, each of which attempted with different levels of success to manage its own economy and system of welfare. Only a few remaining colonies stood outside this framework; in the rest of the world, citizenship and nationhood had come of age. But at the same time there were other processes undermining the symbiotic relationship between capitalism, industrialism and statehood.

The main economic factor involved here was the growing internationalization of production and finance, symbolized in its early stages by the growth of the US and then European and Japanese multinationals, and in its more recent stages by the development of international financial dealing. Both of these phenomena have started to remove the bases of the stable relationship between face-to-face interactions and national institutions that previously existed. Multinational organizations have choices: they can look to their head office, above and separate from any nation state; the head office in turn has choices about appropriate locations for production or appropriate currencies for investment, purchase and payment. To this extent, particular nation states are no longer essential to particular organizations. Whereas the nation state may previously have been an arbiter between organizations or between managers and employers within organizations, it can no longer rely upon playing that role. Indeed, the extent to which nation states are necessary is questionable. Key decisions, for instance over currency, regulation of multinationals, etc., come in the main at a supranational level if they are going to be effective. Whilst political institutions and social loyalties remain to the state, the reality of power is that it has vacated the national space.

There is a significant sense in which this process has been aided

by international political relations. The formation of politico-
military blocs such as NATO and the Warsaw Pact has locked
individual nation states outside the two main protagonists into
relationships that surpass old nation-state loyalties. The fact that
nuclear explosions recognize no national limits to their devastation
means that a nuclear war is a matter for all people of the world, not
just those at the centre of the conflict. This in turn raises the
question of what can possibly justify a handful of nations, for
interests that are not even 'national' but 'supranational', launching
nuclear weapons that have effects beyond the boundaries of the
so-called allied powers. The impact of these processes on defini-
tions of the rights and duties of citizens and states is yet to be
worked out. Whilst the image of 'nation at war' can still be
powerfully evoked on an ideological level and in practice, as the
frequent conventional wars in the nuclear age demonstrate, there
remains a growing sense that the nation state is outmoded.

At both an economic and a political level the nation state is no
longer able to deliver to its members their expectations of stability
and welfare. Powerful forces which cross national boundaries are
shaping the direction of the future. Does it make sense to seek to
bolster the nation state? Is that in fact possible, or will new
supranational institutions and resources of power develop, building
on those that already exist, such as the UN, the EEC, NATO? Will
a new set of relationships develop between individuals and supranational regulatory bodies that will once again generate a symbiotic
relationship of control and growth between companies and political
power? Organizations have been central to this process of change.
To what extent will they develop alternative forms to the nation
state which provide a focus for economic and social well-being *and*
emotional identification?

Conclusion

The future of society and the future of organizations are intricately
bound together. Organizations have provided us with an abund-
ance of material goods and services that 200 years ago would have
been unimaginable. It may be that many of these goods and
services are trivial; it may be that they have cost an unforeseeable
price in human suffering; it may be that the unimaginable end of

humanity itself has now come into the realm of the all too imaginable. These things, however, are not the results of organizations *per se*, but of the way human beings have designed and used them. This is not to say that organizations can somehow be redesigned and restructured tomorrow and everything will suddenly be sweetness and light. On the contrary, our world is now far too complex for that, and the interactions of organizations and states go far beyond what can be predicted by any model of social consequences. It is necessary to reiterate that what happens, does so because people make it happen. Social life is a continuous series of choices. Most of them for most of the time we hardly notice we are taking. For many of the rest, we take the line of least resistance, doing what comes easiest, what is expected. Occasionally we may resist, throw down the gauntlet and challenge the expected. More often, however, things change when problems come at us in a new way, making the old routines less relevant. We therefore act in new ways, almost in spite of ourselves; in most organizations, it is impossible to act in the same way all one's working life. New challenges arise that call for new adaptions which in turn provide an altered environment for others, who in their turn also have to change. Change and continuity are inextricably intertwined.

It is at these times that a sociology of organizations has most to contribute. It can help us to analyse where we are and where the roads may lead; it can help us to consider the consequences for ourselves and others. It can locate us in the sum of human history and the potential future of society. In periods of rapid change such as we are living in at present, it is essential that we are not simply blown into following the current fashions. Our choices need to be informed both by a certain distance from the everyday hurly-burly of organizations and at the same time by an engagement with these processes. Sociology's strength is that at its best it can provide both that distance and that engagement. Without it the study of organizations is continually in danger of becoming nothing more than a set of techniques for management. With it, the study of organizations is undoubtedly less comfortable for many of its practitioners, but potentially more exciting and relevant for society in general.

Bibliography

Abercrombie, N. and Urry, J. (1983) *Capital, Labour and the Middle Classes* (London: Allen and Unwin).

Abegglen, J. C. (1958) *The Japanese Factory* (New York: Free Press).

Ackroyd, S., Burrell, G., Hughes, M. and Whitaker, A. (1988) 'The Japanisation of British Industry', *Industrial Relations Journal*.

Abla, R. (1982) 'Taking Stock of Network Analysis', in Bacharach, S., *Research in the Sociology of Organizations*, vol. 1, (Greenwich, Conn.: Jai Press).

Albrow, M. (1970) *Bureaucracy* (London: Pall Mall Press).

Aldrich, H. (1979) *Organizations and Environment* (Englewood Cliffs: Prentice Hall).

Aldrich, H. and Whetten, D. (1981) 'Organization-sets, Action-sets and Networks', in Nystrom, P. and Starbuck, W., *Handbook of Organizational Design*, vol. 1 (London: Oxford University Press).

Aldrich, H. and Auster, E. (1986) 'Even Dwarfs Started Small: Liabilities of Age and Size and their Strategic Implications', *Research in Organizational Behavior*, 3.

Aldrich, H. (1988) 'Paradigm Warriors: Donaldson versus the Critics of Organization Theory', *Organization Studies*, 9, 1.

Allatt, P., Keil, T., Bryman, A. and Bytheway, B. (eds) (1988) *Women and the Life Cycle* (London: Macmillan).

Allen, M. P. (1974) 'The Structure of Interorganizational Elite Cooptation', *American Sociological Review*, 39.

Allen, S. (1980) 'Perhaps a Seventh Person?', *Women's Studies International Quarterly*, 3.

Allen, S., Bentley, S. and Bornat, J. (1977) *Work, Race and Immigration* (Bradford: University of Bradford).

Allen, S., Waton, A., Purcell, K. and Wood, S. (eds) (1986) *The Experience of Unemployment* (London: Macmillan).

Allen, S. and Wolkowitz, C. (1987) *Homeworking: Myths and Realities* (London: Macmillan).

Allen, V. S. (1981) *The Militancy of British Miners* (Shipley: Moor Press).

Altschuler, A. *et al.* (1984) *The Future of the Automobile* (London: Allen and Unwin).

Anderson, B. (1983) *Imagined Communities* (London: Verso).

Anderson, P. (1974) *Lineages of the Absolutist State* (London: New Left Books).

Ansoff, I. (1968) *Corporate Strategy* (Harmondsworth: Penguin).

Anthony, P. D. (1986) *The Foundation of Management* (London: Tavistock).

Aris, S. (1985) *Going Bust: Inside the Bankruptcy Business* (London: Deutsch).

Armstrong, P. (1984) 'Competition between the Organized Professions and the Evolution of Management Control Strategies', in Thompson, K. (ed.).

Armstrong, P. (1987a) 'Engineers, Managers and Trust', *Work, Employment and Society*, 1, 4.

Armstrong, P. (1987b) 'The Rise of Accounting Controls in British Capitalist Enterprises, *Accounting, Organizations and Society*, 12, 5.

Armstrong, P., Glyn, A. and Harrison, J. (1984) *Capitalism since World War Two* (London: Fontana).

Astley, W. G. (1984) 'Toward an Appreciation of Collective Strategy', *Academy of Management Review*, 9, 3.

Astley, W. G. (1985) 'The Two Ecologies: Population and Community Perspectives on Organizational Evolution', *Administrative Science Quarterly*, 30.

Astley, W. G. and van de Ven, A. (1983) 'Central Perspectives and Debates in Organization Theory', *Administrative Science Quarterly*.

Astley, W. G. and Fombrun, C. J. (1983) 'Collective Strategy: Social Ecology of Organizational Environments', *Academy of Management Review*, 8, 4.

Atkinson, J. (1984) 'Manpower Strategies for Flexible Organizations', *Personnel Management*, August.

Atkinson, J. (1987) 'Flexibility or Fragmentation: The United Kingdom Labour Market in the Eighties', *Labour and Society*, 12, 1.

Baldamus, W. (1961) *Efficiency and Effort* (London: Tavistock).

Barker, J. and Downing, H. (1985) 'Word Processing and the Transformation of Patriarchal Relations in Control', in Mackenzie and Wajcman (eds).

Barrett, M. (1980) *Women's Oppression Today* (London: Verso).

Batstone, E. (1984) *Working Order* (Oxford: Blackwell).

Beardsworth, A., Bryman, A., Ford, J. and Keil, T. (1983) 'Employers' Strategies in relation to Their Demand for Labour', *Industrial Relations Journal*.

Beechey, V. and Perkins, T. (1987) *A Matter of Hours: Women, Part-Time Work and the Labour Market* (Cambridge: Polity Press).

Beetham, D. (1987) *Bureaucracy* (Milton Keynes: Open University Press).

Benson, J. K. (1977) 'Organizations: A Dialectical View', *Administrative Science Quarterly*, March, 22.

Benson, J. K. (1985) 'Paradigm and Praxis in Organizational Analysis', *Research in Organizational Behaviour*, vol. 5.

Bernstein, B. (1971) *Class, Codes and Control*, vol. 1 (London: Routledge and Kegan Paul).

Beynon, H. (ed.) (1985) *Digging Deeper: Issues in the Miners' Strike* (London: Verso).

Blackburn, R. M. and Mann, M. (1979) *The Working Class in the Labour Market* (London: Macmillan).

Blau, P. (1956) *Bureaucracy in Modern Society* (New York: Random House).

Blau, P. (1964) *Exchange and Power in Social Life* (New York: Wiley).

Blau, P. and Scott, W. (1963) *Formal Organizations* (London: Routledge and Kegan Paul).

Boland, R. J. (1987) 'Discussion of "Accounting and the Governable Person"', *Accounting, Organizations and Society*, 12, 3.

Boreham, P. (1983) 'Indetermination: Professional Knowledge, Organization and Control', *Sociological Review*.

Bowles, S. and Gintis, H. (1976) *Schooling in Capitalist America* (London: Routledge and Kegan Paul).

Brake, M. (1980) *The Sociology of Youth and Youth Sub-cultures* (London: Routledge and Kegan Paul).

Braverman, H. (1973) *Labor and Monopoly Capital* (New York: Monthly Review Press).

Brittain, J. and Freeman, J. H. (1980) 'Organizational Proliferation and Density Dependent Selection', in Kimberly, J. *et al.*

Brown, C. (1984) *Black and White Britain* (London: Heinemann).

Brown, P. and Ashton, D. (eds) (1987) *Education, Unemployment and the Labour Market* (London: Falmer Press).

Brunsson, N. (1986) *The Irrational Organization* (New York: Wiley).

Burawoy, M. (1979) *Manufacturing Consent* (Chicago: University of Chicago Press).

Burawoy, M. (1985) *The Politics of Production* (London: Verso).

Burawoy, M. and Lukacs, J. (1985) 'Mythologies of Work: A Comparison of Firms in State Socialism and Advanced Capitalism', *American Sociological Review*, 50.

Burns, A., Feickert, D., Newby, M. and Winterton, J. (1983) 'The Miners and New Technology', *Industrial Relations Journal*, 14, 4.

Burns, A., Newby, M. and Winterton, J. (1985) 'The Restructuring of the British Coal Industry', *Cambridge Journal of Economics*, 9.

Burns, T. and Stalker, G. M. (1961) *The Management of Innovation* (London: Tavistock).

Burrell, G. (1980) 'Radical Organization Theory', in Dunkerley, D. and Salaman, G. (eds).

Burrell, G. (1984) 'Sex and Organizational Analysis', *Organization Studies*, 5, 2.

Burrell, G. (1987) 'No Accounting for Sexuality', *Accounting, Organizations and Society*, 12, 1.

Burrell, G. and Morgan, G. (1979) *Sociological Paradigms and Organizational Analysis* (London: Heinemann).

Burt, R. S. (1983) *Corporate Profits and Cooptation* (London: Academic Press).

Cameron, K. S., Kim, M. U. and Whetten, D. (1987) 'Organizational

Effects of Decline and Turbulence', *Administrative Science Quarterly*, 32.

Carchedi, G. (1977) *On the Economic Identification of Social Classes* (London: Routledge and Kegan Paul).

Carey, A. (1967) 'The Hawthorne Studies: A Radical Criticism', *American Sociological Review*, 32.

Carney, M. G. (1987) 'The Strategy and Structure of Collective Action', *Organization Studies*, 8, 4.

Carpenter, M. (1976) 'The New Managerialism and Professionalism in Nursing', in Stacey, M. *et al.* (eds).

Carroll, G. R. (1984) 'Organizational Ecology', *Annual Review of Sociology*, 10.

Carroll, G. R. and Delacroix, J. (1982) 'Organizational Mortality in the Newspaper Industries of Argentina and Ireland', *Administrative Science Quarterly*, 27.

Castles, S. with Booth, H. and Wallace, T. (1984) *Here for Good: Western Europe's New Ethnic Minorities* (London: Pluto).

Centre for Contemporary Cultural Studies (1982) *The Empire Strikes Back* (London: Hutchinson).

Chandler, A. D. (1962) *Strategy and Structure* (Cambridge, Mass.: MIT Press).

Chandler, A. D. (1977) *The Visible Hand* (Cambridge, Mass.: Harvard University Press).

Chandler, A. D. and Daems, H. (1980) *Managerial Hierarchies* (Cambridge, Mass.: Harvard University Press).

Channon, D. F. (1977) *The Strategy and Structure of British Enterprise* (London: Macmillan).

Child, J. (1984a) *Organization: A Guide to Problems and Practice* (2nd edn) (London: Harper and Row).

Child, J. (1984b) 'Managerial Strategies, New Technology and the Labour Process', in Knights, D. *et al.* (1984).

Child, J., Fores, J., Glover, I. and Lawrence, P. (1983) 'A Price to Pay? Professionalism and Work Organization in Britain and West Germany', *Sociology*, 17, 1.

Clark, P. (1985) 'A Review of Theories of Time and Structure for Organizational Sociology', *Work Organization Research Centre*, Working Paper no. 6.

Clegg, S. (1975) *Power, Rule and Domination* (London: Routledge and Kegan Paul).

Clegg, S. (1979) *The Theory of Power and Organization* (London: Routledge and Kegan Paul).

Clegg, S. (1981) 'Organization and Control', *Administrative Science Quarterly*, 21.

Clegg, S. and Dunkerley, D. (1979) *Organizations, Class and Control* (London: Routledge and Kegan Paul).

Clegg, S., Boreham, P. and Dow, G. (1986) *Class, Politics and the Economy* (London: Routledge and Kegan Paul).

Clegg, S. and Higgins, W. (1987) 'Against the Current: Organizational Sociology and Socialism', *Organization Studies*, 8.

Coates, K. and Topham, T. (eds) (1970) *Workers' Control* (London: Panther).

Cockburn, C. (1983) *Brothers: Male Dominance and Technological Change* (London: Pluto).

Cockburn, C. (1985) *Machinery of Dominance: Women, Men and Technical Know-How* (London: Pluto).

Cockburn, C. (1987) *Two-Track Training: Sex Inequalities and the YTS* (London: Macmillan).

Cohen, B. G. and Jenner, P. J. (1968) 'The Employment of Immigrants; A Case Study Within the Wool Industry', *Race*, X, 1.

Cohen, M. D., March, J. G. and Olsen, P. (1972) 'A Garbage Can Model of Organizational Choice', *Administrative Science Quarterly*, 17.

Cole, R. E. (1979) *Work, Mobility and Participation* (Berkeley: University of California Press).

Cook, K. S (1977) 'Exchange and Power in Networks of Interorganizational Relations', in Benson, J. K. (1977) *Organizational Analysis* (London: Sage).

Coombs, R., Saviotti, P. and Walsh, V. (1987) *Economics and Technological Change* (London: Macmillan).

Cooper, D. J. and Hopper, T. M. (1987) 'Critical Studies in Accounting', *Accounting, Organizations and Society*, 12, 5.

Cooper, R. and Burrell, G. (1988) 'Modernism, Postmodernism and Organizational Analysis', *Organization Studies*, 9. 1.

Corina, M. (1973) *Trust in Tobacco* (London: Allen and Unwin).

Cousins, C. (1986) 'The Labour Process in the State Welfare Sector', in Knights, D. and Willmott, H. (eds) (1986a).

Cousins, C. (1987) *Controlling Social Welfare: A Sociology of State Welfare Work and Organization* (Brighton: Wheatsheaf).

Coyle, A. (1985) 'Going Private: The Implications of Privatisation of Women's Work', *Feminist Review*, 21 Winter.

Crompton, R. (1987) 'Gender, Status and Professionalism', *Sociology*, 21, 3.

Crompton, R. and Jones, G. (1984) *White Collar Proletariat: Deskilling and Gender in the Labour Process* (London: Macmillan).

Crompton, R. and Mann, M. (1986) *Gender and Stratification* (Cambridge: Polity Press).

Crompton, R. and Sanderson, K. (1986) 'Credentials and Careers: Some Implications of the Increase in Professional Qualifications Amongst Women', *Sociology*, 20, 1.

Crouch, C. (ed.) (1979) *State and Economy in Contemporary Capitalism* (London: Croom Helm).

Crowther, S. and Garrahan, P. (1988) 'Corporate Power and the Local Economy', *Industrial Relations Journal*.

Crozier, M. (1964) *The Bureaucratic Phenomenon* (Chicago: University of Chicago Press).

Crozier, M. and Friedberg, E. (1980) *Actors and Systems* (Chicago: University of Chicago Press).

Cusumano, M. (1985) *The Japanese Automobile Industry* (London: Harvard University Press).

Cutler, A. *et al.* (1978) *Marx's Capital and Capitalism Today* (London: Routledge and Kegan Paul).

Dahrendorf, R. (1959) *Class and Class Conflict in Industrial Society* (London: Routledge and Kegan Paul).

Dastmalchian, A. (1984) 'Environmental Dependencies and Company Structures in Britain', *Organization Studies*, 5, 3.

Davies, C. (1987) 'Things to Come; The NHS in the Next Decade', *Sociology of Health and Illness*, 9, 3.

Davies, C. and Rosser, J. (1986) 'Gendered Jobs in the Health Service', in Knights, D. and Willmott, H. (eds).

Deem, R. and Salaman, G. (eds) (1985) *Work, Culture and Society* (Milton Keynes: Open University Press).

Derber, C. (1983) 'Managing Professionals', *Theory and Society*, 12.

Dick, B. and Morgan, G. (1987) 'Family Networks and Employment in Textiles', *Work, Employment and Society*, 1, 2.

Dickens, P. and Savage, M. (1988) 'The Japanisation of British Industry', *Industrial Relations Journal*.

DiMaggio, P. J. and Powell, W. W. (1983) 'The Iron Cage Revisited: Institutional Isomorphism and Collective Rationality in Organizational Fields', *American Sociological Review*, 48.

Doeringer, P., Moss, P. I. and Terkla, D. G. (1986) 'Capitalism and Kinship: Do Institutions Matter in the Labour Market', *Industrial and Labor Relations Review*, 40, 1.

Donaldson, L. (1985) *In Defence of Organization Theory* (Cambridge: Cambridge University Press).

Dore, R. P. (1974) *British Factory – Japanese Factory* (London: Allen and Unwin).

Dore, R. P. (1983) 'Goodwill and the Spirit of Market Capitalism', *British Journal of Sociology*, 34, 4.

Douglas, J. D. (1967) *The Social Meanings of Suicide* (Princeton: Princeton University Press).

Doyal, L., Hunt, G. and Mellor, J. (1981) 'Migrant Labour in the Health Service', *Critical Social Policy*, 1, 2, Autumn.

Du Boff, R. B. and Herman, E. S. (1980) 'Alfred Chandler's New Business History', *Politics and Society*, 10, 1.

Dunkerley, D. and Salaman, G. (1980) *The International Yearbook of Organization Studies 1979* (London: Routledge and Kegan Paul).

Durkheim, E. (1951) *Suicide* (Glencoe, Ill.: Free Press).

Durkheim, E. (1968) *The Division of Labour in Society* (New York: Free Press).

Earl, M. J. (ed.) (1983) *Perspectives on Management* (Oxford: Oxford University Press).

Edstrom, A. *et al.* (1984) 'Alternative Explanations of Interorganizational Linkages', *Organization Studies*, 5, 2.

Edwards, R. (1979) *Contested Terrain* (London: Heinemann).

Edwards, R. C., Reich, M. and Gordon, D. (1975) *Labour Market Segmentation* (Lexington: D. C. Heath).

Edwardes, M. (1984) *Back from the Brink* (London: Fontana).

Elbaum, B. and Wilkinson, F. (1979) 'Industrial Relations and Uneven

Development; A Comparative Study of the American and British Steel Industries', *Cambridge Journal of Economics*, 3.

Ellman, M. (1979) *Socialist Planning* (Cambridge: Cambridge University Press).

Etzioni, A. (1970) *Modern Organizations* (Englewood Cliffs: Prentice Hall).

Fennell, G., Phillipson, C. and Evers, H. (1988) *The Sociology of Old Age* (Milton Keynes: Open University Press).

Fevre, R. (1984) *Cheap Labour and Racial Discrimination* (London: Gower).

Fielding, A. G. and Portwood, D. (1980) 'Professions and the State', *Sociological Review*, 28.

Fligstein, N. (1985) 'The Spread of the Multidivisional Form among Large Firms', *American Sociological Review*, 50.

Ford, J., Keil, T., Bryman, A., Beardsworth, A. and Jenkins, R. (1983) 'Internal Labour Market Processes', *Industrial Relations Journal*.

Foucault, M. (1979) *Discipline and Punish* (Harmondsworth: Penguin).

Foucault, M. (1981) *The History of Sexuality, Vol. 1* (Harmondsworth: Penguin).

Foucault, M. (1980) *Power/Knowledge* (Brighton: Harvester Press).

Francis, A. *et al.* (1983) *Power, Efficiency and Institutions* (London: Heinemann).

Freedman, M. (1976) *Labor Markets: Segments and Shelters* (New York: Allanheld Osman Universe).

Friedman, A. L. (1977) *Industry and Labour* (London: Macmillan).

Froebel, F., Heinrichs, J., Kreye, O. (1980) *The New International Division of Labour* (Cambridge: Cambridge University Press).

Frost, P. *et al.* (1985) *Organizational Culture* (London: Sage).

Gamarnikow, E. (1978) 'Sexual Division of Labour: The Case of Nursing', in Kuhn, A. and Wolpe, A. (eds).

Garnsey, E., Rubery, J. and Wilkinson, F. (1985) 'Labour Market Structure and Workforce Divisions', in Deem, R. and Salaman, G. (eds).

George, S. (1988) *A Fate Worse Than Debt* (Harmondsworth: Penguin).

Gerth, H. H. and Mills, C. W. (1948) *From Max Weber* (London: Routledge and Kegan Paul).

Giddens, A. (1971) *Capitalism and Modern Social Theory* (Cambridge: Cambridge University Press).

Giddens, A. (1976) *New Rules of Sociological Method* (London: Hutchinson).

Giddens, A. (1979) *Central Problems in Social Theory* (London: Macmillan).

Giddens, A. (1980) *Sociology: A Brief but Critical Introduction* (London: Macmillan).

Giddens, A. (1981) *A Contemporary Critique of Historical Materialism*, vol. 1 (London: Macmillan).

Giddens, A. (1982) 'Power, the Dialectic of Control and Class Structuration', in Giddens, A. and Mackenzie, G. (eds) (1982).

Giddens, A. (1984) *The Constitution of Society* (Cambridge: Polity Press).

Giddens, A. (1985) *The Nation State and Violence* (Cambridge: Polity Press).

Giddens, A. and Mackenzie, G. (eds) (1982) *Social Class and the Division of Labour* (Cambridge: Cambridge University Press).

Gleeson, D. (1983) *Youth Training and the Search for Work* (London:

Routledge and Kegan Paul).
Glover, I. (1985) 'How the West was Lost? Decline in Engineering and Manufacturing in Britain and the United States', *Higher Education Review*, 1985.
Glover, I. and Kelley, M. P. (1987) *Engineers in Britain* (London: Allen and Unwin).
Goffman, E. (1968) *Asylums* (Harmondsworth: Penguin).
Goffman, E. (1971) *The Presentation of Self in Everyday Life* (Harmondsworth: Penguin).
Goldthorpe, J. (1982) 'On the Service Class: Its Formation and Future', in Giddens, A. and Mackenzie, G. (eds).
Goldthorpe, J., Lockwood, D., Bechofer, F. and Platt, J. (1968) *The Affluent Worker: Industrial Attitudes and Behaviour* (Cambridge: Cambridge University Press).
Gorz, A. (ed.) (1976) *The Division of Labour* (Hassocks: Harvester).
Gorz, A. (1982) *Farewell to the Working Class* (London: Pluto Press).
Gough, I. (1979) *The Political Economy of the Welfare State* (London: Macmillan).
Gouldner, A. (1954) *Patterns of Industrial Bureaucracy* (New York: Free Press).
Graham, I. (1988) 'Japanisation as Mythology', *Industrial Relations Journal*.
Gregory, D. and Urry, J. (eds) (1985) *Social Relations and Spatial Structures* (London: Macmillan).
Grieco, M. (1987) *Keeping it in the Family: Social Networks and Employment Chance* (London: Tavistock).
Gutman, H. (1977) *Work, Culture and Society in Industrializing America* (Oxford: Blackwell).
Hakim, C. (1979) *Occupational Segregation* (London: HMSO).
Hakim, C. (1987a) *Home-Based Work in Britain* (London: HMSO).
Hakim, C. (1987b) 'Trends in the Flexible Workforce', *Employment Gazette*, November.
Hales, C. (1986) 'What Do Managers Do?', *Journal of Management Studies*, 23.
Hall, J. (1985) *Powers and Liberties* (Oxford: Blackwell).
Hall, J. (1988) 'Classes and Elites, Wars and Social Evolution', *Sociology*, 22, 3).
Hamilton, A. (1986) *The Financial Revolution* (Harmondsworth: Penguin).
Hannah, L. (1976) *The Rise of the Corporate Economy* (London: Methuen).
Hannan, M. T. and Freeman, J. H. (1977) 'The Population Ecology of Organizations', *American Journal of Sociology*, 82.
Hannan, M. T. and Freeman, J. H. (1983) 'Niche Width and the Dynamics of Organizational Populations', *American Journal of Sociology*, 88, 6.
Hannan, M. T. and Freeman, J. H. (1984) 'Structural Inertia and Organizational Change', *American Sociological Review*, 49.
Hannan, M. T. and Freeman, J. H. (1987) 'The Ecology of Organizational Founding', *American Journal of Sociology*, 92, 4.
Harazti, M. (1977) *A Worker in a Worker's State* (Harmondsworth: Penguin).
Harris, L., Coakley, J., Croasdale, M. and Evans, T. (1988) *New*

Perspectives on the Financial System (London: Croom Helm).

Harris, N. (1983) *Of Bread and Guns* (Harmondsworth: Penguin).

Harris, N. (1986) *The End of the Third World* (Harmondsworth: Penguin).

Harris, R. (1987) *Power and Powerlessness in Industry* (London: Tavistock).

Hearn, J. (1982) 'Notes on Patriarchy, Professionalization and the Semi-Professions', *Sociology*, 16, 2.

Hearn, J. and Parkin, W. (1983) 'Gender and Organizations', *Organization Studies*, 4, 3.

Hearn, J. and Parkin, W. (1987) *'Sex' at 'Work'* (Brighton: Wheatsheaf).

Heath, A. (1976) *Rational Choice and Social Exchange* (Cambridge: Cambridge University Press).

Henderson, J. and Castells, M. (eds) (1987) *Global Restructuring and Territorial Development* (London: Sage).

Herzberg, F. (1966) *Work and the Nature of Man* (Cleveland: World Publishing Co.).

Heyderbrand, W. (1977) 'Organizational Contradictions in Public Bureaucracies', in Benson, J. K. (ed.) (1977) *Organizational Analysis* (Beverly Hills: Sage).

Hickson, D. J. (1987) 'Decision Making at the Top of Organizations', *Annual Review of Sociology*, 13.

Hickson, D. J., Hinings, C. R., Lee, C. A., Schneck, R. E. and Pennings, J. M. (1971) 'A Strategic Contingencies Theory of Intraorganizational Power', *Administrative Science Quarterly*, 16.

Hickson, D. J. and McMillan, C. J. (eds) (1981) *Organization and Nation: the Aston Programme IV* (Aldershot: Gower).

Hickson, D. J., Butler, R. J., Cray, D., Mallory, G. R. and Wilson, D. C. (1986) *Top Decisions: Strategic Decision-Making in Organizations* (Oxford: Blackwell).

Hines, R. (1988) 'Financial Accounting: In Communicating Reality, We Contruct Reality', *Accounting, Organizations and Society*, 13, 3.

Hochschild, A. (1983) *The Managed Heart: Commercialization of Human Feeling* (Berkeley: University of California Press).

Hopper, T., Cooper, D., Lowe, T., Capps, T. and Mouritsen, J. (1986) 'Management Control and Worker Resistance in the National Coal Board', in Knights, D. and Willmott, H. (eds) (1986a).

Hopper, T., Storey, J. and Willmott, H. (1987) 'Accounting for Accounting: Towards the Development of a Dialectical View', *Accounting, Organizations and Society*, 12, 5.

Hopwood, A. G. (1987) 'The Archaeology of Accounting Systems', *Accounting, Organizations and Society*, 12, 3.

Hoskin, K. W. and Macve, R. H. (1986) 'Accounting and the Examination: A Genealogy of Disciplinary Power', *Accounting, Organizations and Society*, 11, 2.

Hoskin, K. W. and Macve, R. H. (1988) 'The Genesis of Accountability: the West Point Connection', *Accounting, Organizations and Society*, 13, 1.

Hosking, G. (1985) *A History of the Soviet Union* (London: Fontana).

Hounshell, D. A. (1984) *From the American System to Mass Production 1900–1932* (Baltimore: Johns Hopkins University Press).

Humphries, J. (1977) 'Class Struggle and the Persistence of the Working Class Family', *Cambridge Journal of Economics*, 1.

Husband, C. (ed.) (1982) *'Race' in Britain* (London: Hutchinson).

Huws, U. (1982) *New Technology and Women's Employment* (Manchester: Equal Opportunities Commission).

Hyman, R. and Brough, I. (1975) *Social Values and Industrial Relations* (Oxford: Blackwell).

Ingham, G. K. (1984) *Capitalism Divided?* (London: Macmillan).

Jenkins, R. (1983) *Lads, Citizens and Ordinary Kids* (London: Routledge and Kegan Paul).

Jenkins, R. (1985) *Racism and Recruitment: Managers, Organizations and Equal Opportunities in the Labour Market* (Cambridge: Cambridge University Press).

Jenkins, R., Bryman, A., Ford, J., Keil, T. and Beardsworth, A. (1983) 'Information in the Labour Market: The Impact of Recession', *Sociology*, 17, 2.

Jessop, B. (1982) *The Capitalist State* (Oxford: Martin Robertson).

Jewson, N. and Mason, D. (1986) 'The Theory and Practice of Equal Opportunities Policies', *British Journal of Sociology*.

Johnson, T. (1972) *Professions and Power* (London: Macmillan).

Kimberly, J. (1980) *The Organizational Life-Cycle* (San Francisco: Jossey-Bass).

Knights, D. (1985) 'The State, the City and Life Insurance in the UK', paper presented to the European Group on Organization Studies, June.

Knights, D. (1989) 'Subjectivity, Power and the Labour Process', in Knights, D. and Willmott, H. (eds) *Labour Process Theory* (London: Macmillan).

Knights, D. and Roberts, J. (1983) 'Understanding the Theory and Practice of Management Control', *Employee Relations*, 5, 4.

Knights, D., Willmott, H. and Collinson, D. (eds) (1984) *Job Redesign* (London: Gower).

Knights, D. and Willmott, H. (eds) (1986a) *Managing the Labour Process* (London: Gower).

Knights, D. and Willmott, H. (eds) (1986b) *Gender and the Labour Process* (London: Gower).

Knights, D. with Tinker, T. (1988) 'Risk, Financial Self-Discipline and Commodity Relations', *Advances in Public Interest Accounting*, vol. 2.

Kotter, J. P. (1981) *The General Managers* (New York: Free Press).

Kuhn, A. and Wolpe, A. (eds) (1978) *Feminism and Materialism* (London: Routledge and Kegan Paul).

Lammers, C. J. and Hickson, D. J. (eds) (1979) *Organizations Alike and Unalike* (London: Routledge and Kegan Paul).

Lane, D. (1987) *Soviet Labour and the Ethic of Communism* (Brighton: Wheatsheaf).

Lash, S. and Urry, J. (1987) *The End of Organized Capitalism* (Cambridge: Polity Press).

Lavigne, M. (1974) *The Socialist Economies* (Oxford: Martin Robertson).

Larson, M. S. (1980) 'Proletarianization and Educated Labor', *Theory and Society*, 9.

Lawrence, P. R. and Lorsch, J. W. (1967) *Organization and Environment* (Cambridge, Mass.: Harvard University Press).

Leadbetter, C. and Lloyd, J. (1987) *In Search of Work* (Harmondsworth: Penguin).

Lee, G. and Loveridge, R. (1987) *The Manufacture of Disadvantage* (Milton Keynes: Open University Press).

Lincoln, J. (1982) 'Intra- (and Inter-) Organizational Networks', in Bacharach, S. (ed.) *Research in the Sociology of Organizations*, vol. 1 (Greenwich, Conn.: Jai Press).

Lindblom, C. (1959) 'The Science of Muddling Through', *Public Administration*, 19.

Linstead, S. (1985) 'Jokers Wild: The Importance of Humour in the Maintenance of Organizational Culture', *Sociological Review*.

Littlejohn, G. (1985) *A Sociology of the Soviet Union* (London: Macmillan).

Littler, C. (1980) 'Internal Contract and the Transition to Modern Work Systems: Britain and Japan', in Dunkerley, D. and Salaman, G. (eds).

Littler, C. (1982) *The Development of the Labour Process in Capitalist Societies* (London: Heinemann).

Littler, C. (1984) *Soviet Type Societies and the Labour Process*, in Thompson, K. (ed.).

Littler, C. and Salaman, G. (1982) 'Bravermania and Beyond', *Sociology*, 16, 2.

Littler, C. and Salaman, G. (1984) *Class at Work* (London: Batsford).

Loft, A. (1986) 'Towards a Critical Understanding of Accounting', *Accounting, Organizations and Society*, 11, 2.

Longstreth, F. (1979) 'The City, Industry and the State', in Crouch, C. (ed.).

Lukes, S. (1974) *Power: A Radical View* (London: Macmillan).

McGrath, J. E. and Rochford, N. L. (1983) 'Time and Behaviour in Organizations', *Research in Organizational Behaviour*, 5.

McKelvey, B. (1982) *Organizational Systematics* (Berkeley: University of California Press).

McKelvey, B. and Aldrich, H. (1983) 'Populations, Natural Selection and Applied Organizational Science', *Administrative Science Quarterly*, 28.

McKendrick, N., Brewer, J. and Plumb, J. H. (1983) *The Birth of a Consumer Society: The Commercialization of Eighteenth Century England* (London: Hutchinson).

McKinlay, W. (1987) 'Complexity and Administrative Intensity: The Case of Declining Organizations', *Administrative Science Quarterly*, 32.

McMillan, C. J. (1985) *The Japanese Industrial System* (Berlin: de Gruyter).

Macdonald, K. (1984) 'Professional Formation: The Case of Scottish Accountants', *British Journal of Sociology*, 25.

Mackenzie, D. and Wajcman, J. (eds) (1985) *The Social Shaping of Technology* (Milton Keynes: Open University Press).

Malcolmson, R. (1981) *Life and Labour in England 1700–1780* (London: Hutchinson).

Mallett, S. (1975) *The New Working Class* (Nottingham: Spokesman).

Mandel, E. (1968) *Marxist Economic Theory* (London: Merlin Press).

Mandel, E. (1969) *An Introduction to Marxist Economic Theory* (New York: Pathfinder Press).

Mann, M. (1970) 'The Social Cohesion of Liberal Democracy', *American Sociological Review*, 35.

Mann, M. (1983) *The Student Encyclopaedia of Sociology* (London: Macmillan).

Mann, M. (1986a) *The Sources of Social Power*, vol. 1 (Cambridge: Cambridge University Press).

Mann, M. (1986b) 'War and Social Theory', in Shaw, M. and Creighton, C. (eds) *The Sociology of War and Peace*, (London: Macmillan).

Mann, M. (1987) 'Ruling Class Strategies and Citizenship', *Sociology*, 21, 3.

Manson, T. (1976) 'Management, the Professions and the Unions: A Social Analysis of Change in the NHS', in Stacey, M. *et al.* (eds).

Manwaring, T. (1984) 'The Extended Internal Labour Market', *Cambridge Journal of Economics*, 8.

Manwaring, T. and Wood, S. (1984) 'The Ghost in the Labour Process', in Knights, D. *et al.* (eds).

March, J. G. (1981) 'Footnotes to Organizational Change', *Administrative Science Quarterly*, 26.

March, J. G. (1988) *Decisions and Organizations* (Oxford: Blackwell).

Marginson, P., Edwards, P. K., Purcell, J. and Sisson, K. (1988) 'What Do Corporate Offices Really Do?', *British Journal of Industrial Relations*, 26, 2.

Marsden, D. *et al.* (1985) *The Car Industry* (London: Tavistock).

Marshall, G. (1982) *In Search of the Spirit of Capitalism* (London: Hutchinson).

Marshall, T. H. (1963) *Sociology at the Crossroads* (London: Heinemann).

Martin, J. and Roberts, C. (1984) *Women and Employment: A Lifetime Perspective* (London: HMSO).

Marwick, A. (1970) *Britain in the Century of Total War* (Harmondsworth: Penguin).

Marx, K. (1970) *Capital*, vol. 1 (London: Lawrence and Wishart).

Maslow, A. (1970) *Motivation and Personality* (New York: Harper and Row).

Massey, D. (1984) *Spatial Divisions of Labour* (London: Macmillan).

Mathias, P. (1969) *The First Industrial Nation* (London: Methuen).

Merton, R. (1952) 'Bureaucratic Structure and Personality', in Merton, R. (ed.) *Reader in Bureaucracy* (Glencoe: Free Press).

Merton, R. K. (1982) 'Alvin W. Gouldner: Genesis and Growth of a Friendship', *Theory and Society*, 11.

Merton, R. K. (1987) 'Three Fragments from a Sociologist's Notebooks', *Annual Review of Sociology*, vol 13.

Meyer, J. W. (1986) 'Social Environments and Organizational Accounting', *Accounting, Organizations and Society*, 11, 4/5.

Meyer, J. W. and Rowan, B. (1977) 'Institutionalized Organizations: Formal Structure as Ceremony and Myth', *American Journal of Sociology*, 83, 2.

Meyer, J. W. and Scott, W. R. (1983) *Organizational Environments: Ritual and Rationality* (Beverly Hills: Sage).

Meyer, M. W. (ed.) (1980) *Environments and Organizations* (San Francisco: Jossey-Bass).

Meyer, M. W. (1987) 'The Growth of Public and Private Bureacuracies', *Theory and Society*, 16.

Meyer, M. W. and Brown, M. C. (1977) 'The Process of Bureaucratisation', *American Journal of Sociology*, 83, 2.

Meyer, M. W. *et al.* (1985) *Limits to Bureaucratic Growth* (Hawthorne, NY: de Gruyter).

Michels, R. (1921) *Political Parties* (Chicago: Free Press).

Miles, R. and Phizacklea, A. (1984) *White Man's Country* (London: Pluto).

Miller, P. and O'Leary, T. (1987) 'Accounting and the Construction of the Governable Person', *Accounting, Organizations and Society*, 12, 3.

Mills, C. W. (1970) *The Sociological Imagination* (Harmondsworth: Penguin).

Minns, R. (1980) *Pension Funds and British Capitalism* (London: Heinemann).

Minns, R. (1982) *Take Over the City* (London: Pluto).

Mintz, B. and Schwartz, M. (1985) *The Power Structure of American Business* (London: University of Chicago Press).

Mintzberg, H. (1973) *The Nature of Managerial Work* (New York: Harper and Row).

Mintzberg, H. (1978) 'Patterns in Strategy Formation', *Management Science*, 14.

Mintzeberg. H. and McHugh, A. (1985) 'Strategy Formation in an Adhocracy', *Administrative Science Quarterly*, 30.

Mintzberg, H. and Waters, J. A. (1985) 'Of Strategies, Deliberate and Emergent', *Strategic Management Journal*, 6.

Mizruchi, M. (1982) *The American Corporate Network* (London: Sage).

Mizruchi, M. and Schwartz, M. (1988) *Intercorporate Relations* (Cambridge: Cambridge University Press).

Moran, M. (1983) 'Power, Policy and the City of London', in King, R. (ed.) *Capital and Politics* (London: Routledge and Kegan Paul).

Moran, M. (1986) *The Politics of Banking* (2nd edn) (London: Macmillan).

Morgan, Gareth (1980) 'Paradigms, Metaphors and Puzzle Solving in Organization Theory', *Administrative Science Quarterly*, 25.

Morgan, Gareth (1986) *Images of Organization* (Beverly Hills: Sage).

Morgan, Glenn and Hooper, D. (1982) 'Labour in the Woollen and Worsted Industry', in Day, G. *et al. Diversity and Decomposition in the Labour Market* (London: Gower).

Morgan, Glenn and Hooper, D. (1987) 'Corporate Strategy, Ownership and Control', *Sociology*, 21, 4.

Morris, J. (1988) 'The Who, Why and Where of Japanese Manufacturing Investment in the UK', *Industrial Relations Journal*.

Murray, F. (1987) 'Flexible Specialization in the Third Italy', *Capital and Class*, Winter, no. 33.

Nichols, T. (1986) *The British Worker Question* (London: Routledge and Kegan Paul).

Nichols, T. and Beynon, H. (1977) *Living with Capitalism* (London: Routledge and Kegan Paul).

Nisbet, R. (1967) *The Sociological Tradition* (London: Heinemann).

Noble, D. (1977) *America by Design* (New York: Knopf).

Noble, D. (1984) *Forces of Production* (New York: Knopf).

Nove, A. (1977) *The Soviet Economic System* (London: Allen and Unwin).

Nove, A. (1983) *The Economics of Feasible Socialism* (London: Allen and Unwin).

Nystrom, P. and Starbuck, W. (1981) *Handbook of Organizational Design*, 2 vols (London: Oxford University Press).

O'Connor, J. (1973) *The Fiscal Crisis of the State* (London: St. James' Press).

Offe, C. (1984) *Contradictions of the Welfare State* (London: Hutchinson).

Offe, C. (1985) *Disorganized Capitalism* (Cambridge: Polity Press).

Ornstein, M. (1984) 'Interlocking Directorates in Canada', *Administrative Science Quarterly*, 29.

Osterman, P. (1983) 'Employment Structures within Firms', *British Journal of Industrial Relations*.

Osterman, P. (ed.) (1984) *Internal Labour Markets* (Cambridge, Mass.: MIT Press).

Osterman, P. (1987) 'Choice of Employment Systems in Internal Labor Markets', *Industrial Relations*, 26, 1.

Ouchi, W. G. (1980) 'Markets, Bureaucracies and Clans', *Administrative Science Quarterly*, 20.

Ouchi, W. G. (1981) *Theory Z: How American Business Can Meet the Japanese Challenge* (Reading, Mass.: Addison-Wesley).

Ouchi, W. G. (1984) *The M-Form Society* (Reading, Mass.: Addison-Wesley).

Pahl, R. (1984) *Divisions of Labour* (Oxford: Blackwell).

Palmer, D. (1983a) 'Broken Ties: Interlocking Directorates and Intercorporate Coordination', *Administrative Science Quarterly*, 28.

Palmer, D. (1983b) 'Interpreting Corporate Interlocks from Broken Ties', *Social Science History*, 7.

Pascale, R. T. (1984) 'Perspectives on Strategy; The Real Story behind Honda's Success', *California Management Review*, XXVI, 3.

Peet, R. (ed.) (1987) *International Capitalism and Industrial Restructuring* (Boston: Allen and Unwin).

Penn, R. (1985) *Skilled Workers in the Class Structure* (Cambridge: Cambridge University Press).

Penn, R. and Scattergood, H. (1985) 'Deskilling or Enskilling', *British Journal of Sociology*, XXXVI, 4.

Penn, R. and Simpson, R. (1986) 'The Development of Skilled Work in the British Coal Mining Industry 1870–1985', *Industrial Relations Journal*.

Penn, R. and Scattergood, H. (1988) 'Continuities and Change in Skilled Work', *British Journal of Sociology*, XXXIX, 1.

Pennings, J. (1980) *Interlocking Directorates* (San Francisco: Jossey-Bass).

Pennings, J. (1981) 'Strategically Interdependent Organizations', in Nystrom, P. and Starbuck, W. (eds).

Pennings, J. *et al.* (1984) 'Interorganizational Dependence and Forward Integration', *Organization Studies*, 5.

Perrow, C. (1981) 'Markets, Hierarchies and Hegemony', in Van de Ven, A. and Joyce, W. F. (eds).

Perrow, C. (1984) *Normal Accidents* (New York: Basic Books).

Perrow, C. (1988) *Complex Organizations* (3rd edn) (New York: Scott, Foresman).

Peters, T. J. and Waterman, R. H. (1982) *In Search of Excellence* (New York: Harper and Row).

Pettigrew, A. (1973) *The Politics of Organizational Decision Making* (London: Tavistock).

Pettigrew, A. (1985) *The Awakening Giant: Continuity and Change in ICI* (Oxford: Blackwell).

Pfeffer, J. (1981) *Power in Organizations* (Marshfield, Mass.: Pitman).

Pfeffer, J. (1982) *Organizations and Organization Theory* (Boston: Pitman).

Pfeffer, J. (1983) 'Organizational Demography', *Research in Organizational Behaviour*, 5.

Pfeffer, J. and Salancik, G. (1978) *The External Control of Organizations* (New York: Harper and Row).

Phillipson, C. and Walker, A. (1986) *Ageing and Social Policy* (London: Gower).

Phizacklea, A. (ed.) (1983) *One Way Ticket: Migration and Female Labour* (London: Routledge and Kegan Paul).

Phizacklea, A. and Miles, R. (1980) *Labour and Racism* (London: Routledge and Kegan Paul).

Piore, M. J. (1979) *Birds of Passage: Migrant Labour and Industrial Societies* (Cambridge: Cambridge University Press).

Piore, M. J. (1986a) 'Perspectives on Labour Market Flexibility', *Industrial Relations*, 25, 2.

Piore, M. J. (1986b) 'The Decline of Mass Production and the Challenge to Union Survival', *Industrial Relations Journal*.

Piore, M. J. and Sabel, C. F. (1984) *The Second Industrial Divide* (New York: Basic Books).

Pollert, A. (1981) *Girls, Wives and Factory Lives* (London: Macmillan).

Pollert, A. (1988a) 'Dismantling Flexibility', *Capital and Class*, Spring, 1988, no. 34.

Pollert, A. (1988b) 'The Flexible Firm: Fixation or Fact?', *Work, Employment and Society*, 2, 3, Sept.

Porter, M. E. (1985) *Competitive Advantage* (London: Collier Macmillan).

Porter, R. (1983) *English Society in the Eighteenth Century* (Harmondsworth: Penguin).

Pugh, D. S. and Hickson, D. (eds) (1976) *Organizational Structure: The Aston Studies*, vol. I (Farnborough: Saxon House).

Pugh, D. S. and Hinings, C. R. (eds) (1976) *Organizational Structure: The Aston Studies*, vol. II (Farnborough: Gower).

Pugh, D. S. and Payne, R. L. (1977) *Organizational Behaviour in its Context: The Aston Programme III* (London: Saxon House).

Pugh, D. *et al.* (1987) *Writers on Organizations* (3rd edn) (Harmondsworth: Penguin).

Purcell, J. (1985) 'Is Anybody Listening to the Corporate Personnel

Department?', *Personnel Management*, Sept.

Purcell, J. and Gray, A. (1984) 'The Management of Industrial Relations in Multidivisional Firms in Britain', paper presented to the BSA Annual Conference, April.

Purcell, J. and Gray, A. (1986) 'Corporate Personnel Departments and the Management of Industrial Relations', *Journal of Management Studies*, March.

Purcell, K., Wood, S., Waton, A. and Allen, S. (eds) (1986) *The Changing Experience of Employment* (London: Macmillan).

Quinn, R. E. (1977) 'Coping with Cupid: The Formation, Impact and Management of Romantic Relationships in Organizations', *Administrative Science Quarterly*, 22.

Rainnie, A. F. (1984) 'Combined and Uneven Development in the Clothing Industry', *Capital and Class*, 22.

Reed, M. I. (1986) *Redirections in Organizational Analysis* (London: Tavistock).

Rex, J. (1983) *Race Relations in Sociological Theory* (2nd edn) (London: Routledge and Kegan Paul).

Rex, J. (1986) *Race and Ethnicity* (Milton Keynes: Open University Press).

Rex, J. and Tomlinson, S. (1979) *Colonial Immigrants in a British City* (London: Routledge and Kegan Paul).

Roberts, B., Finnegan, R. and Gallie, D. (eds) (1985) *New Approaches to Economic Life* (Manchester: Manchester University Press).

Roethlisberger, F. J. and Dickson, W. (1964) *Management and the Worker* (New York: Wiley).

Rose, M. (1985) *Reworking the Work Ethic* (London: Batsford).

Rose, M. (1988) *Industrial Behaviour* (2nd edn) (Harmondsworth: Penguin).

Rosenbloom, R. S. and Cusumano, M. A. (1987) 'Technological Pioneering, and Competitive Advantage: The Birth of the VCR Industry', *California Management Review*, XXIX, 4.

Ross, J. and Staw, B. (1986) 'Expo 86: An Escalation Prototype', *Administrative Science Quarterly*, 31.

Roy, D. (1973) 'Banana Time: Job Satisfaction and Informal Interaction', in Salaman, G. and Thompson, K. (eds).

Rubery, J. (1978) 'Structured Labour Markets, Worker Organization and Low Pay', *Cambridge Journal of Economics*, 2.

Sabel, C. and Stark, D. (1982) 'Planning, Politics and Shop-Floor Power: Hidden Forms of Bargaining in Soviet Imposed State Socialist Societies', *Politics and Society*, 11.

Saks, M. (1983) 'Removing the Blinkers? A Critique of Recent Contributions to the Sociology of Professions', *Sociological Review*.

Salaman, G. (1979) *Work Organizations* (London: Longman).

Salaman, G. and Thompson, K. (eds) (1973) *People and Organizations* (London: Longman).

Sampson A. (1975) *The Seven Sisters* (London: Coronet).

Sato, K. and Hoshino, Y. (1984) *The Anatomy of Japanese Business* (London: Croom Helm).

Scott, J. (1982) *The Upper Classes* (London: Macmillan).

Scott, J. (1985) *Corporations, Classes and Capitalism* (2nd edn) (London: Hutchinson).

Scott, J. (1986) *Capitalist Property and Financial Power* (Brighton: Wheatsheaf).

Scott, J. (1988) 'Social Network Analysis', *Sociology*, 22, 1, Feb.

Scott, J. and Griff, C. (1984) *Directors of Industry* (Cambridge: Polity Press).

Scott, W. R. (1987) 'The Adolescence of Institutional Theory', *Administrative Science Quarterly*, 32.

Selznick, P. (1966) *TVA and the Grass Roots* (New York: Harper).

Shrivastava, P., Mitroff, I. and Alvesson, M. (1987) 'Nonrationality in Organizational Actions', *International Studies of Management and Organization*, XVII, 3.

Silverman, D. (1970) *The Theory of Organizations* (London: Heinemann).

Singh, J., House, R. J. and Tucker, D. J. (1986a) 'Organizational Change and Organizational Mortality', *Administrative Science Quarterly*, 31.

Singh, J., Tucker, D. J., and House, R. J. (1986b) 'Organizational Legitimacy and the Liability of Newness', *Administrative Science Quarterly*, 31.

Skocpol, T. (1979) *States and Social Revolutions* (Cambridge: Cambridge University Press).

Smith, D. (1988) 'The Japanese Example in South West Birmingham', *Industrial Relations Journal*.

Spencer, A. and Podmore, D. (1987) *In A Man's World* (London: Tavistock).

Stacey, M. (1984) 'Who are the Health Workers?', *Economic and Industrial Democracy*, 5.

Stacey, M. *et al.* (eds) (1976) *Health and the Division of Labour* (London: Croom Helm).

Starbuck, W. (1982) 'Congealing Oil: Inventing Ideologies to Justify Acting Ideologies Out', *Journal of Management Studies*, 19, 1.

Starbuck, W. (1983a) 'Organizations and their Environments', in Dunnette, M. D. (ed.) (1983) *Handbook of Industrial and Organizational Psychology* (New York: Wiley).

Starbuck, W. (1983b) 'Organizations as Action Generators', *American Sociological Review*, 48.

Stark, D. (1980) 'Class Struggle and the Transformation of the Labour Process', *Theory and Society*, 9.

Stark, D. (1986) 'Rethinking Internal Labor Markets: New Insights from a Comparative Perspective', *American Sociological Review*, August, 51.

Staw, B. (1976) 'Knee Deep in the Big Muddy: A Study of Escalating Commitment to a Chosen Course of Action', *Organizational Behaviour and Human Performance*, 16.

Staw, B. (1980) 'Rationality and Justification in Organizational Life', *Research in Organizational Behaviour*, 2.

Staw, B. (1984) 'Counterforces to Change', in Goodman, P. *et al.* (1984).

Staw, B., Sandilands, L. E. and Dutton, J. E. (1981) 'Threat-Rigidity, Effects in Organizational Behaviour: A Multilevel Analysis', *Administrative Science Quarterly*, 26.

Stewart, A., Prandy, K. and Blackburn, R. (1980) *Social Stratification and*

Occupations (London: Macmillan).

Stewart, R. (1983) 'Managerial Behaviour: How Research Has Changed the Traditional Picture', in Earl, M. (ed.).

Stokman, F. *et al.* (1985) *Networks of Corporate Power* (Cambridge: Polity Press).

Stone, K. (1975) 'The Origins of Job Structures in the Steel Industry', in Edwards, R. *et al.* (eds).

Storey, J. (1983) *Managerial Prerogative and the Question of Control* (London: Routledge and Kegan Paul).

Storey, J. (1985a) 'The Means of Management Control', *Sociology*, 19, 2.

Storey, J. (1985b) 'Management Control as a Bridging Concept', *Journal of Management Studies*, 22, 3.

Strange, S. (1986) *Casino Capitalism* (Oxford: Blackwell).

Strauss, A., Fagerhaugh, S., Suczek, B. and Weiner, C. (1982) 'Sentimental Work', *Sociology of Health and Illness*, 4, 3.

Sutton, R. I. (1987) 'The Process of Organizational Death: Disbanding and Reconnecting', *Administrative Science Quarterly*, 22.

Sweezy, P. (1939) 'Interest Groups in the American Economy', in Sweezy, P., *The Present as History* (New York: MR Press).

Therborn, G. (1976) *Science, Class and Society* (London: New Left Books).

Thompson, D. (1987) 'Coalitions and Conflicts in the National Health Service', *Sociology of Health and Illness*, 9, 2.

Thompson, E. P. (1971) 'Time, Work Discipline and Industrial Capitalism', *Past and Present*, 50.

Thompson, G. (1977) 'The Relationship between the Financial and Industrial Sector in the UK Economy', *Economy and Society*, 6, 3.

Thompson, G. (1978) 'Capitalist Profit Calculation and Inflation Accounting', *Economy and Society*, 7, 4.

Thompson, G. (1982) 'The Firm as a Dispersed Social Agency', *Economy and Society*, 11, 3.

Thompson, J. D. (1967) *Organizations in Action* (New York: McGraw Hill).

Thompson, K. (ed.) (1984) *Work, Employment and Unemployment* (Milton Keynes: Open University Press).

Thompson, P. (1983) *The Nature of Work* (London: Macmillan).

Tinker, T. (1985) *Paper Prophets* (London: Rinehart and Winston).

Tolbert, P. S. and Zucker, L. G. (1983) 'Institutional Sources of Change in the Formal Structure of Organizations', *Administrative Science Quarterly*, 2.

Tomlinson, J. (1982) *The Unequal Struggle? British Socialism and the Capitalist Enterprise* (London: Methuen).

Turnbull, P. J. (1986) 'The Japanisation of Production and Industrial Relations at Lucas Electricals', *Industrial Relations Journal*.

Turnbull, P. J. (1988) 'The Limits to "Japanisation" – Just-in-Time, Labour Relations and the UK Automotive Industry', *New Technology, Work and Employment*.

Useem, M. (1984) *The Inner Circles* (London: Oxford University Press).

Van de Ven, A. and Joyce, W. F. (eds) (1981) *Perspectives on Organizational Design and Behaviour* (New York: Wiley).

Van de Ven, A. H. and Walker, G. (1984) 'The Dynamics of Interorganizational Coordination', *Administrative Science Quarterly*, 29.

Van Gennep, A. (1977) *Rites of Passage* (London: Routledge and Kegan Paul).

Walby, S. (1983) 'Patriarchal Structures: The Case of Unemployment', in Gamarnikow, E. *et al.* (eds).

Walby, S. (1986) *Patriarchy at Work* (Cambridge: Polity Press).

Walker, A., Noble, I. and Westergaard, J. (1985) 'From Secure Employment to Labour Market Insecurity: The Impact of Redundancy on Older Workers in the Steel Industry', in Roberts B. *et al.* (eds).

Wallace, C. (1987) *For Richer, For Poorer; Growing Up In and Out of Work* (London: Tavistock).

Wallerstein, I. (1974) *The Modern World System*, vol. 1. (New York: Academic Press).

Wallerstein, I. (1980) *The Modern World System*, vol. 2 (New York: Academic Press).

Wallis, R. (1984) *Elementary Forms of the New Religious Life* (London: Routledge and Kegan Paul).

Warner, M. (ed) (1987) *Management Reform in China* (London: Francis Pinter).

Warr, P. (1987a) *Work, Unemployment and Mental Health* (Cambridge: Cambridge University Press).

Warr, P. (ed) (1987b) *Psychology at Work* (Harmondsworth: Penguin).

Weber, M. (1949) *The Methodology of the Social Sciences* (Glencoe, Ill.: Free Press).

Weick, K. (1976) 'Educational Organizations as Loosely Coupled Systems', *Administrative Science Quarterly*, 21.

Weick, K. (1982a) 'Management of Organizational Change among Loosely Coupled Elements', in Goodman, P. *et al.* (eds) (1982) *Change in Organizations* (San Francisco: Jossey-Bass).

Weick, K. (1982b) 'Enactment Processes in Organizations', in Staw, B. and Salancik, G. (eds) (1982) *New Directions in Organizational Behaviour* (Malabar, Florida: Kreiger).

Weick, K. (1985) 'Sources of Order in Underorganized Systems: Themes in Recent Organizational Theory', in Lincoln Y. S. (1985) *Organizational Theory and Inquiry* (Beverly Hills: Sage).

Westney, D. (1980) 'Patterns of Organizational Development in Japan', in Dunkerley, D. and Salaman, G. (eds).

Whetten, D. A. (1987) 'Organizational Growth and Decline Processes', *Annual Review of Sociology*, 13.

White, M. and Trevor, M. (1983) *Under Japanese Management* (London: Heinemann/PSI).

Whiteley, R. (1988) 'The Management Sciences and Managerial Skills', *Organizational Studies*, 9, 1.

Whiteley, R., Thomas, A. and Marceau, J. (1981) *Masters of Business?* (London: Tavistock).

Wickham, A. (1986) *Women and Training* (Milton Keynes: Open University Press).

Wilkins, A. L. and Ouchi, W. G. (1983) 'Efficient Cultures; Exploring the Relationship between Culture and Organizational Performance', *Administrative Science Quarterly*, 28.

Wilkinson, B. and Oliver, N. (1988) 'Editorial', *Industrial Relations Journal*.

Williamson, O. (1975) *Markets and Hierarchies* (New York: Free Press).

Williamson, O. (1981) 'The Economics of Organization', *American Journal of Sociology*, 87.

Williamson, O. and Ouchi, W. G. 'The Markets and Hierarchies and Visible Hand Perspectives', in Van de Ven and Joyce (1984).

Willis, P. (1978) *Learning to Labour* (Farnborough: Saxon House).

Willis, P. (1988) *Social Conditions of Young People in Wolverhampton* (London: Gower).

Willman, P. and Winch, G. (1985) *Innovation and Management Control* (Cambridge: Cambridge University Press).

Wilson, B. (1961) *Sects and Society* (London: Heinemann).

Wilson, B. (1969) *Religion in a Secular Society* (Harmondsworth: Penguin).

Wilson, E. K. (1985) 'What Counts in the Death or Transformation of an Organization?', *Social Forces*, 64, 2.

Witz, A. (1986) 'Patriarchy and the Labour Market: Occupational Control Strategies and the Medical Division of Labour', in Knights, D. and Willmott, H. (eds) (1986b).

Wood, S. (ed.) (1982) *The Degradation of Work* (London: Hutchinson).

Woodward, J. (1965) *Industrial Organization* (Oxford: Oxford University Press).

Wright, P. (1987) *Spycatcher* (Sydney: Heinemann).

Zeitlin, J. (1979) 'Craft Control and the Division of Labour: Engineers and Compositors in Britain 1890–1930', *Cambridge Journal of Economics*, 3.

Zucker, L. (1987) 'Institutional Theories of Organization', *Annual Review of Sociology*, 13.

Index

David Fickling Books

The comics in this book were originally published in The Phoenix Comic.

Adaptation, additional artwork and colours by Sammy Borras.
Cover design by Paul Duffield and Jamie Smart.

Bunny vs Monkey: Rise of the Maniacal Badger
is a
DAVID FICKLING BOOK

First published in Great Britain in 2022 by
David Fickling Books,
31 Beaumont Street,
Oxford, OX1 2NP

Papers used by David Fickling Books are from well-managed forests
and other responsible sources.

MIX
Paper from
responsible sources
FSC™ C130176

DAVID FICKLING BOOKS Reg. No. 8340307

A CIP catalogue record for this book is available from the British Library.

Printed by Grafostil, Slovenia.